Global Perspectives in Family Therapy

THE FAMILY THERAPY AND COUNSELING SERIES

Consulting Editor

Jon Carlson, Psy.D., Ed.D.

Ng	*Global Perspectives in Family Therapy: Development, Practice, and Trends*
Erdman and Caffery	*Attachment and Family Systems: Conceptual, Empirical, and Therapeutic Relatedness*

Global Perspectives in Family Therapy

Development, Practice, and Trends

Edited by

KIT S. NG

Brunner-Routledge
New York and Hove

Published in 2003 by
Brunner-Routledge
29 West 35th Street
New York, NY 10001
www.brunner-routledge.com

Published in Great Britain by
Brunner-Routledge
27 Church Road
Hove, East Sussex
BN3 2FA
www.brunner-routledge.co.uk

Brunner-Routledge is an imprint of the Taylor & Francis Group.
Printed in the United States of America on acid-free paper.

10 9 8 7 6 5 4 3 2 1

Library of Congress Cataloging-in-Publication Data

Global perspectives in family therapy : development, practice, trends / edited by
Kit S. Ng.
p. cm. — (The family therapy and counseling series)
Includes bibliographical references and index.
ISBN 1–58391–311–4
1. Family psychotherapy—Cross-cultural studies. 2. Cultural psychiatry.
3. Psychiatry, Transcultural. I. Ng, Kit S. II. Series.

RC488.5 .G565 2003
616.89'156--dc21

200201427 6

Contents

From the Series Editor

How could the drops of water know themselves to be a river?
Yet the river flows on.

Antoine De Saint Exupery

Through considerable luck and good fortune I have been able to visit countries and cultures. As a youngster I saw other cultures and countries as people in need of enlightenment. I saw that the world's population was eager to be more like those in the West. I later learned that this was called globalization. I thought it was important for others to be like us. I studied hard to improve my English skills—after all, the Bible was in English!—and never learned foreign languages.

Somewhere during my development, my views changed from conquest to appreciation. My travels took on new meaning and substance. I began to understand the importance of gender, ethnicity, and culture. Many may find my epiphany silly, because they have always known such things. However, I was raised a White privileged male of European heritage. I was raised Christian, but taught to look down on others. I was not very different from others I met in my North American travels.

This monograph offers a global perspective. This is something that I believe is imperative. This perspective seems revolutionary to those of my background and "old hat" to others. Whether you are learning a new perspective or finding support for your old one, this important book has merit.

An essential aspect of family therapy, whatever the school of therapy, is a negotiation directly or indirectly of the structures of family relationships among family members. The therapist plays an active part in furthering, facilitating, forcing, and directing these negotiations in the family. In the process, the therapist engages in negotiations between himself and herself and the family through his or her personal and professional incursions into the family's relations. The family structures that are being negotiated are not simply personal arrangements among family members. They are manifestations of the values of the cultural groups to which the family belongs. The therapies employed also reflect the cultural values that are inherent in their historical development. The personal interpretations and applications of the therapy by clinicians are filtered through the personal and cultural perspectives of the therapist. Cultural values that shape the relationships between family and therapist, which influence their respective perception of self and others, and affect their manner of communication, occupy space at the core of family therapy. It is imperative that we understand various cultures in order to be effective negotiators.

As you read the book, be aware that studies show that people from different cultures differ in the following:

1. Experience of pain
2. What is labeled as a "symptom"
3. How they communicate about their pain or symptoms
4. Their beliefs about cause
5. Their attitudes towards helpers, doctors and therapists, the treatment they desire or expect (McGoldrick, Giordano, & Pearce, 1996, p. 9)

Kit Ng and his contributors have developed a gem of a book. They have described family therapy in Asia, Europe, Africa, and other countries. As Fred Piercy describes in the Foreword, this book has value both historically as well as in terms of self-reflection. The impact of culture upon our lives is becoming more and more understood. Much behavior that we consider pathological in Western society would be deemed as healthy in other cultures. I hope that readers purchase this book, read it in its entirety, and develop a new understanding and appreciation for the different cultural possibilities.

Jon Carlson

REFERENCE

McGoldrick, M., Giordano, J., & Pearce, J. (1996). *Ethnicity and family therapy* (2nd ed.). New York: Guilford.

Foreword

In an old comic strip two toads, father and son, were talking to one another.

The younger toad asked his father, "Pop, what's the smartest creature on earth?"

Father toad responds, "Well . . . Let's see. . . . I know *we're* right up there. . . . It's either dolphins, toads, or chimps. . . . No! I think it goes toads, then chimps, *then* dolphins!"

"What about human beings?" asks the younger toad.

"Oh, yeah . . . can't leave them out," says Father. "They came up with the light bulb!"

"Why is *that* so great?" says Junior.

"Are you kidding? They attract bugs like you wouldn't believe" (Tribune Media Services, 1988).

We all see the world from our unique vantage point, and it's easy to see the way we do things as the only way.

Americans are particularly good at this. American family therapists were the original definers of family therapy. But as family therapy travels across the globe, it is changing to fit unique cultures and circumstances. The authors of this volume chronicle this change.

Few things are as universal as the importance of families. How one works with families, however, is shaped by cultural, economic, religious, social, and political constraints. This book chronicles the growth of family therapy—and sometimes the challenges that restrict growth—in a wide range of countries. We learn how family therapy permutations are evolving across the world.

This book can be read on several levels. On one, we learn about the history of family therapy across the globe. On another, we vicariously feel the enthusiasm of those forging this new profession. We learn that politics and repression are alive and well, and have their influence on both the price of bread and the family that buys it.

This book also stimulates self-reflection. When we learn about different ways of doing things—and of seeing the world—we remember how much we are imbedded in our own way of seeing and doing. This realization makes it harder to sleepwalk through a day.

I remember teaching family therapy to an Indonesian audience a few years ago. After my presentation, one member of the audience pointed out the high divorce rate in America and worried that American values of individual freedom would contaminate what he saw as the traditional religious and cultural values that support family togetherness in Indonesia. I talked about family therapy in terms of helping all family members have a voice. He talked about the importance of individual sacrifice and the greater good. Perhaps our conversation stretched us both. Regardless, it was clear that he would be the architect of family therapy in Indonesia, not me. This is the legacy of any family. The second generation bears the counsel of their elders, but applies it in a manner true to themselves and their context.

Kit Ng has brought together advocates of family therapy from different lands. The story of each is one of courage, innovation, and enthusiasm for a powerful movement. We will never have a homogenous, one-size-fits-all profession, nor should we. Kit has brought together for us a work in progress, with all the enthusiasm and flaws of the unfinished project called family therapy. I applaud him and stand in awe of his contributors' pioneering efforts. To be sure, there are still uncharted waters and unexplored lands. Thanks to Kit for his efforts to capture the passion, forms, and influence of this exciting movement.

Fred Piercy, Ph.D.
Professor and Chair
Department of Human Development
Virginia Polytechnic Institute & State University
Blacksburg, VA

Preface

This book is intended to serve as a basic and yet informative text for individuals who seek to understand the "growing pains" of family therapy from a global context. This context poses very different types of family dynamics, presenting problems, intervention techniques, cultural variations, and clinical diagnoses compared to the United States.

Even though some of the originators of family therapy have their roots in other countries (i.e., Minuchin, Boszormenyi-Nagy, Madanes), the development of family therapy was primarily confined to the United States until a couple of decades ago. Possibly, the earliest group that engaged family members in treatment outside of the United States was the Milan group from Italy. They developed a unique blend of family therapy and training. Further north, the Norway group developed their Scandinavian style of conducting family therapy and the internationally known "Reflection Team" approach to clinical supervision. Moving to the west, English therapists have historically developed their own brand of family therapy, influenced primarily by psychiatry and psychoanalysis. Other European countries witnessed the emergence of family therapy with their traditional individualistic approach to clinical work.

In Asia, the Japanese struggled to integrate systemic family therapy with their homogeneous culture. Family therapy has indeed been a very slow moving force in Asia. A couple of thousand miles south, the development of family therapy took on a very exciting genesis. In Australia, White, Epston, and Durrant at the Dulwich Family Center developed the "Narrative Approach" to family therapy, which eventually dominated the postmodern clinical practices. The New Zealanders also developed a multicultural approach to treating families with initial work with the Maori families. In every aspect, the push for the development of family therapy beyond the boundaries of North America has been both gradual and challenging.

Historically, because most, if not all family therapy training institutions started in the United States, trainees from abroad flocked here to receive the best training in some of the more traditional systemic (i.e., structural, strategic) approaches to therapy. The trend began to reverse in the 1980s and

1990s when trainees from the United States received training in Europe and Australia or attended workshops conducted by presenters from overseas.

In my opinion, even though there has been a surge of interest in family therapy outside of the United States with the introduction of various conferences and organizations, there is still a lot to be done. In this book, we attempt to touch the "tip of the iceberg" in terms of the developments and trends in family therapy around the globe. Here, my colleagues and I provide the readers with information on the "labor pains" of family therapy in numerous countries. Some of these countries are often besieged by political uncertainties; bureaucratic barriers; limited financial support; inadequate faculties; and the lack of adequate texts, journals, and reference books in their own languages. This may be a surprise to therapists in America because we are often flooded by volumes of family therapy books. In spite of all the odds, my colleagues have detailed the development of family therapy in their own homelands.

The purpose of this book is not to point readers to another textbook on systems theory. We have a lot of them in the market today. With the exception of Italy, which has a more developed family therapy history, the rest of the countries mentioned in this book are basically countries where family therapy is either very new, or developing. This presents the challenging task to my colleagues to "bear the torch" to the readers concerning the needs for family therapy in the less developed countries.

This book is basically divided into four major sections. Each section consists of the different aspects of family therapy in a cluster of countries. Chapter 1 introduces a global view, which depicts the different family structures and complex practices of family therapy in the global community.

Each of the next four chapters (Chapters 2 through 5) presents different aspects of family therapy in Asia. Readers will find this section fascinating, with its diverse cultures, languages, and religious beliefs. The countries presented in these chapters range from very homogenous (Japan, India) to rather heterogeneous (Singapore, Malaysia). The contributors also delineated some of the difficulties of performing family therapy in most Asian cultures, which are rooted in centuries of tradition.

Chapters 6 through 10 usher the readers through the second world countries, which are more developed. The practice of family therapy in a very diverse setting is discussed in these chapters. In most instances, the contributors also traced the historical development of family therapy and the influence of American trainers. The historical impact that political unrest, communism, lack of resources, poverty, and economic depression have on the family and family therapy is felt in some of these countries.

Chapters 11 and 12 are two contrasting chapters, even though they are from the same continent. The development of family therapy in South Africa is more contemporary and diverse, whereas in Nigeria it is more homogenous and tradition-based. However, the ultimate goal remains one of helping the family in need through different means.

The last three chapters delineate family therapy in Israel and South America as a growing movement. Even though some of the earliest cyberneticians (i.e., Varela, Maturana) were from South America, family therapy as a practice has yet to mature. The encouraging news is that these are individuals who are committed to paving the way for family therapy at all cost.

ACKNOWLEDGMENT

The process of working on this book has been a meaningful learning experience for me. I wish to express my gratitude to Kean University for the release time, the psychology department for encouragement, Jon Carlson for his patience and support, and Margaret Chooi for her understanding because I spent much of my summer vacations editing the manuscripts. Last, but not least, I want to thank all the contributors around the globe for their hard work and faith in me to complete this project. I especially thank those who have to go through the painful process of translation because English is either their third or fourth language.

Kit S. Ng
West Orange, New Jersey

CHAPTER 1

Toward a Global View of Family Therapy Development

KIT S. NG

It is impossible to talk about family therapy development without talking about the family. Without the development of family, there is no need for family therapy. In this chapter, an overview of the development of the family and the problems that they have to deal with in different cultural contexts is introduced. Some key areas that therapists need to focus on while working with families across the globe are also suggested. The remaining chapters expand on the different aspects of the historical beginning, current developments, training issues, theoretical variations, future trends, and research potential in family therapy in 14 different countries. We understand that there are other countries in which family therapy is growing, but on the other hand it is not possible to represent all the countries in the world written in one single volume.

IN THE BEGINNING

The beginning of the family is tied to the beginning of the human race. No one actually knows the beginning of the family. It is not hard to develop a strong curiosity about the beginnings of the family. What, indeed, was the family like in the Old Stone Age before humans knew how to create fire? Were the roles of husbands and wives as relatively fixed, and were families as relatively stable as they are today? What were some common domestic problems? What was the position of women? And when did men begin to live in families? These questions appear to be very fundamental and yet necessary as we examine the family from a global perspective.

The evolution of family has historically played an extremely vital part in the life and development of different people and nations. The genesis of family dates back to prehistoric times with the development of the original family unit. The adults maintained their roles as hunters, parents, partners, and protectors, whereas the children served as links to another generation. This seems to have carried the human race for ages. The sense of community also played an important element in survival. Besides that, the different systems provide oases for love, intimacy, devotion, attachment, and a sense of belonging (Adams, 1995).

In Eastern societies, the family, rather than the individual is highly prized and honored. The individual is seen as a product of all the generations of his or her family. This concept is often reinforced by ancestor worship, family rituals, funeral ties, mythologies, and festivity celebrations. Because of this continuum, each individual action reflects not only themselves but also their extended family and ancestors (Lee, 1996). The individual is also expected to have very clearly defined roles and positions based on age, gender, and social class. There is a strong emphasis on harmonious relationships, interdependence, loyalty, and respect to achieve a peaceful coexistence within the family and community at large. In this way, the family serves as the backbone for family development to provide guidance, support, and help for its members. Because of this, it is important to keep the family name, a close family unit, and family honor to improve the family's social status (Hu & Chen, 1999). Consequently, marriages are often arranged in some parts of Asia.

In Europe, different generations of monarchs accumulated wealth and social status. Therefore, the families went through periods of religious, political, cultural, and intellectual changes. Men and women often were expected to be independent and strong. European families as a whole tend to highly value self-control, dealing with suffering in silence and covering over conflict in public. They are less likely to give time, money, and assistance to a family member who needs it (Giordano & McGoldrick, 1996). Children are often taught to be self-reliant, responsible, and independent. The more their children are able to demonstrate that they are self-reliant, the more successful the parents feel.

Middle Eastern families contributed to some of the mystical and earliest developments of family life. The culture of modern Arabs has been impacted by different historical events, such as the founding of the Islamic religion in the seventh century, the division of the different Middle Eastern countries after the Ottoman Empire, the partition of Palestine in the twentieth century, and most recently, the Gulf War. Despite environmental, historical, and sociological changes, the Middle Eastern culture has emerged as a group with its own unique values and norms. The Arabic family is both hierarchical and patriarchal with regard to sex and age. The extended family remains a very important part of the family system. Although the family may have established their own household, they usually are very loyal to their kin and consider them as part of their own.

In South America, the family has had to deal with different political, social, and economic changes for generations. They represent a highly complex culture affected by European colonialism, separated by diverse geography, climate, and languages. Like other families around the globe, families in South America cherish the importance of family unity, religious commitment, welfare, and respect for each other. There is a strong sense of family commitment, obligation, and mutual responsibility. The family is rather protective of its members as long as they stay in the system. The family as a whole is usually an extended system, which often includes adopted children and godparents. Compared to others, these families have to deal with the added stress of political oppression, social isolation, and immigration issues.

The pages of history continue to depict how different families, in different parts of the globe, are impacted by culture, time, religion, and economic changes. To the intellectually curious, the universality of the family institution and its society-to-society variations demand explanations. Part of the dichotomy of the family unit is that it is exclusive and inclusive, rigid and flexible, stable and changing. Most of all, it is unique and has proven to be extremely resilient against all external forces.

GLOBAL FAMILY STRUCTURES

Various types of family structures have long existed in different cultures and the reasons for their existence are innumerable. In a way, the structures operate uniquely in a complex environment consisting of external and internal challenges that include economic, social, religious, educational, political, and technological elements. As the structures deal with such challenges, they become specialists in a world of specialists. They develop their own norms, hierarchies, subsystems, boundaries, and beliefs to carry on their traditions from one generation to another. Some structures tend to change slower than others. Their all-encompassing function since the beginning of humankind is to meet their members' need for love, safety, and a sense of belonging.

Nuclear Family

The basic family system across the globe has indeed gone through enormous changes after World War II because of migration, economic and social development, technologic innovation, and political revolution, but in most cases the nuclear family structure remains intact, of course with exceptions. Family researchers have long debated whether the nuclear family is universal. In general, the opinions are divisive on the definition of the nuclear family, whereas most agree that the universal functions of the nuclear family are socialization, reproduction, economic cooperation, and sex relations (Adams, 1995; Hareven, 1988).

Countries that are more developed and industrialized tend to have more nontraditional family systems compared to Third World countries. For example, in Hong Kong, Singapore, Japan, France, and England, the divorce rates are as high if not higher than in the United States (Binner & Dnes, 2001; Lester & Abe, 1998). In most developed countries, there is also a marked increase in blended families, cohabitating heterosexual couples, dual-career marriages, and single parenthood (Rajadhyaksha & Bhatnagar, 2000; Smith, 1997).

Less developed countries tend to maintain more traditional nuclear families than industrialized countries. Often, the man is the main breadwinner, whereas the woman is the homemaker. The man is also head of the household and is responsible for its support. The woman, on the other hand, is responsible for domestic services and child care. This is especially true for agricultural countries, which tend to have bigger families. In most parts of rural China, India, Africa, South America, and Eastern Europe, nuclear families are still very intact. They are often maintained by centuries-old hierarchical orders. Patriarchy, or father rule, is the most familiar pattern historically, although in some cases women wield the authority.

Marriage Arrangements

Unlike most marriages in the United States, which are an exercise of personal choice, the practice of arranged marriage is still a common practice in some parts of the Middle East, Africa, India, China, and some other Asian countries. Arranged marriages are essentially an institutional device to ensure the perpetuation of the family and its property (Slater, 1984). Often, this form of a family structure provides a solution to the problem of the preservation of property and attainment of social status. Arguably, this type of arrangement fails to offer very much in the way of personal or emotional satisfaction. In some societies, in which marriages represent more than an alliance of two individuals, the expansion of social connections through arranged marriage can offer a benefit that figures prominently in the desire to obtain a spouse.

In most Eastern cultures, unmarried adults are considered to be failing their family or "losing face" if they do not contribute to the expansion of the social contacts of their immediate family (Bhopal, 1997). Since marriage expands the network of relations, it is significant in a patronage society.

In those societies, it is also considered a great favor to match unmarried adults. There is also a financial consideration in arranged marriages. It is generally the responsibility of the bride's father to provide her with a sizable cash amount called a dowry, which is usually paid to the groom's parents (Bhopal, 1997). They, in turn, are expected to provide their daughter-in-law with an annual allowance. If the groom is the eldest son, it is the usual practice to settle the family estate just before they get married. These settlements are essentially designed to preserve the family patrimony intact by limiting the ability of the heir to dispose of his inherited property. This can get very complex and cumbersome. It is safe to say that most modern-day arranged marriages evolve to a more mutual agreement with less complexity.

Extended Family

Extended family involves living with other blood kin, and sometimes extends to three generations. This is possibly the most common form of family structure found outside of the United States. Families in India, China, Africa, the Middle East, and South America are known to have included extended households since the beginning of time. In fact, in most of these societies, not living with extended family is considered breaking cultural norms.

There are numerous ways to categorize possible kinds of extended families. The three most common extended family systems are the stem family, lineal family, and fully extended family. The stem family occurs when one child and only one child remains a member of his or her parents' family after marriage, bringing his or her spouse to this home and raising the children as members of the family. The lineal family occurs when all the children of one sex remain in their parents' home after marriage. Such is common in the Indian family. It is typical for brothers to form their own families after the death of their parents. If they remain together, the result is a fully extended family system, which consists of two or more related nuclear families in each of at least two adjacent families (Lee, 1988).

What keeps some extended families together? One reason appears to be economic. In order to survive and keep their prosperity going, the father must keep the members together to participate in their share of work. In such a family structure, the males usually inherit the wealth after the death of the father if they stay subordinate to the father's authority during his lifetime. This method of pulling their resources together helps both the rich and poor. The Chinese family usually consists of the grandparents, their sons and their wives, and their sons' children. The three generations indeed create a formidable workforce. Ideally, the grandparents and wives work at home doing chores such as taking care of the children and cooking. The men work long hours in the workplace.

Residential Clustering

This form of a structure is common in most societies, especially in Europe. Some of the earliest known residential clustering was found among the Slavs. Societies of those days had to keep the clan members together to protect themselves from foes. It was known that if a clan had to move for economic reasons, they would bring all their immediate and extended family members with them. As societies have become more urban-industrial, the basic characteristics of clustering by families basically have remained unchanged.

In modern times, the newly married couple creates a "new" (i.e., separate) residence from their family of origin. Eventually, they locate near his, her, or both their kin. In Western society the most frequent form of clustering residence is the "neolocal type." This permits the couple to choose a place of residence separate from either set of parents but still within the locality (Adams, 1995). This pattern is common in the West but rare in the rest of the world. In some cases, they may spend part of their married life near his and part near her kin. This practice of "patrilocality" is also another age-old living arrangement. In this situation, the newlywed couple lives close to the home or compound of the parents of the groom or other close male relative of the father's generation. "Patrilocality" is the residence form associated with a strong majority of societies that feature patrilineal descent. This type of residence is most common in polygamous hunting-and-gathering societies throughout Asia, Africa, and Latin America. The clustering of "matrilocality," which is settling near the wife's mother or other close female relative of the mother's generation is also a common practice in most parts of Central America and the Caribbean (Adams, 1995; Marciano & Sussman, 1991). About half of all societies that feature matrilineal descent organization also feature matrilocal residence. This created what researchers called the "matrilineal puzzle" model. The question most often asked is, How do the matrilineal group's males govern if they are separated spatially by matrilocal residence? This structure creates a residential clustering with close proximity and yet maintains adequate space between the different members. This pattern helps the family maintain their ties and communication from one generation to another.

Other aspects of residential clustering involve not only the location of the family but of such persons as retiring parents, single adults, divorced siblings, and so on. This type of family setting is largely impacted by economic change, family restructuring, and family life cycles.

FAMILY-RELATED PROBLEMS

Increasingly, therapists who work with families are recognizing the complexity of treating problems that are rooted in the family, often for generations. When an individual is treated separately from the context of the family, changes may occur, but the client often has to deal with the dysfunctional patterns of the other family members. If the behavior patterns of the rest of the family members remain constant, the client will likely revert back to former dysfunctional patterns that are reinforced by the family. This may result in frustration and cause an impasse in treatment from the therapist's standpoint. From this perspective, it makes sense to involve this often "untapped" resource as a viable channel to change. In working with different families, certain family-related problems appear to be a general representation, some of which are similar to problems faced by families in the United States.

Care for Aging Parents

One of the paramount issues that most therapists have to deal with is the ever-increasing interaction of aging parents with the immediate family. This often puts stress on the marriage, parenting issues, and financial matters. As people are living longer, many young families are feeling obligated to take care of their parents (Stockman, Bonney, & Sheng, 1995). Contributing to this stress is the notion that in most societies it is considered a "societal taboo" to place aging parents in retirement homes. Therapists have to find creative ways to help the family work through differences to ease tensions in the marriage and the family. It is definitely helpful to involve the aging parents in therapy in order to gain their input and perspective on what is needed in order to deal with the tension.

Dealing with Adult Children Leaving Home

Because of the availability of jobs and the promise of a better future, migration to the bigger cities by single young adults is a trend repeating itself in most developed countries since the beginning of the technology age. Skilled and educated adults left the rural countryside and their agricultural heritage, which was there for generations, behind them. This local "brain drain" caused an emotional and economic toll on the family. In most cases, the family has the intention of passing what is left to them to another generation. This often creates a crisis for the elderly parents, who know their physical limitations without the help of their children. In certain parts of China, India, and Africa, there have been reports of elderly farmers burning their farms and committing suicide after their children left. Therapy here involves a negotiated departure by both parties and assurance that the elderly parents will be assisted when the younger generation is gone.

School Management Problems

Many school problems have to do with the value of education placed by parents from across the globe. This often creates a high level of stress for the child to perform well in school. In certain developed countries teen suicide caused by school-related stress has doubled in the last 15 years (Curtright & Fernquist, 2001). In these cases, working with the child alone is highly ineffective. The family needs to participate in therapy to find creative ways to establish effective communication between the school and the family in order to support the changes made by the identified patient. Because of the notion that the family wants the child to excel in school, most family members will do anything to help the child, and in this case, this may mean coming to intensive therapy. The therapist must find ways to work effectively with the two systems in order to facilitate effective change and provide ongoing support for the student.

Parenting Issues

In the United States, the issue of parenting is often aided by workshops, seminars, video tapes, and professional family educators, whereas in other societies, parenting skills appear to come from what was learned from the previous generation. There are very few workshops or books written on parenting outside of the United States. Strict, disciplinarian, and authoritarian types of child rearing characterize how children are raised in other societies, with the exception of certain European countries.

Strict discipline only works when the child is young; when the child grows to be older and more independent, he or she will act out by either running away or getting into trouble. In most cases, this form of acting out is a way the child deals with dysfunction and tries to escape family stress (Horne, 2000). Frequently this type of misbehavior promotes discord between the parents about how to manage and discipline the child. Family therapy at this point can help the family change dysfunctional patterns. Issues such as setting limits and parent–child negotiations are crucial for the family members to understand.

Chemical Abuse Problems

Abuse of drugs such as cocaine, morphine, and crack appears to be a major concern primarily of young people in many parts of the world. The rate of drug abuse has mushroomed despite stiff penalties in some countries. Alcohol is more appealing to older and upper-class working adults, whereas cocaine and other related substances are more common with teens and younger adults (Davies, 1983). Regardless of their drug of choice, addiction has adverse effects on the family and produces severe health problems in individuals. When one member of the family is using, other members are affected as well. In some countries, the use, possession, or trafficking of controlled substances has very severe punishments, from jail time to death. Family members often experience shame and disruption to their daily routine as they deal with another family member who has an addiction problem.

Pattison (1982) identified some themes in dealing with the effects of addiction within the family. First, because of the stress produced by alcoholic members, other family members may have to adapt their roles in order to cope with the alcoholic member in ways that are not in their own best interest. Second, the therapist must understand the effect the family has on the alcoholic. Conflict in the marriage or with children may perpetuate excessive drinking. Third, family participation in the treatment of alcoholism improves the prognosis. Often, it takes more than simply working with the family to deal with alcoholism in the family. In most cases, physical, emotional, social, and vocational issues must be dealt with. Particularly, in many cultures, the community often brands a recovered addict as an outcast. This makes it harder for the recovering individual to mainstream back into society, obtain decent employment, and become self-sufficient. Research has suggested that family therapy is an effective method for treating chemical abuse. This approach is based on the perception that chemical abuse is a part of a dysfunctional family system and that drug use is a way to cope with that system.

Marital and Divorce Issues

The marriage and divorce trend in some countries is very much like that in the United States, whereas others are different. In general, young adults tend to marry much later in life because of their interest in pursuing higher education, achieving career goals, and exercising their need for independence after having arrived at a certain socioeconomic status (Jones, 1994). In most cases, young adults from this cohort are more demanding and have higher expectations toward commitment in long-term relationships.

In the past, the divorce rate was relatively low in most countries compared to the United States. But that demographic has changed quite a bit during the last 20 years. Divorce rates in most developed countries have seen a sharp rise. In most situations, the divorce rate is highest among the educated middle- to upper-middle-class and young adults (Kanazawa, 2001; Phillips, 1988). This is the same age group that would likely seek marital therapy, or divorce if therapy did not work. Most couples who seek therapy dealing with divorce will end up getting divorced. This is because most couples seek therapy only as their last resort. In this regard, most often it is too late to save the troubled marriage.

Researchers postulate different divorce trends in different cultures. In some Eastern cultures the reasons for divorce evolve around the in-laws and children much more than in Western cultures (Jones, 1994). In Western cultures divorce issues have more to do with personality differences and socioeconomic issues (Phillips, 1988). Common therapeutic issues facing divorce include: (a) marital and divorce therapy dealing with immediate issues; (b) marital therapy with discussion about the children; (c) therapy with the children and only one spouse on issues that parents have with the children (Patel, 2001); and (d) therapy with post-divorce issues.

Suicide and Depression

Most countries are developing at an enormous pace, and so are their social problems. The stress and pressure of modern civilization often catch the vulnerable unaware. Studies have shown that suicide and depression in most developed countries have increased significantly. Individuals who are most vulnerable are those with a history of chemical abuse, the currently unemployed, and teenagers (Curtright & Fernquist, 2001; Heuveline & Slap, 2002). Teenagers appear to be greatly affected by the education system and parents who hold excessively high expectations for their school performance. When teens are not able to live up to those expectations, often they either commit suicide or experience depression.

In the case of teenage depression or suicide, therapy with the whole family is an excellent treatment method. On the other hand, adult suicide is a more complex issue to deal with. Most adults, commonly in Asia, who plan to commit suicide, are often successful in their attempts. This is largely because of the cultural sanction that it is better to end one's life than bring shame to one's whole family or community. Therapy with a suicidal adult client is a very challenging task indeed. One of the keys is to assure the client of complete confidentiality. The "duty to warn" takes on a very different meaning for therapists working with suicidal clients outside of the United States. The only people who need to be warned concerning risk of suicide are the family members.

IMPLICATIONS FOR THERAPY

Most therapists need to understand the complexity and difficulty of treating families from other cultures and societies. The variations in language, religion, socioeconomic status, race, and so on often seem enormous and could easily discourage therapists who have little or no exposure to the global community. On the other hand, therapists must look at the global community as their next-door neighbor, because our world is getting smaller as each generation of technology gets more sophisticated.

How then can therapists develop a global framework in which to work with diverse families? I recommend the following suggestions in working with families from different cultural contexts.

1. *Understand how culture influences what we perceive.* Our experiences with other cultures shape our perceptions and often create unreasonable expectations. For example, when we encounter an unpleasant experience with that culture, we tend to generalize and stereotype. For a long time, the issue was raised concerning cultural differences between African Americans and European Americans. African Americans tend to excel in auditory tasks, whereas Europeans do better with visual stimuli. This hypothesis further postulates that African Americans appear to have difficulty with the study of mathematics, and this is compensated for by a good sense of music and rhythm. This assumption is intriguing; however, there are little empirical data to support the theory of the sensory differences between Africans and Europeans (Shiraev & Levy, 2001). Therapists especially must avoid such stereotyping of families. Each family must be carefully understood within their cultural, ethnic, and religious context; for example, an Iranian family may not speak Farsi, and an Indian family may not necessarily be Hindu.
2. *Avoid "pathologizing" the family that seeks help.* Most families that seek help are not interested in being told what is wrong with them or being labeled as having a "manic depressive" father or a "bipolar" mother. Psychological pathologies are unique for each culture and cannot be understood without the social context in which they develop. In one way, pathology is culturally specific and has different meanings in different societies. Other factors such as the religious, social, political, and spiritual norms of each society therefore should determine the way mental

disorders are understood and treated. It is vital for therapists to investigate different cultural interpretations of social stressors and supports such as family, religion, community networks, and levels of functioning. As an example, one could find that prejudice and hostility against a neighboring tribe or ethnic group could have significant impact on the development and treatment of posttraumatic stress disorder in victims of "ethnic cleansing" (Shiraev & Levy, 2001):

3. *Always start with the key member(s) of the family.* Perhaps in most cases, the most significant value shared in the global community is the importance placed on family unity, welfare, and honor. This emphasis is very much on a collective group rather than the individual. There is a deep sense of family commitment, obligation, and responsibility from the parents to their children and the children to their parents. The family, in a very intimate way, guarantees protection and caretaking for life as long as the person stays in the system. Locating the key member(s) and respectfully engaging the decision maker of the family in therapy and information gathering appears to be isomorphic to the community at large. It denotes respect for all levels of authority. In some societies, the man is the head, whereas in others the woman makes the key decisions. It is also important to keep in mind the different communicative aspects of family dynamics, such as language barriers, the cultural significance of seeking therapy, the level of disclosure and confrontation, and the understanding of interventions. In some societies, young female clinicians may have to deal with rejection and mistrust in a male-dominated society. In other situations, an ethnic or religious match is crucial between the clinician and family members.
4. *Provide information and teaching.* Therapists who have experience working abroad understand the need to be "multitask" oriented. Therapists abroad do not have the luxury of seeing clients one after another, as in some clinics in the United States. One of the therapist's roles is to provide information to family members about medical information, social services, governmental agencies, and community networking information. This may be time consuming but is necessary in order to help the family. This holistic approach is often needed in developing countries where resources are scarce and difficult to locate. Families are often locked up within the walls of bureaucratic fortresses. In some cases, this may mean months of waiting to get to certain resources. An Indian family therapist, a friend of mine, experienced culture shock when I told her that in America we rarely help our clients locate government agencies. They have to do it by themselves. Her immediate response was, "if the client knows how to do it (in India), he or she will not need to come and see me." Families that seek therapy usually have more than just family problems. Often, they need help with referrals to resources not known to them.

5. *Action-oriented techniques appear to work best.* Talk therapy has severe limitations in most societies. In quite a few societies, therapy is often equated with medical help. In this context, clients expect a time frame whereby the presenting problem should be fixed. This may appear to be unrealistic to most outsiders, but the reality is that problem solving that leads to a decision-making process type of approach to treatment is most appealing and effective. Often reorientation and education encourage clients to develop goals and put them into action. In most cases, the therapist needs to offer clear and concrete directives in order to render effective therapy. Other techniques such as giving advice, asking for forgiveness, role-playing, homework, and task setting are additional ways to help the family change. The overall goal here is much more than to help clients gain awareness about themselves. It should include concrete behavioral change and new alternatives to make better choices.
6. *Counter metaphors with metaphors.* One of the effective ways of working with families is to use what they bring to therapy. Insoo Kim Berg called it the "gifts" from the family. In this case, the family may bring the gift of metaphor to the therapy room. Metaphors are common ways whereby clients can express their complex, abstract ideas and uncommon experiences. They provide a context for the family's problems and limit the ways in which the family comes to terms with its problems. They are in essence symbolic representations that capture essential features of an object or expression by using descriptions of a completely different class of objects (Constantine, 1986). The use of metaphors has historically been a part of everyday conversation since the birth of languages in societies in the Middle East, Asia, Africa, South America, and parts of Europe. By using metaphors, the family expresses different aspects of complex and obscure communications that otherwise might be missed. When a therapist uses the right metaphor to work with the family, the therapist in a way has altered the family's realities and influences what they do and experience. Metaphors also convey more information than they contain because they are accurate or appropriate to many levels of implications. In a broader sense, families use different types of metaphors such as gender structure, family coalition, triangulation, family rules, negative and positive feedback, and control and power to delineate their daily existence (Rosenblatt, 1994).
7. *The therapist is a cultural mediator.* Often therapists are perceived and accepted as professionals along with other authority figures such as "doctors" in many societies. This is especially true in countries where family therapy organizations are well established and recognized by the government as providers of mental health services to its citizens. Most often, the therapist's graduate training is also highly respected and valued. This can become leverage for change. Besides working with the family in the

assigned sessions, most often therapists educate and engage the family members to other outside resources to work out their problems. It is not uncommon for the therapist to accompany family members to courts, hospitals, and governmental agencies as part of helping the family to deal with their presenting problems. In this sense, the therapist takes on the role of a mediator. The therapist also becomes a mediator of differences between communities. This is more true in different African communities. In this regard, the ability to negotiate and speak different dialects is highly valued.

CONCLUSION

In this chapter, we focused on the need and necessity for therapists to understand the complex cultural context that each family has been immersed in for centuries. It is also very necessary for therapists to obtain detailed knowledge about the presenting problems before any interventions are suggested. Often, therapy may be more than work done inside the four walls of the office. It often involves being an advocate of the family to deal with the establishment, provide information regarding resources, deal with the legal system, and protect the rights of the family. Not only are clients different throughout the global community, but also the roles of therapists are different, in that they have to be multitask oriented. Taking on several roles—therapist, advocate, legal advisor, health educator, and resource expert—is necessary to provide the help needed for the family.

REFERENCES

Adams, B. (1995). *The family: A sociological interpretation* (5th ed.). Belmont, CA: Wadsworth.

Bhopal, K. (1997). South Asian woman with households: Dowries, degradation and despair. *Women's Studies International Forum, 20*(4), 484–492.

Binner, J., & Dnes, D. (2001). Marriage, divorce, and legal change: New evidence from England and Wales. *Economic Inquiry, 39*(2), 298–306.

Constantine, L. (1986). *Family paradigms: The practice of theory in family therapy*. New York: Guilford.

Curtright, P., & Fernquist, R. M. (2001). The age structure of male suicide rates: Measurement and analysis of 20 developed countries. *Social Science Research, 30*(4), 627–648.

Davies, P. (1983). *Alcohol problems and alcohol control in Europe*. New York: Amereon Press.

Giordano, J., & McGoldrick, M. (1996). European families: An overview. In M. McGoldrick, J. Giordano, & J. Pearce (Eds.), *Ethnicity & family therapy* (2nd ed., pp. 427–441). New York: Guilford.

Hareven, K. T. (1988). Historical analysis of the family. In M. Sussman & S. Steinmertz (Eds.), *Handbook of marriage and the family* (pp. 37–57). New York: Plenum Press.

Heuveline, P., & Slap, G. B. (2002). Adolescent and young adult mortality by cause, age, gender and country, 1955-1994. *Journal of Adolescent Health, 30*(1), 29–34.

Horne, A. (2000). *Family counseling and therapy*. Itasca, IL: F. E. Peacock.

Hu, X., & Chen, G. (1999). Understanding cultural values in counseling Asian families. In K. Ng (Ed.), *Counseling Asian families from a systems perspective* (pp. 27-37). Washington, DC: American Counseling Association.

Jones, W. G. (1994). *Marriage and divorce in Islamic Southeast Asia*. London: Oxford University Press.

Kanazawa, S. (2001). Why father absence might precipitate early menarche: The role of polygyny. *Evolution and Human Behavior, 22*(5), 329–334.

Lee, E. (1996). American Asian families: An overview. In M. McGoldrick, J. Giordano, & J. K. Pearce (Eds.), *Ethnicity and family therapy* (2nd ed., pp. 227–248). New York: Guilford.

Lee, G. (1988). Comparative perspectives. In M. Sussman & S. Steinmetz (Eds.), *Handbook of marriage and the family* (pp. 59–77). New York: Plenum.

Lester, D., & Abe, K. (1998). The suicide rate by each method in Japan: A test of Durkheim's theory of suicide. *Archives of Suicide Researchers, 4*(3), 281–285.

Marciano, T., & Sussman, M. (1991). *Wider families: New traditional family forms*. New York: Haworth Press.

Patel, R. (2001). Separation and divorce. In I. Glick, E. Berman, J. Clarkin, & R. Douglas (Eds.), *Marital and family therapy* (4th ed., pp. 417–435). Washington, DC: American Psychiatry Press

Pattison, E. M. (1982). Family dynamic and interventions in alcoholism. In A. S. Gurman (Ed.), *Questions and answers in the practice of family therapy* (vol. 12, pp. 158–162). New York: Brunner/Mazel.

Phillips, R. (1988). *Putting asunder: A history of divorce in Western society*. Cambridge: Cambridge University Press.

Rajadhyaksha, U., & Bhatnagar, D. (2000). Life role salience: A study of dual-career couples in the Indian context. *Human Relations, 53*(4), 489–511.

Rosenblatt, P. C. (1994). *Metaphors of family systems theory: Toward new constructions*. New York: Guilford.

Shiraev, E., & Levy, D. (2001). *Introduction to cross-cultural psychology*. Needham Heights, MA: Allyn & Bacon.

Slater, M. (1984). *Family life in the 17th century: The Verneys of Claydon House*. Boston: Routledge & Kegan Paul.

Smith, C. R. (1997). Career transistions of dual-career couples: An empirical study. *Career Development International, 2*(5), 229–237.

Stockman, N., Bonney, N., & Sheng, X. (1995). *Women's work in East and West: The dual burden of employment and family life*. Portland, OR: Book News, Inc.

PART I

The History of Family Therapy in Asia

CHAPTER 2

The Development of Family Therapy and the Experience of Fatherhood in the Japanese Context

TAKESHI TAMURA

JAPANESE CULTURE AND FAMILY

To understand Japanese families in the cultural and historical context, two kinds of social regime have to be taken into account; (a) the era of militarism before and during Word War II: and (b) the economic growth or expansion after the war (Kitaoji, 1971; Morioka, 1990). The society was very hierarchical under the military regime. Chinese teaching of Confucianism was used as a framework of discipline that people had to obey. The emperor was the top figure and whatever passed down from him had to be obeyed to the letter. The relationship in any kind of group was also defined in the hierarchical order. For example, in schools, teachers exercise authority and students are not allowed to challenge or question at all. So are family relationships. The senior man is called *master* or a *head of the family*, and holds an extreme power over the members of the family. The division of labor between the genders is clearly defined; men stay out of the family and are involved with work and women are expected to stay home and do the household chores and childrearing.

Democracy was gradually introduced after World War II. The militarism had shifted to democracy, but group orientation and hard-working ethics remained the same. People worked hard for the nation before the war and for their companies after the war. This was the key to establishing a successful economy in the last 50 years. The demand for productivity, time, and loyalty was paramount from all employees, particularly men in managerial positions. But the shortcomings were the distortion and stress on the family structure.

The gender pattern has always remained the same. Men are supposed to work hard, staying late at night during the weekdays, and playing golf with work colleagues on weekends to entertain their business partners. As a result, mothers take on the major responsibility in childrearing and maintain very close (often enmeshed) relationships with their children throughout the childhood years and into adolescence and young adulthood (up to their twenties). On the other hand, the father remains a peripheral figure in the family, but is still expected to function as head of the family. He is like the president of a poorly-functioning company or organization. The head of the organization has to be a leader even though he may not know what is going on within the system.

The Japanese are highly group-oriented, which can be contrasted with the individualism of the Western culture. Japanese people value *dependence* more in a positive way (Doi, 1973). It may be just a matter of balancing the opposite ends of the scale in regard to personal closeness. People are connected to each other and at the same time separated from each other. These elements have been a part of Japanese families for generations. Too much independence (separateness) causes isolation, just as too much dependence (connectedness) causes enmeshed relationships (Tamura & Lau, 1992). The point where people feel most comfortable on the separated/connected continuum may differ by individual, gender, and culture. The Western culture values separateness and independence, whereas Japanese culture values connectedness and closeness.

The differences came from the different view of the world according to their religious backgrounds. The Judeo-Christian religion is very much a "father-like" religion, whereas Buddhism and Shintoism are much more "mother-like" religions (Doi, 1973). In Christianity, the most important relationship is between God and the individual. This relationship is said to be manifested in one's daily life and is observed by others. Western theology teaches that one needs to be conscious of God watching over humankind, and doing good deeds defines how good one is.

On the other hand, reincarnation is one of the most important messages of Buddhism. One is to be born, die, and be reborn. This belief perpetuates the need to relate meaningfully to all existing elements in this world, particularly with other human beings. The focus is on relatedness and connectedness (Tamura & Lau, 1992). For example, the mosquito that annoys you or the cow that you are eating may be your friend from previous lives. So the most important relationship is not with any form of deities, but with all the living creatures around you. Therefore, people are taught for generations to live in harmony. They must watch over each other. One is taught that he or she need not be conscious of the watching eyes of Buddha, but rather be aware of the people who are around him or her. Good deeds in this sense are deeds defined in relational terms. People who can stay harmonious with others are most valued and respected.

UNDERSTANDING THE JAPANESE FAMILY

Families as Closed Systems

Eastern tradition defines the man as the head of the family. The old family law postulated that men could divorce their wives but women could not divorce their husbands. They have to define the boundary of the power to maintain their power. Therefore, family boundaries are very rigid. The boss takes all the responsibilities for whatever happens in the family (Kitaoji, 1971). Outside agencies are not allowed to intervene in family matters. This creates difficulties for any third parties (therapists, social workers, etc.) who intervene with the families in crisis.

In the traditional Japanese extended family, the tie and loyalty within the family system are extremely strong and well protected. The family boundary is closed to outsiders. Each family puts on a brave face to keep information and secrets among itself. It is a cultural shame to speak about negative aspects of family life (e.g., mental illness, suicide, and divorce) outside of the family. This patriarchal family system is very much characterized by the father being the boss who expects orders to be obeyed at all cost by the family members. To maintain the father's image as an authority figure, he generally remains distant from the family's daily life. The traditional assumption is that if fathers become close to children like mothers, then children will treat fathers like friends and their authority eventually will be undermined.

Strong Parent–Child Bond

The most important relationship in the modern Western nuclear family is believed to be between the husband and wife. There should be clear generational boundaries, and any close relationship that overrides the boundaries (e.g., mother–child) is regarded as *enmeshed* or a *coalition* (Minuchin, 1974). In some instances, enmeshed relationships are considered to be unhealthy, which affects the growth of an individual.

In Japanese traditional families, the most important relationship is the cross-generational relationship between the parent and child. The mother is expected to meet the physical and psychological needs of the child. Physical needs here refer to cooking, clothing, helping the child with schoolwork, and so forth. It is especially so for sons, because the oldest son eventually will become the head of the family for the next generation and the aged parents will have to depend on him for future care. On the other hand, the father–child relationship tends to be more distant, but still important for the succession of family leadership. Sons also are expected to obtain their fathers' occupational skill.

It used to be the family's obligation to look after the elderly in the family. When the children are in their thirties or forties and their parents are in their sixties, their elderly can still live on without any help. Because the children are busy working and raising their own children, the elderly parents can live separately. When the parents grow old and weak and need to be looked after by others, they often decide to live together so that the younger generation can care for the parents or parents-in-law. This rejoining is very much a part of Confucian teaching about honoring one's parents at all costs. The parents look after children when they are young, so the children have the obligation to respect and look after them when they become old. One can imagine the stress on both generations, as they have to readjust to each other. The emotional ties (loyalty, obligation, dependency) stay very strong throughout their life cycles. This appears to be very different from families in the West where retirement homes and communities grow at a phenomenal rate.

Divided Gender Role

Oftentimes, Japanese families consist of a close mother and a distant father. Generally, men have to spend a lot of time at work and leave their wives and children at home. This lifestyle has been changing rapidly in the last 100 years, partly because it put a lot of stress on the family and caused many social ills. At least up until the end of World War II, the Japanese believed that women ought to be subordinate to men. The concept of gender equality was gradually introduced by the Western influence. On the surface, people accept gender equality as the ideal, but at the deeper level they still find it hard to change their traditional beliefs. Therefore, when the Japanese economy started to grow rapidly in the early 1960s, men gave themselves permission to leave the home and devote their lives to their work, almost as though they were married to the company. Women also accepted society's norm, stayed submissive to their husbands, gave up their social status, and became housewives. In a larger context, the gender divide is still rather distinct at all levels.

DEVELOPMENT OF FAMILY THERAPY IN JAPAN

The traditional form of psychotherapy in Japan has very close links to Buddhism. The "Self" is defined in relationship with Mother Nature and the ultimate goal in life is the integration of the self and the world. Societal problems arise only when one loses touch with the natural flow of wholeness. This is often in contrast with the value of self-encapsulated ego or individuality in the West.

Morita therapy and Naikan therapy are the two major schools of therapy that originated in Japan. Their underlying theory of change is very much influenced by Buddhism. Both of these approaches assume the need to find and hear one's own voice while tuning out outside voices. The voice from within oneself is considered innately good. Morita, a turn-of-the-century Japanese philosopher-psychiatrist, applied Buddhist thinking while treating neurotic patients, which later became known as Morita therapy around 1920 (Reynolds, 1980).

The main influence from the Western schools of psychotherapy had been primarily Carl Rogers' client-centered therapy. It has some similarities with the Japanese traditional therapies in that it accepts clients the way they are and avoids direct verbal confrontations. Traditional psychoanalysis, on the other hand, has not gained popularity in Japan compared to other countries. There are just a few institutions with professionals who are trained analysts. The interpretative and insight-oriented approaches do not seem to be appealing to Japanese professionals.

Systemic theory was first introduced in early 1980. The first annual meeting of the Japanese Association of Family Therapy was held in 1984 with Salvador Minuchin as a guest speaker. The number of memberships was around 400 when it started, then rapidly increased, and doubled in the 1990s. There was a period of expansion in the middle and late 1980s. It was a time of euphoria among mental health professionals, who dreamed that every clinical problem could be resolved with the new tool. Unfortunately, the rate of increase dropped in 1990s when they realized that family therapy could be a panacea.

The initial family therapy work was primarily with schizophrenics and their families in the 1970s (Makihara, 1993). Later, it shifted to the more psychoeducational approach that became a fad. Since the early 1980s, family therapy has attempted to apply to a wide variety of illnesses such as eating disorders, conduct disorders, personality disorders, depression, and psychosomatic disorders. Among these, school phobia or behavioral problems in children and adolescents have generated significant professional and social interests. The twelfth congress of the International Association for Child and Adolescent Psychiatry and Allied Professionals was held in Kyoto, Japan in 1990. The issue of school-related problems in children was cross-culturally discussed (Chiland, 1990). Professionals from all different orientations have to grapple with the most effective way to deal with such problems related to the family.

As family therapy struggles out of its infancy in Japan, interest in systemic work is picking up momentum. Interest in family therapy has come from professionals of all orientations, but the actual number of professionals who claimed to practice family therapy has remained the same. Some of the reasons are that:

1. Training in the family system is not very well organized. Family therapy is taught in various settings, such as the National Institute of Mental Health, a few medical schools, child guidance centers, family courts, probation offices, and private practices. Throughout the years, different agencies and institutions have conducted workshops offered by overseas experts. David McGill and Cathy Colman came to Aoibashi Family Service in Kyoto in 1985 to train. Matsuda Clinic in Osaka organized a series of family therapy workshops in affiliation with the U.S. Menninger Clinic. The Institute of Family Systemic Consultation International in Chiba organized annual international workshops where master therapists such as Howard Liddle, Karl Tomm, Bunny Duhl, Maurizio Andolfi, and Jay Haley were invited to conduct numerous workshops. All of these courses and seminars generated curiosity in family therapy, but they are not extensive enough as a training program to train family therapists in Japan. There are very few organized training programs that include various schools of theories and practice, and clinical case supervision.
2. Theories and practices of family therapy are borrowed from Western therapists, and we are unable to integrate some of the ideas and philosophies into Japanese culture. There are reported practices such as *Kan-no-mushi*, which is a unique externalization of the internal conflict (Tomm, Suzuki, & Suzuki, 1990). Other veteran Japanese therapists extended the concept of family boundary to "family membrane" in order to include the ambiguous nature of the relationships (Kameguchi & Murphy-Shigematsu, 2001). Shimosaka, a former president of the Japanese Association of Family Therapy, was influenced by Buddhist philosophy and systemic thinking. He extended the understanding of relationships, not only the relational term "self and others," but all the reciprocal relationships, including even tiny dust in the wholeness. He emphasized the importance of understanding by intuition, not by intellectual and operational terms. He documented all the attitudes that are taken for granted and therefore not articulated, and called it "common sense" family therapy (Shimosaka & Shibusawa, 1996). In Japan, family therapists can get caught up with new theories instead of clinical work, and they can become rather lopsided. From the Universalist position, any theory and practice can be applied to any cultural context. On the other hand, they have to be culturally sensitive to appropriately adapt the different theories. This is a struggle that we have here in Japan. The differences between Japan and the West can be enormous, which makes cultural adaptation a daunting task.

3. There are difficulties in motivating fathers to be involved in therapy. When the idea of family therapy was first introduced in the early 1980s, one main argument among therapists was who should be involved in treatment. Others argued the severe limitations of family therapy without inviting all the members in the family. Most Western therapists without hesitation require the whole family to be involved. In Japan, the mother comes, but not the father. When a child shows any signs of a problem, his or her mother is the first to be involved. The father, on the other hand, is deeply concerned, but unfortunately his primary task is to his work and his involvement is minimal or nonexistent. If the mother accompanies the child to the clinic, the father has no reason to be there as well, because he is not in charge of family affairs. In this sense he knows little about the children and family. This is typical of fatherhood in Japan. Family therapists had to struggle with this pervasive trend in the past, often with much frustration and intimidation. Fortunately, this trend has changed to some extent in the 1990s. Because of the Japanese economic depression, men do not need to work as long as they used to. This forces them to participate more in everyday family matters. This leads to a slight differentiation of role in the family but it is still difficult, especially for men who grew up in a fatherless family.
4. The next two reasons are not specific to family therapy, but can be applied to psychotherapy in general. In Japan, unlike medical doctors or nurses, clinical psychologists or psychotherapists do not have state licenses and their jobs are not recognized as a specialty by the government. It was only a few decades ago that psychotherapists were more employable in hospitals as psychotherapy and counseling became a part of the cultural repertory to deal with emotional problems. Currently, there are quite a few psychologists or psychotherapists who have started their own businesses, and their need in the society has increased in the last 20 years. However, the government is slow to implement new licenses for clinical psychologists and psychotherapists. The Japanese Association of Clinical Psychology is the only gatekeeper that issues the right to practice for qualified psychologists. This lack of recognition by governmental bodies also reflects the people's mistrust in psychotherapy, and holds prejudice toward emotional problems as a sign of weakness or immaturity.
5. The fee for medical doctors is counted by the point system defined by social medical insurance. Psychotherapy, on the other hand, is not properly counted. Some family therapy that takes more than an hour is counted like a complete blood test, which takes less than 5 minutes. Psychiatrists can make more money by prescribing antidepressants than by offering full therapy. This time element in treatment rules out getting reimbursement for family therapy from medical insurances.

CONTEMPORARY FAMILY PROBLEMS

Truancy in the School System

Truancy or refusing to go to school is one of the biggest challenges for Japanese family therapists. In most reported cases, children reject schools during preadolescence because of separation anxiety from their mothers. However, most cases occur after adolescence. In such cases, the child indicates no problem at the beginning of elementary school but eventually completely shuns school. Many family therapists try to explain this problem from the family dynamic perspective. One of the most widely accepted hypotheses is the combination of enmeshed relationships between the child and mother, whereas the father is emotionally distant from the family. Although the identified adolescent has a symbiotic relationship with his or her mother, the fathers in these cases are absent because of work commitments, marital conflict, or difficult in-laws. This creates further difficulties for the child to form personal relationships with people outside the family (Chiland, 1990; Tamura, 1993). It is very interesting that they may not have problems before puberty, but as they advance into adolescence, their relationships with friends suddenly become problematic. They become very self-conscious and have a sense of ambivalence about being accepted and at the same time fear rejection. Those adolescents who have a close relationship with their mothers and a distant relationship with their fathers cannot regulate the distance with other people. Often they have the omnipotent illusion that their close friend can fulfill all their needs like their mothers do.

Part of the reason why school-related problems are so prevalent comes from the development of the Japanese school system, parents, teachers, and the Japanese society as a whole, which sets extremely high academic standards for their children. Children receive a lot of pressure about academic achievement. School rules are very strict. Students have to wear school uniforms and follow many regulations. Many education professionals believe that these are the main reasons students refuse to go to school and find other ways to act out their problems.

Another reason is their limited ability to relate with other people. Most of the children who refuse to go to school are not actually refusing school itself. They feel relatively comfortable during class with their teachers. All they have to do is sit still and passively listen or take notes. When they feel most uncomfortable is during the break and at lunchtime. They have to deal with friends spontaneously. This should be the fun part of school for ordinary children, but some find it to be most difficult to deal with personal relationships with friends.

Family Violence

Violence in the family has also been the focus of interest among family therapists. There are many forms of family violence in Japan. The type of violence that is unique in the Japanese family is the adolescent child beating up his or her parents. Many find reasons not to go to school in spite of strong pressure for academic achievement. The children are frustrated at not being able to socialize in school, and violently release their internal conflict at their parents (often mothers), whom they are most closely attached to (Tamura, 1993).

Another form of family violence is child abuse. This was regarded as a rare phenomenon until the late 1980s (Ikeda, 1982). The abuse cases were kept well under the carpet. Professionals in child guidance centers could not manage the cases properly because of the strong *parental rights* guaranteed by civil law. Things started to change in 1991 when volunteer groups in Osaka and Tokyo set up children's emergency telephone lines for abuse victims. Very interestingly, the most frequent callers were neither abused children nor third parties, but rather perpetrators who were seeking help for themselves. They were typically housewives from intact families, whose husbands worked very hard and offered very little help in raising their children (Tamura, 1993). They were very isolated, and often had been traumatized in childhood by their own parents. The society itself has been sensitized in the last decade by the mass media, which covered many incidents of serious child abuse cases. The number of abuse cases reported to child guidance centers have drastically increased in the last 10 years. A new child protection law was introduced in 2000 that made it easier for professionals such as social workers and police to intervene in such abuses.

Domestic violence (men generally are the perpetrators) came to the public's attention in the last 5 years. Social supports for battered women such as shelters and counseling services have been set up by governmental and nongovernmental groups. Support treatment groups for women and men have sprung up as well. The increase in domestic violence seems to relate to the economic depression that Japan is going through. The loss of jobs or demotions have increasingly been key stress factors in the Japanese family.

THE EXPERIENCE OF FATHERHOOD

The Traditional Father

From the 1960s to the early 1980s, the Japanese collectively believed that economic success was the top priority for men. The definition of masculinity then was measured primarily by their success in the workplace. The purpose and satisfaction of men's life came solely from their work. Capable and successful persons (mostly men) were and are expected by their companies to spend long hours at work. They normally come home very late at night, only to sleep and leave early in the morning. Some even sleep in quarters provided by their companies. Even on weekends, there are work-related activities. This leaves them little time to spend with their family. But the fathers and members of the family do not see this as a problem. The absent father in a way is a sign of a successful man. This idea became a Japanese subculture. The mother has the unspoken responsibility of taking charge of everything in the family, including childrearing. She may not feel supported by her husband, but it is regarded to be something she has to put up with.

Husbands' relationships with their wives are rather distant as well. They spend a small amount of time together. However, they can trust each other, and believe they can understand each other without words and without seeing each other very much.

The father–child relationship is often very distant. They spend very little time together, but children can still hold a positive and intimate image of the absent father. After all, it is the mother's job to help children create that positive image. There is a saying that children grow up by watching the "back" of their father. Children may not be able to see their father's face, but they imagine their relationship with father by just looking at his back. This has been successful to some extent, and it was the cultural norm at that time.

A New Type of Father

In the early 1990s when the Japanese economy began to fall apart, people suddenly realized that working too much created problems such as suicide in middle age and *karo-shi,* or sudden death syndrome, among workaholic men. Men came to the realization that work commitment did not provide their purpose in life anymore. They looked at family life as a possible source of happiness. However, they had not learned how to communicate as an active member of the family because most of *their* fathers were also absent when they were young.

Most of the men I encounter in family therapy appear to lose confidence and do not know how to take on the role of husband and father in the family. He may try to be nice to the family and become a *friend* to his children. As a result, he cannot exercise any authority, and becomes overindulgent with the children. On the contrary, he may believe a father must be aggressive to be respected by the children, so he becomes abusive to the children and rejected by them and his wife.

His wife, on the other hand, may still hold the image of the traditional family that a wife and mother needs to be in charge of the family and should not ask her husband for help. In this kind of family, the husband may try to be involved in childrearing, but his wife dominates. As a result, the husband gradually becomes peripheral. The father's difficulty continues when the children grow to adolescence. The children become rebellious against the father's authority. It is a very difficult job for the father to set the right limits with the growing adolescents; unfortunately, Japanese fathers tend to have a hard time.

Solutions to the Absent Fathers

It is very difficult to engage the peripheral fathers in family therapy. They tend to be absent not only from family life, but also from therapy. They are not included in a problem-solving system at home. In other words, once the system has changed its configuration and the father is invited, the family problem seems to resolve automatically. It is a new experience for them to talk in the family with the father being included. This "third" factor sometimes stiffens the progress the family makes in therapy.

At times, the wife resents her husband's involvement. His involvement could confuse her role. If the father is involved, she will have to minimize her role as the primary caregiver of the children, and this can be stressful for her. The question is, Why does she need the father now? It is certainly a hard task to share her power with her partner. For the housewife who stays home all the time, her children are the only beings over whom she can exercise her power.

Therapists need to understand the structure of the Japanese family without a father. Men do not come to therapy, either because they are busy working or because of their immature personalities. It is characteristic of the system that fathers are excluded from solving the family's problem. Family members often invalidate any action of the therapist to include the father in therapy. Therapists have to bear this in mind; otherwise they might misunderstand the reason why men do not come for family therapy.

CONCLUSION

I have outlined some of the tasks of family therapists for the survival of Japanese families in the twenty-first century. One needs to devise a cultural model that is congruent to the Japanese value, not just a carbon copy of the Western model. They have to be sensitive to the traditions and nature of relationships in the Japanese family. The unique gender pattern of the Japanese family also needs to be taken into account, as well as ways of integrating it into modern family life.

Family therapy and other forms of psychotherapy will take time to be more socially accepted. State qualification for the clinical psychologist and training courses at a master level aimed for experienced therapists are definitely needed for the future. The social insurance system also needs to change so that people can comfortably consult family therapists with less financial stress.

Finally, helping professionals need to work as a united front to solve the complicated issues in modern Japanese families. For example, mental health professionals, school teachers, and school nurses need to work together as a team in order to deal with school-related problems. Powerful intervention by social workers, the police, and other legal authorities is needed to deal with domestic violence in the family. Therapists need to work collaboratively with the family courts and probation officers to deal with juvenile delinquencies and marital discord. At the moment, these professionals are isolated and work on their own.

The development of family therapy in Japan has been gradual and to a large degree significant compared to other Asian countries. We have the luxury of attracting some of the best family therapist trainers and maintain an infrastructure that the next generation of family therapists can build on. We still have a lot to accomplish but "a journey of a thousand miles begins with the first step."

REFERENCES

Chiland, C. (1990). *Why children reject school: Views from seven countries*. New Haven, CT: Yale University Press.

Doi, L. T. (1973). *The anatomy of dependence* (John Bester, Trans.). Tokyo: Kodansha International.

Ikeda, Y. (1982). A short introduction to child abuse in Japan. *Child Abuse and Neglect, 6,* 487–490.

Kameguchi, K., & Murphy-Shigematsu, S. (2001). Family psychology and family therapy in Japan. *American Psychologist, 56*(1), 65–70.

Kitaoji, H. (1971). The structure of the Japanese family. *American Anthropologist, 73,* 1036–1057.

Makihara, H. (1993). Reflections on the tenth anniversary of the founding of JAFT (in Japanese). *Japanese Journal of Family Therapy, 10*(2), 85–91.

Minuchin, S. (1974). *Families and family therapy*. London: Tavistock Publications.

Morioka, K. (1990). Demographic family changes in contemporary Japan. *International Social Science Journal, 42*(4), 511–522.

Reynolds, D. K. (1980). *The quiet therapies. Japanese pathways to personal growth*. Honolulu: University of Hawaii Press.

Shimosaka, K., & Shibusawa, T. (1996). Present situation of family therapy: Japan and the U.S. (in Japanese). *Seishin Igaku (Psychiatry), 38*(10), 1022–1034.

Tamura, T. (1993). Child abuse versus school refusal: Contrasting family crisis in Britain and Japan. *Bulletin of Tokyo Gakugei University VI, 45,* 113–123.

Tamura, T., & Lau, A. (1992). Connectedness vs. separateness: Applicability of family therapy to Japanese families. *Family Process, 31*(4), 319–340.

Tomm, K., Suzuki, K., & Suzuki, K. (1990). The kan-no-mushi: An inner externalization that enables compromise? *Australian and New Zealand Journal of Family Therapy, 11*(2), 104–107.

CHAPTER 3

Family Therapy in Malaysia

An Update

KIT S. NG

Malaysia is a culturally and religiously diverse country of about 19 million people consisting of 59% Malays and other indigenous groups, 32% Chinese, and 9% Indians/others. Most Malays (Bumiputras) are Muslims and most Chinese are Buddhists. A minority of the Indians, Chinese, and Eurasians are Christians; however, Hinduism is also a noticeable religion in Malaysia. Each ethnic group strongly adheres to its religious and cultural beliefs. Although the English language is widely used in Malaysia, the official language is Malay. Malaysians are accustomed to using several languages in their school systems and in official business. Malaysia is one of the fastest growing countries in Southeast Asia and is rapidly becoming a major economic force. The escalated growth toward urbanization during the last 30 years has mobilized concentrated efforts toward adequate social welfare and human service programs by the Malaysian government. This trend is clearly evident in the country's massive drug rehabilitation programs and its emphasis on reducing juvenile delinquency (Scorzelli, 1986, 1992). Although the efforts have significantly reduced drug abuse, there are still questions regarding juvenile delinquency.

THE NEW MALAYSIA

Malaysia has been very fortunate compared to other developing countries. With vast natural resources and steady economic growth, Malaysians have enjoyed a very comfortable standard of living. Because of consistent economic growth, Malaysians are also forced to adjust to many socioeconomic changes. For the last 15 to 20 years, there has been a mass migration of the different ethnic groups to bigger cities for better and more lucrative jobs. The side effects have been the mushrooming of numerous suburbs on the outskirts of some cities, primarily Kuala Lumpur and Johor Bahru. This, in turn, has intensified the need for more and better psychological services to handle the stress of the urban lifestyle. To answer this challenge, the Malaysian government has made a long-term commitment to deal with these problems to build a safer Malaysia for future generations. This has resulted in the government's commitment to train counselors for drug rehabilitation and school counseling. Currently, about one-third of all Malaysian universities have different counseling programs to train local counselors that emphasize primarily school and community counseling. Both the Ministry of Social Welfare and the Ministry of Home Affairs have been instrumental in planning training programs for community counseling. Recently, the Minister of Education, Datuk Seri Najib Abdul Razak, challenged human service professionals to move into uncharted territories such as research and industry to boost productivity and efficiency (Najib, 1996). Malaysia's mental health workers and human rights advocates also have organized programs to deal with domestic violence, incest, marital discord, parenting issues, relationship enhancement, stress management, and family conflict. As the Malaysian society grows to be more complex and sophisticated, there is a definite need for a more comprehensive mental health program to promote its services to the general public.

CONTEMPORARY MALAYSIAN FAMILIES

Malaysian family systems are the byproducts of a complex mixture of Malay, Chinese, Indian, and Eurasian influences from different historical and cultural backgrounds. Each family has its roots in different civilizations and has required long periods of cultural adaptation to the local environment. The Malay and other related indigenous families have long inhabited Malaysia. In most cases, Malay families adhere to Islam. However, a small percentage of the indigenous families are practicing Protestants or Roman Catholics. Malay families have traditionally established themselves in the rural areas of Malaysia. Chinese families have their historical roots mostly in Southern China. Their migration efforts brought them to larger towns and cities, where they have traditionally been involved in tin mining, trading, and commerce. The Chinese have always maintained their own cultural identities and strictly adhered to Confucian ethics. Most Indian ancestors were from Southern India; they came to work in rural rubber plantations during the colonial days. Like other immigrants, the Indians have followed their religious beliefs for generations.

The contrast of Malaysian family systems of a decade ago with those of today is striking in some ways and nil in others. The different families have come a long way from the days when working in the villages and rice fields was an acceptable way of life. Today, especially the second- and third- generation families have migrated to sizable towns and cities to seek a better way of life. Families in general have become more affluent. It is not an uncommon sight to see families having two cars, dining in expensive Western restaurants, planning luxurious vacations, and shopping for niceties to decorate their homes.

There are also significant changes in the perception of mental health by contemporary Malaysian families. In the past, seeking mental health treatment was considered a cultural taboo and ethnic shame. Today, it seems to be a more acceptable alternative to holistic health. Recently, there have been numerous advertised workshops, open discussions, and seminars on enhancing self-esteem, parenting issues, stress management, positive body image, and mate selection. There was even an open forum on how to handle chronic student dropouts and truancy problems in the public school systems ("In place," 1996). Some educators advocated the traditional use of "caning" and others suggested therapy involving the parents. A few years ago, educators suggested the use of family therapy to deal with elementary and secondary students with chronic behavioral problems. Those suggestions were not adequately followed through on for a few years because of the lack of familiarity with therapy techniques that involved other family members. In June 1996, once again, the issue of family therapy was brought up by some concerned educators in a written debate on the caning of problematic students. Numerous key educators advocated the idea of utilizing family therapy in addition to individual therapy to deal with chronic behavioral problems. Currently, there seems to be renewed interest in looking at family therapy as a viable alternative to dealing with school problems.

RELIGIOUS PRACTICES VERSUS MENTAL ILLNESSES

Mental illness has long been a part of Malaysian folk history. As far back as 1846, when Malaysia was still a British colony, there were reports of individuals having public psychotic outbreaks in rural villages. This was often called "amok" and usually occurred among Malay men (Ee, 1991). Other mental illnesses, such as mass hysteria, "latah" (a conditioned behavioral response to a variety of external stimuli characterized by coprolalia, automatic obedience, and hypersuggestibility), and "Koro" (psychosomatic complaints that death will result once the genital is fully retracted) have been topics of investigation by sociologists, anthropologists, and mental health professionals in Malaysia (Bartholomew, 1994a, 1994b). Recently, the concern within the mental health community in modern Malaysia has been that mental illnesses have transcended the ancient cultural norms and are disrupting family units in Malaysia. This is largely because of the stresses of modern living.

Health authorities claimed that an average four to five out of 10 Malaysians suffered some form of psychiatric related disorders ("Expert," 1996). Other experts reported on the rise in the sexual and physical abuse of children (Kasim, Cheah, & Shafie, 1995; Kasim & Kassim, 1995); student truancy and dropouts ("In Place," 1996); domestic violence ("Women Crisis," 1996); divorce and separation; and AIDS. As mentioned, because mental illness is considered a taboo and a shame to the family, those who had mental illness were either sent to one of a few state-supported mental hospitals or sent to consult with a religious medium, shaman, or other form of primitive healer. Malaysian shamanism, often practiced on the east coast of Malaysia, appears to contain mixed elements of possession and exorcism. The patient's involvement with healers and spectators has been thought to provide a cathartic mechanism and heighten the feeling of self-worth (Laderman, 1988). The common belief among Malaysians, which include ethnic Chinese and Malays, is that too much or unexpressed "angin" (wind) within the person will breed pathology and those who possess a large amount of "angin" will be at greater risk compared to those who have a smaller amount. Patients regain health through shamanistic healing. Shamanic healing invokes a trance-like experience for the patient that is a sign that the "angin" has begun to blow freely within the person.

The Malaysian Chinese also have traditionally turned to religious rituals and herbal medicine to deal with their mental illness. Consulting with mediums and eating holy scripts written by the same medium are different ways to drive out the uninvited spirits that cause mental illness according to Chinese traditions.

Indian families have traditionally turned to their holy men for curing mental illness. Often, because of the shame of being possessed with "uninvited spirits," family members tend to hide or deny the existence of problems. Traditional religious ways of dealing with mental illness are very much a part of the Malaysian culture. This is largely owing to the belief by all ethnic groups that the causes of mental illness have their roots in the religious belief that one is being invaded by foreign spirits. In order to be cured, one needs to get help to drive those spirits out of the physical body. Even the very rich and the educated elite of Malaysia are not immune to these traditional beliefs. Recently, a saga entitled "The divorce battle" was disclosed concerning a wealthy Malaysian chief executive who divorced his wife after 18 years of marriage. The plaintiff alleged that her Muslim husband had a habit of abandoning her throughout their married life. She filed for a 200 million dollar settlement. The point of this saga was that in the process of working on their separation and divorce, a famous *bomoh*, or medicine man, was consulted to settle the divorce and deal with other family problems ("Business and Politics," 1996).

Malaysia is constantly struggling to incorporate other forms of therapeutic treatment into the religious, traditional ways. The advanced training of numerous mental health professionals, primarily from abroad, has continued to challenge the traditional methods. Lately, there have been some discussions on an integrated model. Azhar and Varma (1995) advocated the use of a mixture of cognitive and religious therapy for pathological bereavement and depressed patients. The approach seemed to have significant therapeutic effects with Malays from very religious backgrounds. Different ongoing attempts have been made to integrate therapy from an Islamic perspective. Several papers on the various approaches were presented at the Sixth Conference on Islamic Counseling in August, 1996 in Kuala Lumpur. Other experts discovered group therapy for the family to be a viable alternative to helping family members deal with their transitional needs (Anderson, 1990).

THE EMERGENCE OF FAMILY THERAPY

One piece of the jigsaw puzzle that has been missing in the mental health history of Malaysia is the lack of emphasis on systemic family therapy. The training and promotion of human services for the practice of family therapy is very minimal by the different government agencies. Culturally, family therapy is a taboo or shame for all the ethnic groups in Malaysia. The notion that family problems need to be dealt with only within the family is still a widely held tradition. Common interventions such as confrontations, role clarification, and boundary setting may be helpful in Western society but not in Malaysia (Scorzelli, 1987). This may contribute to the lack of interest in systems theory and thinking in the existing training programs. Some of the closest work with families has only involved family members in drug rehabilitation programs in order to educate immediate family members about the treatment milieu. The paradox seems to be that the current emphasis has ignored the family as part of treatment, although traditionally the family is considered an important resource by all Malaysian ethnic groups.

Currently, there is minimal training and practice of systemic family therapy in Malaysia. Some family therapy is done by a few psychologists, mental health counselors, and pastoral counselors in the capital city of Kuala Lumpur. Most of the academic training in the different universities over the last 20 to 25 years has been in counseling education and psychology, with the exception of a new family counseling track in the education department at a local university. This new track is in its infancy and is slowly gaining recognition.

Three Different Levels of Intervention

Intervention by a One-Stop Center

Traditionally, Malaysians who needed mental health services were referred to state-supported mental hospitals. Most of the hospitals were understaffed with very few trained mental health professionals. Medications have been the most common method of treatment besides solitary confinement. Patients who are more functional are introduced to occupational or recreational therapy. The introduction of family therapy and family psychoeducation was initiated in a few church-supported drug rehabilitation centers, primarily in Kuala Lumpur. Family members were encouraged to get involved in counseling education with drug abusers who were undergoing treatment. Lately, because of the concerns about the upsurge in domestic violence, child abuse, and rape, a one-stop center has been initiated by the government. This crisis-related center seemed to work very effectively in Penang Hospital, where it was first started ("Women Crisis," 1996). The victims, mostly women, received counseling, police interviews, and court appearance preparation to help deal with their stress. Some forms of family therapy are also provided as a means of support for the victim. Other major cities have begun to offer mental health services to the public. From this very humble beginning, the role of family therapy is accepted in part as a form of treatment for the victims.

Intervention by the Religious Leadership

This is the most common form of intervention. Parishioners and worshippers feel a strong bond and attachment to the leadership of their places of worship. A senior pastor once expressed privately that he was so glad that finally one of his associates was coming back from Australia with a graduate social work degree to help with the counseling work in his church. The clergy leadership, with minimal or no formal training in family therapy, are often forced to work with the problems of spousal abuse, infidelity, depression, communication, problems with in-laws, and parenting issues of their parishioners. Another pastor took a professional approach by referring one of his male parishioners who had exhibited bizarre behavior to one of the few psychiatrists in town. Most of the work done by religious leaders is generally supportive in nature, usually giving advice. The emphasis is often on making mutual adjustments in order to make the relationship work.

Intervention by the Family Court Systems

Even though the divorce rate in Malaysia is still relatively low compared to most Western countries, divorce is becoming a growing concern of the religious leadership. The Islamic Family Law Act of 1984 is still being reinforced by the Shariah court as the country's law for marriage and divorce. The Shariah court system is the regulatory body of Muslim law concerning marriage and divorce. The law has changed drastically during the last 20 years by making the process of divorce lengthier and more time consuming, aimed at reducing divorce. The court's main focus is to reconcile and settle the differences between the different parties, and divorce is generally not granted until some reconciliatory efforts have been attempted. Some judges even go so far as to require the couple to get counseling for at least 3 months before proceeding to formally hear the case (Jones, 1994). In some cases, the court referred the couples to family counseling by the "Kadi" (court registrar) or social workers appointed by the court. The court-appointed counselors initially interview the husband and wife separately, and later talk with the couple together. Going to divorce court always appears to be the last resort for couples trying to settle their differences and, in most cases, heralds the termination of the marriage. The utilization of family counseling by the court has indicated the need for systemic intervention from a nonpsychiatric point of view.

CONCLUSION

The future of family therapy in Malaysia is very uncertain, partly because of the lack of training and interest of mental health professionals. On the other hand, problems related to the family are surging. In many ways, Malaysia is like the United States in the 1950s to 1960s, when the family therapy movement was in its early development. The rate of growth may never be as fast and extensive because of the primary focus on economic development by the government. Therefore, there is always room for new methods, research development, and other pioneering work. The government has expressed support for a more comprehensive mental health care program for all Malaysians by the year 2020, also called Vision 2020. In light of Vision 2020 the obvious question is, "What role does family therapy play in Malaysia?" This very pressing question confronts mental health professionals within the Malaysian context. The Malaysian mental health community cannot afford to ignore the efficiency and effectiveness of family therapy. The time has come to consider seriously integrating family therapy training and practice into the existing training programs.

REFERENCES

Anderson, J. D. (1990). Group work with families: A multicultural perspective. *Social Work with Groups*, *13*(4), 85–101.

Azhar, M. Z., & Varma, S. L. (1995). Religious psychotherapy as management of bereavement. *Acta Psychiatrica Scandinavica*, *91*, 233–235.

Bartholomew, R. E. (1994a). Disease, disorder, or deception? Latah as habit in a Malay extended family. *The Journal of Nervous and Mental Disease*, *182*(6), 331–337.

Bartholomew, R. E. (1994b). The social psychology of "epidemic" koro. *The International Journal of Social Psychiatry*, *40*(1), 46–60.

Business and politics meet thugs and magic spells in saga coming to trial. (August, 1996). *The Wall Street Journal*, p. A 11.

Ee, H. K. (1991). Amok in nineteenth-century British Malaya history. *History of Psychiatry*, *3*, 429–436.

Expert: More suffer from mental illness. (June, 1996). *The Star*, p. 5.

In place: Counseling for students. (May, 1996). *New Straits Times*, p. 15.

Jones, G. (1994). *Marriage and divorce in Islamic South East-Asia*. Malaysia, Kuala Lumpur: Oxford University Press.

Kasim, S. M., Cheah, I., & Shafie, M. H. (1995). Childhood deaths from physical abuse. *Child Abuse and Neglect*, *19*, 847–854.

Kasim, S. M., & Kassim, K. (1995). Child sexual abuse: Psychosocial aspects of 101 cases seen in an urban Malaysian setting. *Child Abuse and Neglect*, *19*, 793–799.

Laderman, C. (1988). Wayward winds: Malay archetypes and theory of personality in the context of shamanism. *Social Science and Medicine*, *27*(8), 799–810.

Najib, J. (1996, July). Psychology can help boost productivity. *The New Street Times*, p. 8.

Scorzelli, J. F. (1986). Malaysia rehabilitation system: A challenge to the drug problem. *Journal of Applied Rehabilitation Counseling*, *17*, 21–24.

Scorzelli, J. F. (1987). Counseling in Malaysia: An emerging profession. *Journal of Counseling and Development*, *65*, 238–240.

Scorzelli, J. F. (1992). Has Malaysia's antidrug effort been effective? *Journal of Substance Abuse Treatment*, *9*, 171–176.

Women crisis centres at all state hospitals. (May, 1996). *The Sun*, p. 3.

CHAPTER 4

The Emergence of Family Therapy in Postmodern Singapore

AUGUSTINE TAN

This chapter traces the emergence of family therapy in Singapore. After an introductory section, where a brief history of Singapore and some current demographic information are presented, the professional context in which the development of family therapy in Singapore has taken place is discussed.

Singapore, an island republic, is located at the tip of Peninsular Malaysia in Southeast Asia, just north of the equator. Consisting of the main island of Singapore and some 63 offshore islands, Singapore is home to about 3 million people (Singapore Government, 1997).

Historically, Singapore was founded by Sir Stamford Raffles in 1819 as a trading station of the British East India Company. With the opening up of the Suez Canal in 1869, Singapore was able to capitalize on its strategic position to become a major port of call for ships plying between East Asia and Europe. It also became the main sorting and export center in the world for rubber as a result of the development of the rubber planting industry (Singapore Government, 1999b).

By the end of the nineteenth century, Singapore was experiencing "unprecedented prosperity" (Singapore Government, 1999b, p. 19). This prosperity attracted numerous immigrants in search of economic opportunities. Immigrants came from China, India, and nearby Indonesia and Malaysia. It continued as a colony of the British Empire until internal self-government was achieved in 1959. Singapore finally became a fully independent and sovereign nation on August 9, 1965.

With independence, "commenced Singapore's struggle to survive and prosper on its own. It also had to create a sense of national identity and consciousness among a disparate population of immigrants" (Singapore Government, 1999b, p. 22). Thus, it is against this backdrop of a migrant's survival mentality, and the fact of diverse, immigrant, although mainly Asian, cultural identities that the emergence of family therapy has taken place.

Singapore's population is made up of three major ethnic groups: the Chinese, Indians, and Malays. The Chinese and Indians of Singapore today are largely the descendents of migrant workers who came from China and India during the 1800s and early 1900s, respectively. The Malays are people indigenous to the area and are mainly from Malaysia and Indonesia. Four major dialect groups of Chinese came: the Hokkiens, Teochews, Cantonese, and Hakkas. The Indians came from the Indian subcontinent, as well as from Penang and Sri Lanka. When Singapore was made a penal colony by the British in 1823, a few hundred Indian convicts were brought in to help with the work of civil construction. However, the vast majority of Indians who came were brought in as indentured laborers, mostly from South India.

Today, the Chinese are the largest group, making up some 77% of the population. They are followed by the Malays (14%), the Indians (7.6%), and a group consisting of persons from other ethnic groups (1.4%). Among those in the "Others" group are persons of mixed Euro-Asia parentage called Eurasians.

This process of racial integration is likely to be ongoing, especially in light of the government's current strategy of encouraging the inflow of foreign talent to the country. In recent years, the issue of ethnicity in family therapy has gained prominence (Lau, 1984; McGoldrick, 1982). In a sense, Singapore is like the United States, where for over 200 years a "variety of cultural groups from all over the world . . . have coexisted" (McGoldrick, 1982, p. 3). In Singapore too, the various cultures have also not "melded."

McGoldrick (1982) has pointed to the paucity of material on the impact of ethnicity on family therapy. In Singapore, very little has been written about the impact of Western ideas and methods of family therapy on local practice. Blake (1991) has written a seminal article on this issue, in which she discussed the applicability of the Western conceptualization of family therapy, in terms of both theories and techniques, to countries with different social, economic, and political systems. She wrote this article in the hope "that the framework provided in this paper suggests the conceptual base" (Blake, 1991, p. 57) from which analyses on the portability of family therapy to different contexts can be examined. However, hardly any local literature has since emerged from it.

THE PROFESSIONAL CONTEXT FOR THE DEVELOPMENT OF FAMILY THERAPY

The development of family therapy in Singapore cannot be discussed apart from the development of counseling as a profession. It is also of interest that counseling, and therefore, family therapy grew out of the context of social service rather than the hospital or mental health settings. It was among the social workers and those working in social service agencies that family therapy first took roots.

Therefore, for the purpose of this chapter, the emergence of family therapy is discussed within the larger context of counseling and social service development in Singapore.

The Historical Development of Counseling in Singapore

In 1992, Yeo (p. 20) wrote that "Unlike its Western counterparts, family therapy only became part of the mental health scene in recent years; as a professional discipline it is in its infancy." This according to Yeo (1992, p. 20) is "inevitable," given the brief history of counseling and psychotherapy in Singapore.

Counseling as a distinct professional activity had its roots in the mid-1960s with the setting up of the Churches Counselling Service in 1966. This pioneer counseling service was initiated by a group of concerned Christians who saw the need to provide professional help for those with psychological and emotional problems. It is interesting to note that, at that point in time, there were "very few people trained in psychology and most of the counseling was conducted by social workers and religious leaders" (Yeo, 1992).

Counseling as it was practiced then, was very much influenced by the individualistic focus of Western thoughts and tended to exclude the family. This was not surprising given that the early pioneers of professional counseling had their training in the West. However, this created some difficulties, because an Asian tends to see himself or herself first as a member of a family and community, and second as an individual.

This failure to take the family system into consideration may well have an adverse effect on the therapeutic outcome; either alienating the individual from the family or maintaining the problem. The early practitioners of counseling in Singapore adopted counseling orientations that were then established or popular in the West. Many of them were grounded in Rogerian therapy. Other forms of therapy included Gestalt therapy, behavioral therapy, psychodynamic approaches, and transactional analysis. Although the focus was essentially on the individual, some practitioners also did group counseling.

There was clearly no systemic thinking or a family approach in those early days of counseling. Yeo (1992) pointed out that:

> If a child were to be treated for psychological problems, he or she would be seen individually and the focus of therapy would be the child and what goes on inside. Any attention given to family members would often be in order to delve deeper into the child's psyche or behaviour. (p. 20)

It would appear that even "when family problems were treated, the focus was on individual members. Marriage counseling was also conducted in similar fashion" (Yeo, 1992, p. 20). Any family counseling attempted then was conducted based on an understanding of groups and group processes, with the family treated as a group.

The Development of Family Therapy in Singapore

Blake (1991) believes that several factors create a conducive climate for the development of family therapy in Singapore.

First is the multicultural population of Singapore's 3 million people, many of whom live all their lives in this City Island. The three dominant racial/cultural groups, the Chinese-Taoist/Confucian, Indian-Hindu or Muslim, and Malay-Muslim, all have a family orientation "in which the advice of family elders, religious leaders or traditional healers would be sought in the event of family conflict" (Blake, 1991, p. 33).

Second, enormous changes have taken place since Singapore attained independence from Britain in 1965. These changes in social policies and conditions, politics, and the economy have affected family life and expectations in major ways. Blake (1991) pointed out that:

> In recent years, official policy has influenced family size, encouraged women to enter the work force, urged families to look after their elderly, promoted the establishment of child-care centres, and encouraged an extensive parent-education program. A successful public housing scheme provides accommodation to 87% of the population in high-rise flats. These conditions represent a change, in one generation, to the way family members relate to each other and their neighbours. Today's parents are not only more confined within the walls of family residence they have few appropriate models of family life to fit contemporary challenges. (p. 33)

Third, there is the ever-increasing influence of television; families are now more exposed to democratic styles of family communication and Western ideas. Blake (1991) believes that the preceding factors led to a readiness to accept professional expertise for the solution of family stress, possibly even for Western styles of family therapy, particularly among the English-educated middle classes (p. 33). This observation by Blake appears to be supported in a recent study in which the patterns of help-seeking behavior were analyzed. It is interesting to note that "expert assistance" now ranks ahead of "extended families" as a source of help when families face difficulties (Quah, 1999, p. 50).

Up to the Mid-1980s: The Early Development of Family Therapy

The Counselling and Care Centre, which had played a key role in the development of professional counseling and the training of professional counselors, also pioneered the development of family therapy in Singapore.

In one sense, the pioneering role of the Counselling and Care Centre began at its inception. Yeo (personal communication, November 23, 1999) commented that although the Counselling and Care Centre adopted an essentially individual focus in counseling generally, it was also focused on working with couples with marital conflicts. Gunnar J. Teilman, the founding director, was doing marriage counseling even in the early days of the Counselling and Care Centre. According to Yeo (personal communication, November 23, 1999), therefore, the development of family therapy in Singapore started with the practice of marriage counseling.

Subsequent to its founding, Gunnar Teilman was joined at the Counselling and Care Centre by local staff, many of them graduates of the Singapore University's Social Work Department. These early pioneers in professional counseling were very soon caught up with the study and development of family therapy. The Counselling and Care Centre itself appears to have provided a conducive environment and the necessary support for this pioneering effort. According to Yeo (1992), various overseas consultants were engaged to provide expertise and direction in this effort. Among the experts consulted were Myer Katz from McGill University School of Social Work, Montreal, Canada, and Clyde Murthy from Bangalore, India. Clyde Murthy was recruited by the Counselling and Care Centre to help develop a training program in family work for social workers in Singapore.

Although there is no record of the first person to receive formal training in family therapy, the first known counseling professional in Singapore to be admitted as a Clinical Member of the American Association for Marital and Family Therapy was Anthony Yeo from the Counselling and Care Centre in 1980. According to Yeo (personal communication, November 23, 1999), around the late 1970s and early 1980s a few fellow professionals from the Counselling and Care Centre had also received some family therapy training as part of their graduate training in social work.

Also in the early 1980s when the Counseiling and Care Centre was moving toward the practice of family therapy, the Child Psychiatric Clinic under the Ministry of Health sent one of its child psychiatrists, the late Goh Choo Woon, to the Tavistock Institute in the United Kingdom where he studied family therapy for 1 year. He continued to practice family therapy at the Child Psychiatric Clinic until his demise in the late 1980s (Yeo, 1992; Yong, personal communication, May 12, 2000).

Earlier in this chapter I mentioned that family therapy emerged largely in the context of social service rather than the hospital or mental health settings. Earlier it was also highlighted that it was among the social workers and those working in social service agencies that family therapy first took root. Yeo (1992, p. 21) noted that "the key people working with families tended to be social workers rather than psychologists" and that "family casework, as it has been known, has been practised for as long as social work has been a profession in Singapore." Yeo (personal communication, November 23, 1999) is of the opinion that, although in a sense the social workers could be considered the first mental health professionals to look into family dynamics and intervene with the family, what they did could not be considered family therapy, because "it was not a distinctive discipline in the early years of counseling development (which would be the 1960s)".

However, all this was to change in 1985 when an important milestone in the development of family therapy came about with the decision of the Singapore Council of Social Service to appoint a group to "explore the possibility of beginning a program for training social workers to work with families from a systems orientation" (Yeo, 1992, p. 21).

As has been noted, the only mental health center in the early 1980s with an overall focus on the practice and development of family therapy in Singapore was the Counselling and Care Centre. Thus, it was not surprising that the expertise of the Counselling and Care Centre in this area was tapped by the Singapore Council of Social Service. A program known as "Training in Family Work" was conducted by the staff of the Counselling and Care Centre. Some 30 social workers from various agencies came together and were exposed to concepts that allow them to work with families from a systemic focus. It should be pointed out that at that point in time, most of the social workers who attended "Training in Family Work" had no coursework on working with families at the National University of Singapore.

The move by the Singapore Council of Social Service in 1985, in a sense, marks the formal shift toward focusing on the family as a primary unit of intervention. Yeo (1992) reported that:

> Since 1986, family therapy became more accepted as social workers began to work with families and individuals from a systems perspective.

> Though these social workers were not trained to function as family therapists, they were integrating knowledge and skills from this discipline for their work (p. 21).

For the first time, too, family therapy was introduced into the curriculum of the undergraduate degree program in social work at the National University of Singapore.

From the Early 1990s to the End of the 1990s: A Decade of Family Therapy Training in Singapore

Although the first local training program on working with families from a systemic perspective, "Training in Family Work," was conducted in 1986, it was only in the 1990s that formal training in family therapy became available locally in Singapore.

Yeo (1992, p. 22) writing in the early 1990s observed that, "one of the most significant features of the field of psychological counseling is the lack of training programs in Singapore." Counseling was taught as a subject in social work and psychology, in the teacher training program at the National Institute of Education, and at some theological colleges and seminaries. Although the Counselling and Care Centre had initiated the 9-month Counsellor Training Program in 1981, most Singaporeans wanting formal training in counseling had to go abroad.

Yeo (1992, p. 22) noted that "with the lack of training opportunities in counseling it is inevitable that training in family therapy should be excluded from the universities and polytechnics." The few Singaporeans who received formal training in family therapy before 1990 had all been trained abroad in North America, Britain, and Australia. Although the situation today is vastly different in terms of training opportunities for professional counseling, the availability of formal training for family therapy remains rather limited.

Because the government had made strong families a part of the national ideology and pushed for the strengthening of families through various measures, including the development of more Family Service Centres (Singapore Government 1989, Singapore Government, 1995a), there were a flurry of initiatives to provide more training in counseling for Singapore. It must be pointed out, however, that these programs tend to be more entry-level professional counseling training programs than formal family therapy training programs.

The highlighting of the various negative social trends in the local media, such as juvenile delinquency, family violence, rising divorce rates ("Divorce Rate Continues to Climb," 1997), and the resultant stress on families ("More Children Seeing Psychiatrists," 1997), plus the constant call to have more trained counselors, have resulted in a trend in which more and more individuals are seeking professional training in counseling. Many of these are mid-career individuals who have been involved as volunteers and are now seeking to move into full-time work as counselors.

In June 1991, a conference was jointly organized by the Singapore Council of Social Services, The Institute of Policy Studies, and the Community Chest to map out the future direction of social services in Singapore. It was an important conference: Ee Peng Liang, then President of the Singapore Council of Social Services, pointed out that it was the first time "that members of the public and private sectors and the academia came together to discuss the issues and challenges that the disadvantaged and the voluntary welfare organizations serving them faced" (Ee-Choi, 1997, p. 467). Among the issues highlighted was the need for more specialized training to enable professional helpers to function at an optimum level. Another more worrying concern is the overreliance by many mental health agencies on their volunteers, who are sometimes "used to replace the professional personnel providing counseling services to clients" (Machner-Licht, 1991, p. 184).

The Report of the Inter-Ministry Committee on Dysfunctional Families, Juvenile Delinquency and Drug Abuse had also recommended that more counselors need to be trained if family service organizations are to achieve their goal of helping families in Singapore (Singapore Government, 1995a, pp. 7, 25, 65).

Abdullah Tarmugi, Minister for Community Development, on the occasion of the launch of the Specialist Diploma in Counselling and Guidance at Temasek Polytechnic, in 1997 said: "The demand for counsellors has never been greater . . . " (Crying Need for More Trained Counsellors," 1997). Speakers at a panel discussion following the launch also noted a growing need for counselors and expressed their concern that some counselors already working in the field are not properly trained.

Besides the Specialist Diploma in Counselling and Guidance at Temasek Polytechnic, the National Institute of Education, Psychological Studies Division had also, in 1997, launched a master's level program with a focus on either Counselling Psychology or Educational Psychology. The National University of Singapore also began to offer a postgraduate and master's level program in Social Work and Applied Psychology. What is interesting about these programs is that, although each offers some units in family therapy, none are formal family therapy training programs.

In addition to the programs offered by various government sanctioned tertiary institutions, the late 1990s also saw a proliferation of graduate counselor training programs offered by private educational institutions. These programs are usually offered in conjunction with overseas tertiary institutions. At this point in time, the collaborating institutions are all Australian universities. Three programs, all master's level, are either currently available or are soon to be available. The courses offered are the master's in social science (counseling) by the University of South Australia, the master of social science (counseling) by Edith Cowan University, and the master's in counseling by the University of Southern Queensland. An examination of the course curriculum of these programs again indicates that these are generic entry-level professional counseling programs, and not family therapy programs.

To date, only four formal family therapy training programs have been offered in Singapore. At the time of this writing, one of the programs is no longer operating. A brief description of each of the four programs follows:

Postgraduate Diploma in Family and Marital Therapy Offered by the Counselling and Care Centre

It is obvious that although there has been a proliferation of courses in professional counselor training, the same degree of training is not available locally for family therapy. In fact, formal training in family therapy became a reality only in March 1991 when the Counselling and Care Centre took in its first group of 15 trainees for the postgraduate diploma in family and marital therapy. That there is a strongly felt need among the local helping professionals for such a program could be seen by the fact that more than 30 professionals, including social workers, psychologists, religious workers, educational counselors, and even a psychiatrist, applied to enroll in the program.

The postgraduate diploma in family and marital therapy is a part-time, 2-year course designed for mental health professionals who wish to develop skills in family and marital therapy. It was born out of an exploratory meeting between Anthony Yeo of the Counselling and Care Centre and Hugh Jenkins, then Director of the Institute of Family Therapy in London at the Bridges Conference on Family Therapy in Budapest in 1989 (Yeo, 1992).

The postgraduate diploma in family and marital therapy was designed along the lines of the program offered at the Institute of Family Therapy in London. The course is now jointly offered by the Counselling and Care Centre and the Institute of Family Therapy (London) and is cocertified by Birkbeck College, University of London.

Diploma in Family Therapy Offered by the Family Resource and Training Centre

Following the Coopers and Lybrand report of 1993, and the decision of the Ministry of Community and the National Council of Social Services to promote family service centers as a holistic approach to services for the family and to adopt a "family as a primary unit of intervention" approach, the Family Resource and Training Centre was commissioned to run a 2-year family therapy training program leading to a diploma in family and marital therapy. Twenty social workers enrolled in the program. Besides local social work educators, a mix of academics and practitioners, mainly from the United States, were also involved as resource persons in the program. Among the American academics were Jim Moran from the Mental Research Institute (MRI) in Palo Alto, California, Nancy Vosler and Nancy Morrow-Howell from George Warren Brown School of Social Work, Washington University, and Lie Gwat Yong, originally from Singapore, but at that time teaching at the University of Texas. Two American practitioners also taught in the program, Jean Caine and Doris Diamond, both practicing in the St. Louis, Missouri area. Lee Wai-Yung served as the external examiner. The diploma in family and marital therapy conducted by the Family Resource and Training Centre had only been in operation for 1 year.

With the termination of the program offered by the Family Resource and Training Centre, helping professionals interested in family therapy training could only train at the Counselling and Care Centre. Up until 1997, the postgraduate diploma in family and marital therapy, offered by the Counselling and Care Centre, was the only formal family training program available in Singapore.

Postgraduate Diploma in Satir's Brief Systemic Therapy Offered by Choice Makers Consultancy

Training in Virginia Satir's system of family therapy was formally launched in April 1997 with the first intake for the 18-month postgraduate diploma in Satir systemic brief therapy. Twelve trainees, eight of them from Care Corner Family Service Centre, enrolled in the first intake. The remaining four trainees were social workers from other Social Service and Family Service Centres.

Currently, the program is coordinated by Warren Tan of Choice Makers Consultancy. Warren first met John Banmen from the Satir Institute of the Pacific, British Columbia, in April 1994 at a 3-day workshop on Satir's family therapy in Singapore. A social worker by training, Warren continued studying with John Banmen from 1994 to 1997 at the Hong Kong Satir Institute for Human Development. His initial motivation was to introduce Satir's model to social workers then working in the Care Corner Family Service Centre.

The response to the first intake for the postgraduate diploma in Satir systemic brief therapy, where four of the participants were not from Care

Corner Family Service Centre, convinced Warren that there is a demand for helping professionals already in the field for formal training in family therapy. Indeed, the Satir program has seen rising enrollment. In the second intake in October 1998, 17 professionals were accepted into the program. Of these 17, two were not helpers in the "traditional sense," being teachers in the Ministry of Education's gifted program. The third intake in May 2000 saw some 27 participants. The composition was interesting; some 50% were "traditional helping professionals," meaning social workers, psychologists, and professional counselors, and about 50% were nontraditional helpers. In this group were mainly professionals from other disciplines, including accountants, human resource personnel, and even a lawyer; all were actively involved in volunteer counseling work at various social service agencies and educational institutions. Some of them were also preparing for a possible career switch to the helping professions.

From 1997 onward, two 2-day workshops introducing Satir's system of family therapy have been made available each year. Some 30 to 40 participants attend each 2-day workshop, facilitated by John Banmen, where they are introduced to Virginia Satir's ideas, including the importance of open communication and emotional experiencing. The participants are not just the "traditional professional helpers," but also educators, religious leaders, and volunteers from various social services. According to Warren, more than 500 people have experienced these workshops. Given Satir's humanistic focus and emphasis on personal growth and development, it is not surprising that large numbers have been drawn to these workshops. Some of the workshop participants go on to the 18-month postgraduate diploma in Satir systemic brief therapy. Many do not. However, even those who do not have at least been exposed to the systemic thinking and way of working with families.

The Postgraduate Diploma in Solution-Focused Brief Therapy Offered by the Academy of Human Development

In 2000, the Academy of Human Development, affiliated with the Fei Yue Family Service Centre, started another orientation-specific training program in family therapy.

It began to offer a 1-year training program in Steve de Shazer's solution-focused brief therapy. The postgraduate diploma in solution-focused brief therapy is offered in conjunction with the Brief Family Therapy Center in Milwaukee, Wisconsin. More than 35 applications were received and 29 applicants were accepted into the program. All the participants are from the helping professions; although social workers predominate, there are also some psychiatrists.

The Current Situation

Most of those who have been trained in the various formal therapy programs are currently employed by family service centers and other voluntary welfare organizations. The "action" in the field of family therapy is still very much within the social service context. The Child Psychiatric Clinic since the mid-1980s, when Goh Choo Woon was trained, had seen only two other professional staff trained in family therapy. Tian Cheong Sing, a psychiatrist, and Irene Yong, the Chief Medical Social Worker, both trained with the Counselling and Care Centre and received the postgraduate diploma in family and marital therapy. However, Tian Cheong Sing is now in private practice and Irene Yong is now retired. There are only a handful of family therapists in private practice.

CURRENT ISSUES

Software Development

Blake (1991) observed in the early 1990s that conditions were right for the development of family therapy in Singapore.

The Singapore Government's desire is to keep the family strong and adopt a policy of "strengthening the family." The government approached this issue in a systematic way with the appointment of high level committees, such as the Advisory Council on Family and Community Life in 1989, and the Inter-Ministry Committee on Dysfunctional Families, Juvenile Delinquency and Drug Abuse in 1995, to study problems faced by families in Singapore and propose solutions to these problems.

The government also showed its commitment to implementing the solutions proposed by these various committees. Particularly significant is the setting up of a strong network of social services to support families (Singapore Government, 1995a, p. 70). As mentioned, the neighborhood Family Service Centre, with its family focus, will serve as a first stop, and possibly also one-stop center for all family services. Besides prevention and developmental programs, which are essentially educational in nature, Family Service Centres also offer counseling services and casework. This counseling is family-focused and the family is the *primary unit of intervention* (emphasis mine) (Singapore Government, 2000). As of May 2000, 27 Family Service Centres distributed all over the island had been set up. And by end March 2001, the targeted number of Family Service Centres, a total of 34, as recommended by the Inter-Ministry Committee on Dysfunctional Families, Juvenile Delinquency and Drug Abuse (Singapore Government, 1999a), will be set up.

The infrastructure is ready, the focus on the family and the goal to strengthen the family clearly defined. In a way the "hardware" to strengthen the family is present; what seems to be somewhat lacking is the "software."

The need to have more people trained in the helping professions has been recognized for a long time. In the conference "Social Service: The Next Lap" in June 1991, various speakers and panelists highlighted this issue (Machner-Licht, 1991). Even in the Report of the Inter-Ministry Committee on Dysfunctional Families, Juvenile Delinquency and Drug Abuse, numerous references were made to the need for more trained professionals (Singapore Government, 1995a, pp. 7, 25, 65). Tamney (1995) described the Singapore Council of Social Services and its affiliate voluntary organizations as "understaffed and underfunded" (p. 105).

In relation to this issue of not having enough trained individuals is the related issue of retaining those who are already trained. Helping professionals have a very high burnout rate. Although this is caused in part by the nature of their job, burnout also reflects the low status and relatively low remuneration of helping professionals (Kaw, 1991; Phua, 1991; Yee, 1991). Machner-Licht (1991, p. 184) had also suggested that more needs to be done to assist helping professionals to cope with the stress that comes with the job. She also suggested that more specialized training be given to help the professional helper perform at optimum levels.

Manpower development and training of professional helpers must be addressed urgently. With the Family Service Centre having its overall focus on the family as the basic unit of intervention, with the types of problems dealt with being mainly of the "family" type, and with a developmental service aimed at preventing potential family dysfunction, it appears advantageous to have professional staff who have had specific training in family therapy. Yet an examination of the "Staffing and Utilisation" guidelines for Family Service Centres (Singapore Government, 1999a, p. 10) indicates that only one professional on staff, the Senior Social Worker, should "preferably" have "recognised qualifications in family and marital counselling."

There is certainly a need to equip more professionals with skills in family and marital therapy, and there is definitely no shortage of mental health and social work professionals wishing to be trained. That there is a need for more training among helping professionals can be seen by the response to the existing postgraduate diploma in family and marital therapy at the Counselling and Care Centre, which has been running since 1991. There has also been a very positive response to the postgraduate diploma in Satir systemic brief therapy since its launch in 1997, and also more recently to the postgraduate diploma in solution-focused brief therapy.

Besides making more family therapy training programs available, programs must somehow also be made more affordable. High-quality training programs in family therapy are understandably expensive. For example, the 2-year postgraduate diploma in family and marital therapy offered by the Counselling and Care Centre costs S$16,500 (about U.S. $10,000). Social workers and counselors in Singapore, such as those around the world, tend not to be highly remunerated. Also, additional training does not necessarily translate into higher income, unlike, for example, training in information technology, which given Singapore's stress on a knowledge-based economy, frequently translates into significant increases in financial remuneration. Although sponsorships to professional training programs currently are available through the National Council of Social Services, more can be done.

Indeed, if Singapore is to be pro-family because "strong and stable families are central to the well-being of a society" (Singapore Government, 1995b, p. 3), then the development of family therapists, among other helping professionals, must be given some priority. The development of the software, or the "heartware," must support the development of the hardware.

Research

Currently, there is a paucity of material on family and marriage therapy in Singapore. Although some papers have been written as dissertations in formal family therapy training programs (Yong, 1994), generally very little research and writing have taken place. A notable exception is a study conducted by Tan Boon Huat of the Counselling and Care Centre, which examined the therapeutic effectiveness of marital therapy (Tan, 1997).

With more trained family therapists, a "critical mass" hopefully can be achieved and more writing and research on family therapy outcomes and processes be undertaken.

Blake (1991) suggested several issues worth looking into from a local perspective. Among these issues are the place of language and communication, and life cycle stages.

Language and Communication

Singapore's multiracial and multilingual population presents special challenges for the family therapist. Although knowledge of a particular culture alone does not guarantee culturally sensitive therapy, it is frequently the first step.

However, in Singapore's context, the acquisition of such cultural knowledge is complicated by the fact that even within major racial groups there are wide variations in language and cultural norms. For example, within the Chinese community there exists a plethora of dialects and cultural variations among the various dialect groups. Although the situation has improved somewhat over the years, with the annual "Speak Mandarin Campaign" organized by the government, still only 24% of families use Mandarin as their language of communication at home (Singapore Government, 1999b). Even with more Chinese people using Mandarin as a common language of communication, the subtle cultural variations within dialect groups still exist. An interesting example is the wide variation in the marriage customs of the various dialect groups. An appreciation of such subtleties has an impact on the effectiveness of a family therapist.

Another example, as pointed out by Blake (1991, p. 53), is that correct forms of address, which define the hierarchical relationship between the speaker and the other party (e.g., younger brother/sister), are important to all cultural groups in Singapore. Because these rules of courtesy have implications for the definition of positions in the therapeutic interaction, their implications need to be studied.

The situation is further complicated by the fact that many family therapists are more conversant in English than Mandarin, Malay, or one of the Indian languages. With more foreigners working and settling in Singapore, the challenges to the family therapist working in Singapore will mount.

Professional Regulation

The mental health professions are not regulated in Singapore. There are currently no licensure or even certification requirements to practice as a psychologist, social worker, or professional counselor. In fact, with counseling becoming increasingly recognized, the term counselor especially is used very loosely. An example is an advertisement for a matchmaking service in the local newspaper in which the matchmaking agency claims it has in its employ a "marriage counsellor"!

Recent attempts by the Singapore Association of Counselling and the Singapore Association of Social Workers to accredit members of their respective professional associations were unsuccessful. It appears that accreditation is still a long way off. The Singapore Association of Family Therapists has so far not attempted to seek accreditation.

Among the rationale for licensure are that it protects the public by ensuring that only properly qualified practitioners are allowed to practice, and it ensures a minimum standard of service and provides a mechanism for accountability (Corey, Corey, & Callanan, 1998). With the proliferation of counseling programs and the increasing acceptance of counseling as a way to solve problems, the licensure of counseling professionals, including family therapists, must be addressed more seriously.

CONCLUSION

This chapter has attempted to trace the development of family therapy in Singapore. In a country where professional counseling is a relatively recent phenomenon, family therapy as a professional discipline is also in a very early stage of development. Its growth has been sparked by the emphasis on social policies, especially that of "strengthening the family." This policy, together with the creation of a network of Family Service Centres, has created a demand for more professionals who are trained in family work. The 1990s saw increasing availability of training opportunities in family therapy. The professional discipline has much to offer Singapore in its quest for strong families. However, the influence of the profession can only be felt if more people are trained.

Greater financial support for the training of family therapists and other helping professionals, as well as raising the standards of professional delivery through regulation of the professional practice of family therapy, will aid the development of a stronger profession in Singapore.

With a bigger pool of helping professionals who are trained in family therapy, a critical mass hopefully will be reached, and more research can be undertaken, especially into the issues of ethnicity and applicability of Western models of family therapy to the Singapore context. Hopefully also, the use of family therapy will spread beyond the social service context, and become more widespread, with more mental health and hospital settings adopting the use of family therapy as part of their interventions.

Although the field of family therapy in Singapore is less than 30 years old, the early pioneers have laid much of the groundwork, and recent years have seen a growing enthusiasm for the study and use of family therapy. With the country ready for the development of family therapy (Blake, 1991), the time is now ripe for consolidation of the gains we have made, and to further encourage the growth and use of family therapy across disciplines.

REFERENCES

Blake, M. (1991). The portability of family therapy to different cultural and socio-economic contexts. *Asian Pacific Journal of Social Work, 1*(2), 32–60.

Corey, G., Corey, M. S., & Callanan, P. (1998). *Issues and ethics in the helping professions* (5th ed.). Pacific Grove, CA: Brooks/Cole.

Crying need for more trained counsellors. (1997, July 6). *The Sunday Times*, p. 28.

Divorce rate continues to climb. (1997, November 18). *The Straits Times,* p. 39.

Ee-Choi, T. (1997). *Father of charity and . . . my father Ee Peng Liang.* Singapore: SNP Publishing Pte. Ltd.

Kaw, S. (1991). Service directions for voluntary welfare organisations serving disadvantaged families and children. In M. T. Yap (Ed.), *Social service: The next lap* (pp. 87–89). Singapore: Institute of Policy Studies/Times Academic Press.

Lau, A. (1984). Transcultural issues in family therapy. *Journal of Family Therapy*, 6, 91–112.

Machner-Licht, B. (1991). Service directions for voluntary welfare organizations in the mental health field. In M. T. Yap (Ed.), *Social service: The next lap* (pp. 173–187). Singapore: Institute of Policy Studies/Times Academic Press.

McGoldrick, M. (1982). Ethnicity and family therapy: An overview. In M. McGoldrick, J. K. Pearce, & J. Giordano (Eds.), *Ethnicity and family therapy* (pp. 3–30). New York: Guilford.

More children seeing psychiatrists. (1997, June 8). *The Straits Times*, p. 26.

Phua, K. H. (1991). Service directions for voluntary welfare organisations serving the elderly. In M. T. Yap (Ed.), *Social services: The next lap* (pp. 146–152). Singapore: Institute of Policy Studies/Times Academic Press.

Quah, S. (1999). *Study on the Singapore family*. Singapore: Ministry of Community Development.

Singapore Government. (1989). *Towards better family and community life*. Singapore: Singapore Government.

Singapore Government. (1995a). *Report of the inter-ministry committee on dysfunctional families, juvenile delinquency and drug abuse*. Singapore: Ministry of Community Development.

Singapore Government. (1995b). *Singapore: A pro-family society*. Singapore: Ministry of Community Development.

Singapore Government. (1997). *Singapore facts and pictures 1997*. Singapore: Ministry of Information and Arts.

Singapore Government. (1999a). *Guide to setting up family service centres (FSCs)*. Singapore: Ministry of Community Development/National Council of Social Services.

Singapore Government. (1999b). *Singapore 1999*. Singapore: Ministry of Information and The Arts.

Singapore Government. (2000). *Report on a revision of family service centres*. Singapore: Ministry of Community Development and Sports.

Tamney, J. B. (1995). *The struggle over singapore's soul: Western modernization and Asian culture*. New York: Walter de Gruyter.

Tan, B. H. (1997). *Marital therapy: Outcome evaluation of therapeutic effectiveness*. Singapore: Counselling and Care Centre.

Yee, J. (1991). Service directions for voluntary welfare organisations serving disadvantaged families and children. In M. T. Yap (Ed.), *Social services: The next lap* (pp. 90–98). Singapore: Institute of Policy Studies/Times Academic Press.

Yeo, A. (1992). Family therapy in Singapore. *Clinical Psychology Forum, September 1992*, 20–23.

Yong, I. (1994). *Externalising the problem: An impetus for change*. Unpublished dissertation, University of London, London/Counselling and Care Centre, Singapore.

CHAPTER 5

The Beginning of Family Therapy in India

RADHA PRABHU

The Indian civilization is one of the oldest in the world. With a population of nearly 1 billion, India is the largest democratic country in the world. It is a land of multicultures and subcultures with diverse religions, communities, languages, customs, and traditions. This diversity permeates every aspect of life in customs, rituals, selection of marriage partners, childrearing, education, family development, employment, and attitudes (Mullatti, 1995). India is also a land of paradox: although the illiteracy rate is one of the highest in the world, a sizable number of Indians has excelled academically and economically on par with the Western world. Consequently, there is no single approach that can be used in viewing Indian families. There are significant differences in family structure, roles, and traditions based on religion, community, caste, and urbanization. The growth of family therapy in India does not parallel the West because the unique nature of family interrelations, and social and cultural aspects influence the development of this approach.

In the West, the major growth of family therapy began around the 1950s and despite the divergent views on what constitutes family therapy, this approach has become a major therapeutic tool in providing help to families in distress. In India, the field of family therapy has progressed very gradually because of problems such as inadequate training facilities, lack of professional interest, and shortage of trained professionals. Most family therapists in India do not draw from a single theory and technique, even if they are trained in a single school of family therapy, because of cultural differences that include different family relationships, and different socioeconomic and sociocultural norms (Chandiramani, 1995; Shanker & Menon, 1991). In this context, working with families often involves multiple approaches, techniques, and theoretical assumptions. Many of the conference discussions among professionals have more to do with the pragmatics of treating families rather than the theories behind the techniques as compared to the West.

CHARACTERISTICS OF INDIAN FAMILIES

Traditional Indian families generally are comprised of several related individuals and their families living and sharing almost everything under one roof. This "joint" family has been a part of Indian culture for thousands of years. Family has always been at the core of Indian society and the key focus has always been in the centrality of marriage and family life (Mullatti, 1995). The structure of the Indian family is still based very much on a hierarchy determined by gender preferences. The emphasis is on conformity to family goals at the sacrifice of personal autonomy and pursuits. However, over the past few decades, Indian family structures have undergone major changes because of urbanization, migration, women joining the work force, and other social changes (Bharat, 1994).

Indian families also face some very complex problems. The majority of Indian families who live in the countryside and villages are still very poor and isolated from the mainstream. On the other hand, urban dwellers also have to deal with overcrowding, poverty, crime, natural disasters, political instability, poor nutrition, and a host of other problems. These have become the modern-day challenges to traditional family structure, putting marriage and families at risk. Given the difficulties, the future of Indian families is uncertain.

Family Structure

Indian families for thousands of years sought to provide stability and support when confronted with outside problems. Often there are well-defined rules, roles, and rituals that bind the family together. Members share feelings of togetherness and solidarity and strive to uphold family dignity and status within the community. Therefore, family unity and cohesiveness are very necessary for family stability and survival. Traditionally, families still maintain the centuries-old nuclear family structure, even though many Indian traditions have undergone significant changes (Mullatti, 1995).

Another form of family structure commonly seen is the "extended family," where occasionally two to three generations live under the same roof. Indian families often have loose boundaries where aunts and uncles, cousins, and in-laws all participate in family decisions and practices. According to Indian tradition, the principal duty of children, particularly males, is to take care of their parents in old age. A strong sense of duty is embedded in each individual and he (usually the oldest male) is expected to adhere to societal expectations in taking care of elderly parents as well as serving as a parental figure to his younger siblings. He is given a special place in the family and community and is nurtured across the generations in order to maintain the family tradition. Traditional roles are closely observed where men work to support the family and women remain the primary homemakers. This trend has indeed shifted because the number of women entering the workforce has increased greatly in the last few decades. Age is held in high esteem, and the elderly members of the family have more influence on decision making than any other individuals.

Nuclear Family

The gradual shift from the traditional joint family to the nuclear family is a growing phenomenon caused by economic and industrial factors as well as distribution of power and women moving rapidly into the workforce. This happens primarily in urban communities. The impact of urbanization often has negative effects on the nuclear family such as the loss of emotional and social support, and lack of guidance in childrearing and problem solving. This appears to put a lot of stress on young working families with children. Indians believe that elders are also wise men and that if they are not a part of the household, then the younger generation will be without their spiritual leadership and guidance. Bharat (1994) reports that the emerging nuclear family structure in urban India is assumed to favor sharing of roles rather than a hierarchy, a liberal structure rather than role differentiation, and an overall egalitarian outlook rather than a traditional outlook. However, several Indian studies report increased incidences of mental disorders in nuclear families (Agarwal, Mehta, & Gupta, 1978; Verghese & Beig, 1974) in urban communities. Regardless of the pros and cons, the nuclear family has survived over time, and it appears that the present generation is gaining in independence and individuation.

This trend has raised further questions by the younger generation on the roles, obligations, and value of the traditional family structure, which has been nurturing the social fabric of the Indian family. The tension of pursuing personal fulfillment and familial goals can become an important source of stress. This situation calls for a different perspective that balances the old and new. Experts proposed the concepts of integration and negotiation at all socioeconomic levels as viable solutions to the current state of affairs in Indian society (Bharat, 1994).

Another phenomenon that has changed the family structure in India is the ongoing brain drain among young, talented, and highly educated Indians who are emigrating abroad in search of more lucrative job opportunities. This has led to elderly couples living alone with no caregiver, something that was rare a few decades ago. A sharp increase in the number of old age homes also validates this phenomenon.

Marriage Patterns

Most marriages in India are arranged by the elder members of the family. Spouses are generally chosen at a young age. In most cases, family backgrounds, social status, and astrological compatibility are given preference over individual choice. The partners remain strangers until the marriage, and the couple is expected to get to know each other only after their wedding. Consanguinous marriages are also common in the upper caste in India. These marriages are between maternal uncles and nieces, and maternal and paternal cousins. The purposes of such marriages are twofold: to keep family property from being further distributed, and to provide a familiar, supportive environment to the bride (Sareendar, Reddy, & Baburajan, 1992). Love marriages, where individuals choose their own partners, are becoming more common in modern India. Over the last decade, young people, especially those in the urban areas, have sought their own partners, and often do not gain parental approval. Such marriages are typically frowned upon, especially if the two partners come from different communities, castes, and social backgrounds. However, the influence of the West has made this kind of marriage more viable among the young and educated generation. Urban-educated individuals often prefer to select their partners. Marriages, whether arranged or by choice, bring about a series of life changes and if support does not come from the family, the young family experiences a lot of stress. However, as compared to the West, the divorce rate in India is relatively low and varies from 1.6 in 1,000 in the state of Haryana to 34 in 1,000 in Kerla (Sareendar et al., 1992). One reason could be the cultural emphasis on the sanctity and chastity of marriage and the stigma associated with divorced individuals. Similarly, single-parent families are rare—in most cases, the single parent is widowed.

Changing Roles

Women do not have any power or authority in traditional Indian families. The identity of an Indian woman is defined only in the context of her relationship with an adult male. Although the Indian tradition has a place for women, in everyday life their value is not equal to that of men (Almeida, 1996). Males have greater economic, political, physical, and spiritual value than females. Thus, female children are considered to be burdens, and are looked upon as belonging to the households they marry into, but birth of boys is celebrated. Traditionally, women have been the primary homemakers; they are undervalued, not included as decision makers, and provided with fewer opportunities for education and autonomy. However, in modern India, an increasing number of women are receiving more than just a basic education; thus, they are discovering their identities beyond homemaker. With the advent of more women in the workforce, the role of women in the household has become multifaceted and more stressful. Indian women contribute to the economy of the home and often single-handedly manage the entire household. In the traditional household, the role of the male is limited to just providing for the family. However, with smaller families and more women working, men have started contributing toward the maintenance of the household. These role transitions can lead to tremendous stress and role confusion. In a study by Nathawat and Mathur (1993), working women were found to have better marital adjustment and coped well as homemakers in the dual roles. This highlights the point that the role changes have a positive influence on Indian women.

FAMILY THERAPY IN INDIA

Family therapy is relatively new in India. Traditionally, family problems are handled by a priest, friend, relative, or the adult in the family. Those with more severe emotional problems go to native healers, gurus, and exorcists more often than trained mental health professionals (Davar, 1999). Mental health professionals are usually medically trained psychiatrists and general practitioners who prescribe medications. From all directions, the need for mental health has been on the rise. There seems to be an increase in suicide, homicide, rape, and other psychiatric-related problems (Agarwal et al., 1978; Chandra et al., 1995; Davar, 1999), partly because of the compounding stresses of modern living. Overall, seeking help for family problems is considered a foreign idea generally associated with the hospitalization of the mentally and emotionally ill.

Some of the earliest family work was done by Vidyasagar in the Amritsar Mental Hospital. He saw the need for helping individual mental health patients by involving their family members in the treatment process (Vidyasagar, 1971). He reported that involving the family significantly reduced hospital stays, increased acceptance of the patient by the family, and enhanced family coping skills (Bhatti & Verghese, 1995). Involving the family as an ally in therapy helps in the overall improvement of the patient. In a similar vein, the National Institute of Mental Health and Neurosciences (NIMHAN), encourages family members to stay with patients occasionally in the open wards, and this greatly helps in the treatment procedure (Narayan, Embar, & Reddy, 1972). This often serves to educate families about the causes and symptoms of mental illness. Educating family members also helps to dispel myths about the mentally ill and helps in the maintenance of treatment and recognition of the early signs of relapse.

The first center to start living facilities for patients was the Mental Health Center at Vellore, where families were included in the treatment of patients. This system had a dual advantage as families also learned how to cope better with patients and share their experiences. A major family treatment center was started in NIMHAN where the entire family stayed in the hospital and underwent therapy. Other settings where family therapy is practiced include nongovernmental organizations, child guidance clinics, welfare agencies, family courts, and private practice settings. Most of these places involve the education of extended family members rather than emphasizing the therapy and treatment of the existing disorders, as is done in the West.

The SCARF Experience

The Schizophrenia Research Foundation (SCARF) in Chennai, South India is an organization dedicated to the long-term care and rehabilitation of the chronically mentally ill. Rehabilitation programs are offered for the chronic mentally ill in a daycare setting including medical management, vocational rehabilitation, social skills training, and family management. The SCARF family intervention program approach aims to meet the needs of both patients and families. The program includes helping family members develop more effective coping strategies, symptom management, improving social and occupational functioning of the patient, psychoeducation, improving communication within the family, identifying early signs of relapse, and relieving the family's burden. The program has three stages: Documenting family needs, accessing overall coping strategies, and identifying resources in surrounding communities. This program has been implemented for different families and has proven to be effective. The report of the staff members asserted that getting family in treatment has helped the patient to function well in social and occupational settings (personal communication, 1999).

The Family Therapy Center

The Family Therapy Center started by the National Institute of Mental Health and Neurosciences (NIMHAN) is now a successful center in the treatment of families with varying mental illness. An average of 150 to 200 families were referred to the Family Therapy Center annually (Bhatti & Verghese, 1995). The families are initially screened for the purpose for therapy and after that a formal therapy contract is signed. Subsequent appointments are made at convenient dates for outpatient or inpatient therapy. The Family Therapy Center consists of a multidisciplinary team of psychiatrists, clinical psychologists, family counselors, and social workers. A few postgraduate students are also posted to the Center to do their internships. Clients are generally referred from the psychiatry units in the Institute or from similar departments from all over India. Initially, the family goes through a careful screening process as part of assessment. Clients are referred for therapy for various problems such as family or marital discord, juvenile delinquency, family violence, depression, and other related psychiatric illnesses. Others want to understand relapse prevention strategies and other educational resources. Depending on the need of the family, at times, the Center used the "Family Assessment Performance" to further assess the family. This instrument was locally developed by the Center. The instrument assesses several major aspects of family dynamics:

- *Family structure:* Family composition, boundary subsystems, and alignment
- *Leadership patterns:* Power structures and decision making, role structure and functioning, communication patterns, behavior patterns, and cohesiveness
- *Adaptive patterns:* Conflict resolution and social support systems

The information is gathered in consultation with the entire family over a three- to four-session period. Once the therapist finishes gathering the information, the case is presented to the clinical team. The team in turn makes suggestions as to how to deal with the family and makes suggestions about the type of intervention that is most appropriate. Usually, the team starts with a hypothesis and further treatment is based on that hypothesis. In the past, the team has suggested different approaches (behavioral, supportive, system, or eclectic) to meet the needs of the family. The hypothesis may at times undergo changes and modifications during the course of therapy as more and more understanding about the family is gained. Each therapy session is discussed in terms of goals and outcomes and future plans of management. In this case the treatment milieu is very structured and organized.

Indian families have learned to be more encouraging and supportive of a mentally ill member through the years. However, the hierarchical structure of Indian families often hinders free communication of thoughts and feelings; therefore, the therapist often encounters difficulties in improving family communication patterns. During therapy, the therapist may have to deal with the fathers, who often usurp the authority or refuse to allow the rest of the family members to express their feelings. The therapist comes to an impasse if he or she challenges the father's authority or aligns with the wife. Often it takes a lot of sensitivity and cooperation on the part of the therapist with the father to gain his respect and trust.

In India, the therapist is looked upon as charismatic and authoritarian and in control of the session (Chandiramani, 1995). Directive approaches have been found to be more suitable for Indian families (Mohan, 1972). Therapy with Indian families has to be tailored according to the needs of each individual family, and factors such as socioeconomic status and educational levels have to be taken into consideration. There are few studies that have documented the efficacy of including families in the management of patients with specific psychiatric illness such as neurotic disorders and mental retardation. Geetha, Channabasavanna, and Bhatti (1980) compared family treatment of hysteria to other outpatient models. The conclusion was that the rate of recovery was fastest in the family treatment group. Girimaji (1993) reported that family intervention using an educative behavioral approach is highly effective in the management of mental retardation. Chandra et al. (1995) reported three cases of anorexia where family therapy was proven to be highly effective. The role of the family in schizophrenia also has been addressed by studies of expressed emotion (EE). Leff et al. (1987) found significant associations between EE and relapse rates. There are also several reports on the efficacy of family intervention in schizophrenia. The Schizophrenia Research Foundation (SCARF) in Chennai, India stresses the importance of the family playing an active part in the management and rehabilitation of the patient. This foundation has developed several programs based on family psychoeducation approach and has found a better outcome when the family has more knowledge in coping with the patient.

Tools for Family Assessment

Most of the assessment tools used in the clinical practice of aiding formulation and measuring outcome have been developed largely in the West. In the last two decades, attempts have been made to construct culturally sensitive tools to assess Indian families in treatment. The Family Typology Scale is a 28-item scale developed by Channabasavanna and Bhatti (1982), which measures family types: normal cohesive, egoistic, altruistic, and anoxic. The second tool, developed by Bhatti and his colleagues (1986), is called the Family Interaction Pattern Scale and looks into the developmental phases of the family. There are six subscales pertaining to leadership, communication, role, reinforcement, cohesiveness, and social support. Kumar and Rohtagi (1976) developed the Marital Adjustment Questionnaire, which measures seven aspects of the family—such as personality, emotional factors, sexual satisfaction, marital role and responsibility, relationship with in-laws, attitude toward family planning and children, and interpersonal relationships—in order to understand marital adjustment. One of the most comprehensive tools developed in India is called the "Marital Quality Scale" (Shah, 1991). This tool measures 12 aspects: understanding, rejection, satisfaction, affection, despair, decision making, discontent, dissolution potential, dominance, self-disclosure, trust, and role functioning. This tool is being widely used in the understanding of marital relationships. In a way, therapists here are fortunate to have some of these culturally sensitive instruments to work with different families.

Outcome Studies

To date, there has been only one comprehensive study that evaluated the outcome of family therapy in India. In NIMHAN, Prabhu et al. (1988) compared 60 families who had received brief integrative inpatient family therapy combined with group and individual therapies for a period of 2 years. The results of this study postulated that a large percentage (43%) of families in treatment were doing very well. Another 23% reported doing moderately well. Finally, 33% reported no change in relieving symptoms. This study is significant in that it paves a way for mental health professionals in India to consider family therapy as a viable, effective treatment modality before using traditional approaches such as medication or other forms of therapy.

Training

Currently, the training of marriage and family therapists as an individual discipline is not available. Because of numerous causes, family therapy training needs to be integrated into traditional academic programs in universities or other institutes of higher learning and research centers. In fact, some institutions, such as the NIMHAN, of which I was a part, have courses and a clinical emphasis on working with families. As for the future, there is a critical need for well-rounded course content and clinical training programs for family therapists. With the availability of programs, there will be more trained family therapists to offer services to families. The ultimate goal is to license family therapists in the future. Perhaps this will provide credentials and public acceptance of family therapy as an effective treatment modality.

CONCLUSION

Family therapy is still a very new field in India. The changing sociopolitical scenario has put the Indian family under tremendous pressure, and there is a need for family-based approaches in the management of mental health issues. However, the progress made in the last few decades has been minimal and restricted to a few institutions. Problems that hinder the development of a family-based system of therapy include lack of trained personnel, lack of structured research outcome, difficulties in trying to find a comprehensive model for a highly diverse population, and problems in integrating family therapy along with other psychiatric management. Future work should aim to produce methodologically sophisticated outcome research and training units in existing psychiatry departments in the country.

An Indian sociologist once remarked that the Indian family is ready and in need of family therapy. I agree that India is ripe for family therapy as a viable approach in clinical treatment. In spite of scarce resources and the limited number of trained family therapists and training facilities, we need to continue to pave the way for the next generation of family therapists. This stems from my core belief that family therapy holds great promise as a keeper and healer of family units.

REFERENCES

Agarwal, A. K., Mehta, U. K., & Gupta, S. C. (1978). Joint family and neurosis. *Indian Journal of Psychiatry, 20*, 232–236.

Almeida, R. (1996). Hindu, Christian and Muslim families. In M. McGoldrick, J. Giordano, & J. K. Pearce (Eds.), *Ethnicity and family therapy.* New York: Guilford.

Bharat, S. (1994). *Normative family patterns: Correlates, changes and implications in enhancing the role of the family as an agency for social and economic development.* Tata Institute of Social Sciences, Bombay.

Bhatti, R. S., Subbakrishna, D. K., & Ageira, B. L. (1986). Validation of family interaction patterns scale. *Indian Journal of Psychiatry, 28,* 213–218.

Bhatti, R. S., & Verghese, M. (1995). Family therapy in India. *Indian Journal of Social Psychiatry, 11,* 30–34.

Chandiramani, K. (1995). Family therapy: The Indian perspective. *Indian Journal of Social Psychiatry, 11*, 50–52.

Chandra, P. S., Shah, A., Shenoy, J., Kumar, U., Verghese, M., Bhatti, R. S., & Channabasavanna, S. M. (1995). Family pathology and anorexia in the Indian context. *International Journal of Social Psychiatry, 41*, 292–298.

Channabasavanna, S. M., & Bhatti, R. S. (1982). Family therapy of alcohol addicts. In V. Ramachandran, V. Palaniappan, & L. P. Shaw (Eds.), *Continuing medical education programme* (Vol. 1, pp. 17–23). Madras: Indian Psychiatric Society.

Davar, B. V. (1999). *Mental health of Indian women: A feminist agenda.* New Delhi: Sage.

Geetha, P. R., Channabasavanna, S. M., & Bhatti, R. S. (1980). The study of efficacy of family ward treatment in hysteria in comparison with the open ward and the outpatient treatment service. *Indian Journal of Psychiatry, 22,* 317–323.

Girimaji, S. C. (1993). *A study of the evaluation of the effectiveness of brief inpatient family intervention versus outpatient intervention for MR children.* Final report of the India Center for Mental Research Project.

Kumar, P., & Rohtagi, K. (1976). Development of the Marriage Adjustment Questionnaire. *Indian Journal of Psychology, 51,* 346–358.

Leff, J., Wig, N. N., Ghosh, A., Bedi, H., Menon, D. K., Kuipers, L., Korten, A., Ernberg, G., Day, R., & Sartorius, N. (1987). Expressed emotion and schizophrenia in North India. III. Influence of relatives' expressed emotion on the course of schizophrenia in Chandigarh. *British Journal of Psychiatry, 151,* 166–173.

Mohan, D. (1972). *Premarriage and marriage counseling in the Indian family in the change and challenge of the seventies.* New Delhi: Indian Social Institute.

Mullatti, L. (1995). Families in India: Beliefs and realities. *Journal of Comparative Family Studies, 26*(1), 11–25.

Narayan, H. S., Embar, P., & Reddy, G. N. N. (1972). Review of treatment in family ward. *Indian Journal of Psychiatry, 14,* 123–126.

Nathawat, S. S., & Mathur, A. (1993). Marital adjustment and subjective well-being in the Indian educated housewives and working women. *Psychologia, 127*(3), 353–358.

Prabhu, L. R., Desai, N. G. Raguram, A., & Channabasavanna, S. M. (1988). Outcome of family therapy: A 2 year follow up. *International Journal of Social Psychiatry, 34,* 112–117.

Sareendar, S., Reddy, G. C., & Baburajan, P. K. (1992). Divorce in India: A macro-level analysis. *Social Change, 22,* 3–8.

Shah, A. (1991). *Assessment of marital life.* Ph.D. thesis submitted to Bangalore University, Bangalore, India.

Shanker, R., & Menon, S. M. (1991). Family Intervention Programme in Schizophrenics. The SCARF experience. In *Research on families with problems in India* (Vol. 1). Unit for Family Studies, Tata Institute of Social Science, Bombay.

Verghese, A., & Beig, A. (1974). Neurosis in Vellore town: An epidemiological study. *Indian Journal of Psychiatry, 16,* 1–7.

Vidyasagar, A. (1971). *Innovations in psychiatric treatment at Amritsar Mental Hospital: Report on a seminar on the organization and future needs of Mental Health Service.* New Delhi, WHO-SEA/Ment.

PART II

The Development of Family Therapy in Europe

CHAPTER 6

Systemic Family Therapy in Austria

GERDA KLAMMER

Austria is a small country with about 8 million inhabitants in the heart of Europe. Although its capital, Vienna, was once the metropolitan center of a multicultural monarchy, it has been shaken by decades of changes in and around the country since Austria became a republic in 1918. During the last 15 years, the opening of the borders of the Eastern European countries, the wars in former Yugoslavia, the migration of refugees, the joining of the European Union, and the close proximity to the Iron Curtain, have been both stressful and challenging to Austria. Trying to integrate foreigners and immigrants and depending on tourism and international trade continue to create problems Austrians have to deal with on a political, community, family, and personal level.

Currently, Austria is considered one of the richest countries in the world. At the same time, families with lower incomes are severely threatened when economic crises, divorce, unemployment, sickness, and family-related problems affect their social and economic functioning. Although 5% of households without children are close to the poverty line, about 12% of families with one child and 21% with three or more children are close to poverty as well, despite financial aid received from the state (Familienbericht, 1999). Political, legislative, and administrative trends are meant to foster the autonomy and adequate functioning of the family as a unit. Therefore, the state is committed to providing help for families (i.e., educational counseling, family counseling, family therapy training, mediation, and the like), so that family members in need are taught and given resources to solve their problems. Those who have mental health needs are also referred to appropriate professionals (Familienbericht, 1999). The model of the traditional nuclear family (mother spending time at home with the children while father works) still exists, but in reality, as in many other countries in Europe, single-parent households with children are a growing segment of the demographic mosaic of modern Austria. Formerly, the state provided direct aid for those in need, but the state is pushing such families to be self-sufficient.

THE TRADITION AND PRACTICE OF PSYCHOTHERAPY

On the verge of the twentieth century, Sigmund Freud published the "Traumdeutung" in Vienna and it became the cutting edge for the development of "talking cures" by the end of the century. Thus began the revolution of psychoanalysis followed by a long history of followers that started from Vienna and eventually throughout Europe. The development was eventually interrupted by the shadow of World War II. As the result, many had to leave the country, which ultimately broke the tradition and stifled the flourishing of psychosocial activities in Vienna. Friends and colleagues of Sigmund Freud, such as Karl and Charlotte Bühler, Brunswick, Erikson, and Moreno, quickly left the country for their own security. This resulted in a "brain drain" of psychoanalysts for that period, and it took a while to fill the gap.

The student revolution of the late 1960s in Europe and later years somehow created an awareness of the need for psychosocial help for those who could not emotionally care for themselves. As part of the awakening, workshops aimed at raising self-consciousness, well being, and the search for meaning in life continue to spread in different directions. Many became interested in psychology, group dynamics, and therapeutic techniques, and attended personal self-help training workshops and seminars.

Politically, the social democratic governments with people such as Bruno Kreisky in Austria and his friend Olaf Palme in Sweden, and many other socialist leaders in Europe also portrayed a humanistic outlook, which was conducive to the spread of the self-help movement. Other European countries also seemed to follow the trend of allocating enormous amounts of money to help its citizens in need, particularly those who were unemployed, economically deprived, handicapped, and mentally ill. For a while, the mood in some of these countries had become more supportive and lenient instead of criticizing or punishing its citizens for their demise.

For the mentally ill, the government also opened more and bigger psychiatric hospitals and regional psychiatric outpatient clinics. Transitional housing units were also built to minimize longer stays in hospitals. During the same period, there was also a growing market for private practitioners working with families, couples, and individuals. Unlike the United States, there were few full-time private practitioners in Austria. Most of them had other full-time jobs with fixed incomes. It was very difficult to survive financially in full-time private practice. Most therapists worked in institutions such as child guidance clinics, psychiatric units, hospitals, schools, and correctional institutions. A few have since established their own training institutes, whereas others work in agencies part-time or teach part-time besides having their own private practice.

One of the most exciting developments in 2000 was that therapists formally developed contracts with some health insurance companies, similar to the managed care system in the United States. This is a huge victory for therapists working with families as well. This exciting change means that private practitioners have the potential of creating a bigger market for private practice. Part of the contract stipulated that if the clients choose a preferred provider who meets the criteria of the health insurance companies, then the client may receive a refund of 80% of the fee. Some therapists do not want to work under such a contract, because of the regulations and responsibilities set forth by the insurance company. This reimbursement program, nonetheless, redefined the role and identity of the therapist to the public.

Since 1991, psychotherapy has been approved as a profession by the state and has become a protected title by law. This was a great accomplishment for mental health professionals. By November 1999, 5,300 psychotherapists were licensed in Austria, of whom 835 were systemic family therapists. Seventeen training centers were approved to provide training that leads to licensing. To practice psychotherapy in Austria, one has to be licensed by the state. Currently, about 30 institutions are authorized in Austria to provide training for psychotherapy. Family therapists are one of the three largest groups that are licensed under the title of psychotherapist.

Students applying for *fachspezifikum* (graduate training) in one of the 30 state-approved schools must be at least 25 years of age and have passed the *propädeutikum* (undergraduate training) in order to get a special permit from the ministry. They must also have a basic degree in social work, teaching, psychology, or theology. The application process allows candidates and teachers to get more information about what to expect from each other, which presumably helps them to decide if they want to work together for 4 years. The application process appears to be time consuming to some students. The teachers, on the other hand, are very interested in the students' motivation, reasons for training, and their ability and willingness to deal with curriculum requirements. There are also issues of financial burden, demand on time and effort, and interest in working with the clients the way teachers do.

In a larger context, the European Association for Psychotherapy (EAP) was founded in Vienna in 1999. This brought together 182 organizations (including 13 national umbrella organizations) from 28 European countries.

The EAP is concerned with the protection of the interest of the profession and the public it serves. It also acts as a gatekeeper to ensure that the profession follows an appropriate standard of training and practice. In a professional way, EAP continues to legitimize the practice of psychotherapy with the government and public.

In every sense of the words, the growth of psychotherapy in Austria is both painful and slow. We have gone through the "adolescent" phase and hopefully moved to the "adult" phase with much more maturity. In another sense, psychotherapy functionally paved a way for the development of family therapy in Austria. Similar to the United States in the 1950s, family therapy sprung out of psychoanalysis, which was the dominant force during that period. In a similar way, family therapy here was a reaction against psychology and psychoanalysis.

THE BEGINNING OF FAMILY THERAPY

In the last decade of the twentieth century, new technology and political changes in Europe opened up several novel avenues, and in the process adversely affected many people. Cellular phones, answering services, computers, and the internet have provided instant communication with others without seeing, meeting, or hearing them. These avenues of communication have adversely influenced different relationship styles in families and couples. Employment is one of the areas affected. The different working hours, low paying jobs, diminishing trade union protection, and flux in the job market have caused a tremendous amount of stress on the average citizen, which ultimately affects the family. The open borders between East and West Europe (the collapse of the Iron Curtain and Berlin wall) and within the European Union also have created an uncontrollable flow of traffic and new tensions. Furthermore, the wars in the former Yugoslavia have directly created much turmoil and suffering for those who came across the borders into Austria. The distribution of wealth and the availability of resources within the country and Europe have been issues that are constantly challenging the government. Because of the growing scarcity of resources, cutbacks in public financing have become challenges for mental health professionals. These are issues and questions that family therapists and families in Austria grapple with on a daily basis.

In 1974, a *Familienförderungsgesetz* (family referendum) was passed by Austrian government that formed the basis for financing psychological and psychotherapeutic help for families, couples, and psychiatric outpatient clients. As a result of that Act, family therapy centers and child guidance clinics mushroomed (Retzer, 1999). Counseling centers for special clientele, such as families with homosexual members, students, people with sexual problems, and single parents, were provided with highly adequate resources.

Because of the huge demand by the public, some family therapy centers were funded with public money. This new growth provided ample job opportunities for systemic family therapists and other professionals. Drug abuse treatment centers also sprouted and, in most cases, provided mandated treatment with some families. Most *kinderschutzzentren* (child protection centers) and couples and family therapy institutes were usually publicly funded as well. Some of these institutions charged for their services, whereas other institutions offered sliding scale fees for service. Fund raising has become a major activity of institutions providing psychotherapeutic services.

Family therapy as a movement is rather diverse in terms of theories and different models used in working with families. Ongoing voices challenge the establishment. One such voice is Klaus Mücke, who in his article "Verschulung als TotengräberIn der systemischen Psychotherapie" ("Overtraining" is grave-digging for systemic therapy), postulated that the grave of strict regulations was prepared for burying the unique, open, creative, and effective approaches such as solution-focused, competency-focused, or client-oriented therapy (Mücke, 1999). Helm Stierlin, one of the family therapy's trailblazers in German-speaking countries, announced similar views in the introduction to the handbook for systemic therapy and systemic counseling by Von Schlippe and Schweitzer (1996). After 10 years of struggling with fulfilling the requirements without losing systemic identity, the profession seems to have reached a stage that allows therapists to be creative and develop innovative ideas to improve their work with families. Therapists have also adapted to the changes in the markets, working with new managed care regulations, court mandatory therapy, and contracts with social services in an ever-changing environment such as Austria.

FAMILY THERAPY TRAINING WITHIN LEGAL BOUNDARIES

Like other schools of psychotherapy, systemic training is required to fulfill licensing requirements. Systemic training institutes that offered training in the early 1980s had to find ways to identify with some of the mandated teaching elements and adapt their programs and teaching methods to meet the requirements by the law.

Presently, only three institutions are approved by the Ministry of Health, Environment and Traffic to offer systemic therapy training. This shift to formal regulations required uniformity with regard to training, administration, and curriculum. At times this has created turmoil and thus forced the institutions to rethink their teaching methods and training missions. Often, this poses a great challenge to schools and training institutes, because most emphasize collaboration and openness to multiple ways of working with families.

The three programs in family systemic training are somewhat different. The first one is the Fachsektion Sytemische Familientherapie des OAGG (Osterreichische Arbeitsgemeinschaft fur Gruppentherapie und Gruppendynamik) (Systemic Family Therapy Training). This institute operates more from a medical model, even though it has tried to integrate different schools of theories into the curriculum. They existed long before any regulation was needed to monitor mental health practices. Some of the instructors, whom I know personally, worked in psychiatric hospitals and a hospital for children. One of their philosophies is to collaborate with professionals from other parts of the world. They also encourage their students to participate in international conferences. A few instructors have experimented with combining family systems theory with other approaches. Because of the stringent state regulations on specific syllabus and curriculum requirements, they decided to forgo state control and began to run workshops on supervision and see families on their own. In a way, this institution has gone through a lot of changes regulated mostly by the government. Currently, it is a free-standing institute with no support from the government. With a lack of consistent and solid organizational structure, there have been discussions among the staff members as to the role of the institute in the coming years.

The second institute, Lehranstalt fur Systemische Familientherapie der Erzdiozese Wien grew out of a Catholic school for social work with families in their own parishes. There is a strong influence of Catholicism in their curriculum. This school is academically oriented with emphases on exams, written projects, clinical experiences, integration of spirituality, and course fulfillments. They also teach different aspects of systemic theories. Little written information is available about this institute. Of the three institutes, this institute appears to have the fewest students.

Finally, there is the The Austrian Society for Systemic Thinking and Family Therapy (ÖAS model) in Vienna. I provide much more detailed information on this institute since I have been on staff with them for a number of years. OAS requires that students come with some knowledge of therapy, such as theory, human development, personality, assessment and diagnosis, ethics, and basic approaches to psychotherapy. They also require some basic clinical internship (about 200 hours) and passing the propädeutikum (the undergraduate basic training for psychotherapists).

Our institution started with a structural approach 15 years ago and worked with a different systemic framework. Colleagues from the Ackerman Institute, the Milan group, Karl Tomm, Virginia Satir, Steve de Shazer and his team, Harold Goolishian, Tom Anderson, and Kurt Ludewig are only a few who provided us with some direction and sense of identity. The solution-focused approach; the narrative school (ranging from Goolishian, Andersen, and Anderson, to White) and deconstruction approach have been very much a part of our clinical work with families. We have also been influenced somewhat by *Aufstellungen* (systems formation) after Bert Hellinger, a multigenerational approach theorist.

In our program, we started by providing an overview of systemic therapy that eventually leads to more comprehensive course contents. Topics covered are solution-focused approaches (i.e., De Shazer, Kim Berg, Walter, De Jong, Friedman), collaborative language system (i.e., for example, Andersen, Anderson, Goolishian, Ludewig), and narrative therapies (i.e., White, Epston). Students are also exposed to the staff's own theoretical developments based on systems theory, autopoiesis, social constructionism, and performative approaches. Ultimately, students are encouraged to develop their own competency in the style with which they feel most comfortable.

The emphasis in the *first year* is primarily on theoretical background, which includes introduction to systemic thinking and theories, history of systemic therapy, relevant contexts (problem-oriented system, solution-oriented system), family cycles, concepts of family, basics in referral systems, contracting, interviewing, and different types of intervention.

In the *second year*, we teach posturing and practices in various systemic schools and construction of systemic realities emphasizing hypothesizing, exceptions, hypothetical and circular questions, solution talk, intersubjectivity and intercontextuality, deconstruction, and externalizing.

In the *third year*, the students are prepared for practicing therapy under supervision. They are expected to be competent in most of the basic skills by this time and able to work on broadening and learning intermediate and advanced skills. The emphasis here is more on the needs of individual students. Generally, we concentrate on different case settings such as families, children, adolescents, couples, individual sessions, group therapy, client systems and referral, and professional systems.

In the *final year,* we offer specific topics, such as specific therapy concepts and techniques. We also deal with issues in therapy, such as trauma, drugs, psychiatric diagnostics, eating disorders, psychosomatics, gender, and abuse. Often the students choose which topics they wish to focus on. We believe that the task of the teachers is to provide an atmosphere in which learning and growth are possible. We also ensure that the needed skills, learning needs, and learning processes of each student are acknowledged. Each student is treated professionally and encouraged to grow as a person and therapist as much as possible. Also, the instructors are ready to reflect openly on the personal stance, limits, problems, goals, and requests that arise within the student. Each student is encouraged to find his or her individual therapeutic style within the learning context. At the same time, we are conscious that we all create this space together and that everyone takes responsibility for being part of a learning and caring system.

Where do the students come from? I feel the need to expand this section on our students because they are the driving force and future generation of the development of family therapy in Austria. At present, 130 students are enrolled in the ÖAS Institute. The other two institutes have fewer students. The first institute has about 25 trainees, whereas the other program has close to 12 trainees per year. Often our students come from different occupational experiences and have completed basic orientation in psychotherapy (propädeutikum). The students' backgrounds are generally heterogeneous regarding gender, age, family status, personal situation, and professional experience. Out of the current student body of 130 students at the ÖAS, 92 are women and 38 are men. Similar to the United States, we have a very high ratio of women wanting to be trained as family therapists. In our student body, 47 are psychologists, 18 come from the medical profession, 17 are school teachers from different teaching and administrative capacities, 14 are social workers, and nine have academic degrees in pedagogies, whereas 25 students come from different professional backgrounds, such as commerce, computer science, and biology. The high enrollment from psychologists and social workers originated with the closeness of the therapeutic field to their primary professional training (Figure 6.1).

However, they often find that they lack the needed skills to do systemic work and therefore have sought additional training. The negative aspect of

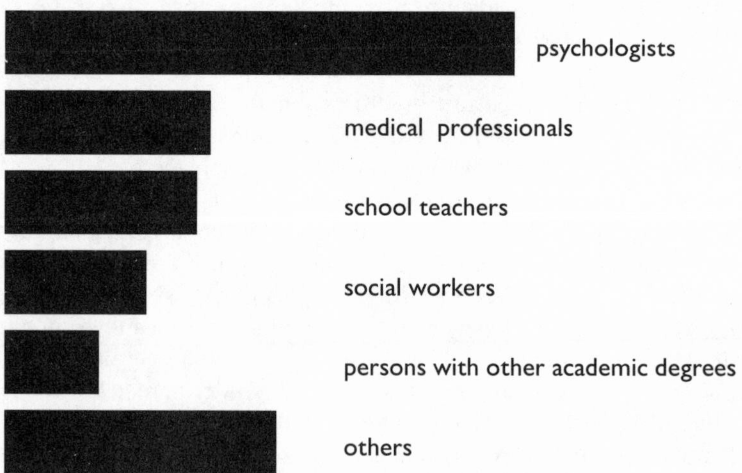

FIGURE 6.1. Occupational experiences of students enrolled in the ÖAS Institute.

seeking additional systemic training is that the students (psychologists and social workers) have a hard time adjusting to their traditional way of working with clients. Their "new way of thinking" can become conflictual in their workplace. These are issues that we often have to handle.

The students' ages vary from 26 to 53 years; about half of the students are between 31 and 40 years; the rest are older than 41 years (Figure 6.2). This distribution clearly shows that becoming a therapist is a second career for most of the students and a well-planned endeavor. Although some younger students are just settling in their private arena, others already are or become parents during the training and some even have grown children. This often brings a rich developmental perspective to the training institute.

Feedback from students shows that listening and attending to their needs calls for much negotiation, reflection, and compromise, which is not always pleasant for everyone. The students have varying degrees of interest in theory. Some find little interest in theories, whereas others perceive it to be highly relevant. For all students, the practice of therapy and supervision is preeminent. One ongoing controversy among students is the issue of how much disclosure is appropriate when conducting therapy and supervision. Although some do not want to spend too much time "talking about ourselves," others feel they do not have enough time for their own personal and group issues. Another debate involves the adequacy of the curriculum and whether instructors from outside with little knowledge of the Austrian lifestyle should be recruited to teach. As in other established institutions across the globe, we constantly have to make adjustments to accommodate changes from different perspectives.

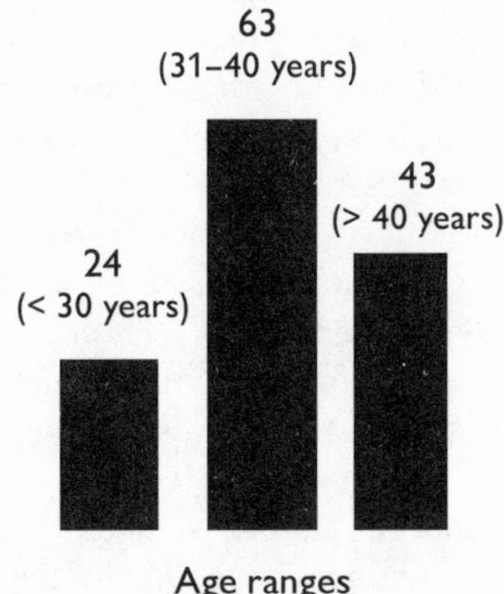

FIGURE 6.2. Age ranges of students enrolled at the ÖAS Institute.

CURRENT DEVELOPMENT IN SYSTEMIC THERAPY

The current systemic movement has created various platforms for open dialogue in Austria. Many local associations and interest groups are organizing regular meetings and setting up workshops, conferences, and discussion groups. Scholars, practitioners, and researchers here seem to prefer dialogue more than empirical research. Only a few systemic therapists hold research or university faculty positions. In German-speaking countries (Germany, Switzerland, Austria, and Lichtenstein), there are a number of systemic-oriented journals, including *Familiendynamik* (23 years old), *Zeitschrift für systemische Familientherapie* (since 1982), *System Familie* (since 1993), *Systema* (since 1986), and *Systeme* (since 1986). Some publishing companies—Karl-Auer-Systeme Verlag, Borgmann Verlag, and Verlag modernes Lernen—specialize in publishing systemic books. Verlag Vandenhoeck & Ruprecht and a few smaller publishing companies publish systemic books among other topics. Most systemic books are translations from the English language.

The first generation of therapists is just about gone. Many of the German trailblazers have formally retired (e.g., Helm Stierlin, Josef Duss von Werdt, Ludwig Reiter, Heimo Gastager, Georgine Steininger, Harry Merl, and Margarete Scholze), whereas others are still active, such as Rosemarie Welter-Enderlin, Jürgen Hargens, Kurt Ludewig, the Milanese Chechin, and Boscolo. At this stage, the second generation has gradually established themselves. This group has grown and expanded rapidly. However, one can only reflect with thankfulness that the first-generation therapists set the stage for systemic therapy in Austria and guided the movement for years. Some years ago, we could refer to only a few people who had given us an identity and a sense of belonging. Now, however, one may speak of a clan, or members of a large extended family with many centers, and diverse emphases on theoretical orientation methods and applications because we have grown so much.

Currently, there is hardly any clear boundary between the different psychotherapeutic schools in Austria, but systemic therapy and thinking have the strongest influence and have deeply permeated other schools of thought. Most mental health professionals have been exposed in one way or another to short-term therapy, hypnotherapeutic techniques, systems work with individuals, and other systemic-influenced clinical techniques. There have been ongoing discussions on who is still included in the systemic arena; the brief therapists, the narrative therapists, the feminist therapists (a rather small group), the systems formation people (*Aufstellungen*), and many more. In this regard, I believe that we need to continue a dialogue on a functional definition of systemic family therapy. In order to accomplish that, we need to engage in meaningful dialogues with each other. Some of the crucial questions are: Where do we go after the postmodern period? Will we turn to other ways or disciplines outside of the systemic therapy arena, or is it time again to deconstruct the format of therapy, because the new regulations are making sweeping challenges regarding mental health practices? These are, indeed, very pressing questions faced by second-generation therapists. In my view, it is a challenging time for systemic therapists in Austria. The movement of systemic therapy and thinking has reached a different stage. It has become a democratic, open, and very diverse field. Some in the past have taken advantage of it, whereas others are struggling to deal with it. Others have tried to provide direction with little or no support. At times, it resulted in chaos, disorientation, and power struggles. In reality, we are much like other organizations having to deal with the joys and woes of maturing.

CONCLUSION

In Austria, the creative expansion of systemic family therapy in the late 1980s was followed by a period of formalizing and restructuring in the 1990s. Now the movement calls for more emphasis on the core commonalities that hold the systemic people together and yet allow flexibility, patience, and open dialogue. This often requires respect and listening to each others' differences.

Some of the twenty-first century challenges for therapists to deal with are the effects of globalization, new communication, and giving up of nationalism in favor of a more open Europe. This has a tremendous impact on family units, systems work, training, and identity. Currently, people in Europe are more flexible in moving from country to country and losing their family roots. The East European countries in particular have undergone drastic changes in ideology, commerce, mobility, and lifestyle. Our southern neighbors also have to deal with many problems, including the long-lasting effects of the wars in Kosovo and Bosnia. The parliaments in Western European countries are constantly moving away from liberal socialism. That in itself may adversely change the available resources and attitudes toward those in need of help even more. Job possibilities and contracts are also undergoing changes that affect the family lifestyle.

All these changes ultimately will redefine the work and mission of systemic therapists in Austria. With regard to the potential families that we work with, we need to be more sensitive to their backgrounds, because we will be seeing families from other regions as well. We also need to revisit the intervention techniques, because there are obvious cultural and language differences. With regard to training, we critically need to assess its usefulness and effectiveness to meet the needs of future generations. The bottom line is that our future is both highly challenging and uncertain. We can always echo Jay Efran's wisdom, who states that change is a part of normality (Efran, 1986).

REFERENCES

Efran, J. (1986). Sprache: Realitäten, illusionen und paradoxa. . . . Ein Gespräch. *Zeitschrift für Systemische Therapie, 4,* 80–88.

Familienbericht, Ö. (1999). *Familie-zwischen Anspruch und Alltag. Zur Situation von familie und familienpolitik in Österreich.* Bundesministerium für Umwelt, Familie und Jugend, Austria.

Mücke, K. (1999). Verschulung als totengräber in der systemischen psychotherapie. *Z für systemische Therapie 17*(2), 94–100.

Retzer, A. (1999). Die zukunft der systemischen familientherapie. *Familiendynamik* 24(4), 200–217.

Von Schlippe, A., & Schweitzer, J. (1996). Lehrbuch der systemischen therapie und beratung. Vandenhoeck & Ruprecht, Göttingen Wanschura Esther (1996) Zur situation der familie und familientherapie in Österreich. *Familiendynamik 21*(1), 85–95.

CHAPTER 7

The Effects of Family Therapy in Italy

PAOLO BERTRANDO

In Italy, as well as in the United States, the birth and proliferation of family therapy has occurred mainly within a psychiatric environment. However, a difference in timing—a delay of 20 years—and different social and political conditions, have engendered a series of peculiarities to which Italian family therapy owes its deeply, in all senses, "national" aspect.

First of all, in this chapter I endeavor to outline the situation of both psychiatry and psychotherapy in Italy at the end of the 1960s, when family therapy was being introduced to our country. I go on to sketch the birth and development of our main schools of family therapy, until the period of its most resolute growth at the beginning of the 1980s. Then I describe the present phase of institutional consolidation in Italian family therapy, which resulted from the legal regulation of psychotherapy as a profession and activity in the schools of psychotherapy. Last I attempt to synthesize the characteristics that distinguish, within the psychiatric whole, the Italian movement of family therapy as opposed to those of other countries.

ITALIAN PSYCHIATRY: BETWEEN TOTAL INSTITUTION AND COMMUNITY

As far as Italian psychiatry is concerned, the period between 1960 and 1970 was one of profound crisis and evolution. Although up to that time Italian psychiatry had been essentially biological and institutional, during those years new concepts came into play, such as sociopolitical critique, antipsychiatry, and psychoanalysis. By 1960, it was abundantly clear that institutional psychiatry was entering its conceptual twilight. In our country it continued nevertheless to rule without interference the lives of most patients and psychiatrists, because psychoanalysis was the preserve of a few, rigorously private specialists, and any sporadic attempt to transfer it to institutions aroused perplexity in the minds of traditional psychiatrists. Community therapy was virtually unknown, and even the introduction of psychotropic drugs had not really altered the existing situation, although it occurred more or less simultaneously with that of other Western countries.

Psychiatric patients continued to be institutionalized, so much so that research statistics show that in Italy the number of patients in psychiatric hospitals increased steadily until the end of the 1960s, remaining unchanged thereafter until the 1978 reform (Canosa, 1979). These data ought not to be wondered at. As Warner's (1985) accurate research has shown, the deinstitutionalization of psychiatric patients both in England and the United States had begun before the introduction of neuroleptic medication, and had simply been amplified and accelerated by it. Deinstitutionalization did not depend either on the discovery or the use of specific categories of drugs, but rather on the attitudes of society or the characteristics of the economy as well as on the choices made by psychiatrists.

In Italy—formerly a peasant, archaic culture that had turned into a strongly industrialized, increasingly dynamic nation—the situation was changing. It follows, then, that the psychiatric situation also could not remain indefinitely stagnant. In 1962, Basaglia inaugurated the first Italian therapeutic community in Gorizia's psychiatric hospital. This experiment was followed soon by other pilot centers in Arezzo, Parma, and Trieste. At the same time, the first therapeutic centers outside hospitals began to be opened, initially in Perugia, in 1968, and 1 year later in Reggio Emilia.

Simultaneously, psychoanalysis found its place both in Italian social life, together with a noticeable increase in the number of private psychotherapists, and in the psychiatric institutions themselves. Besides, on a cultural level, the British authors of antipsychiatry, Ronald Laing, David Esterson, and David Cooper, began to excite the interest of thoughtful readers. Although the answers provided by psychoanalysts and antipsychiatrists to the problems posed by social Italian psychiatry were varied and antithetic in many respects, they contributed nevertheless to a decisive modernization of ancient institutional practices.

Each of these models contained, in more or less explicit form, a reference to relationships, context, and family: It was by working on the most profound implications of the renewal of psychiatry that a fresh interest in the role of the family in all psychopathological models, and therefore the possibility of intervening therapeutically in family matters without mediation, was emerging in Italy. It is no mere chance that *La maggioranza deviante* was written in the early 1970s which was one of the first theoretical texts, should welcome contributions by the founder of antipsychiatry, Ronald Laing, and by Jurgen Ruesch, fellow author, together with Gregory Bateson, of *Communication: The Social Matrix of Psychiatry* (Ruesch & Bateson, 1951).

It is probably here that the origin of the deep tie among family therapy, psychiatry, and social politics in Italy is to be found. In Italy, family therapy occupied a critical place vis-à-vis official psychiatry, which is a common feature of original American family therapy, but in Italy the critique was sociopolitical rather than merely epistemological as had been the case in America.[1] This is how one of the pioneers of Italian family therapy, Luigi Cancrini, as a young psychiatrist undergoing personal analysis, recalls his first encounter with those trends of thought:

> The second "flash of lightning", in 1968, was Franco Basaglia's *L'istituzione negata*; an identity crisis suffered by an only partially trained psychoanalyst who was distressed by the disparity between psychiatric texts and their practical application and was unable to enjoy the rites celebrated by the increasingly tired, marginalized and depressed personnel of the Institute of Psychoanalysis. New therapeutic enthusiasm was aroused by D.D. Jackson's book and Paul Watzlawick, Jay Haley and Sal Minuchin's lively brand of teaching. (Carcrini, 1987, p. 13)

In a sense, our young Italian psychiatrists needed to be furnished with ideas that could go beyond psychoanalytical intuition, however remarkable it may be. Soon the family systems therapy was to become one of the veins they would be able to tap.

THE BIRTH OF ITALIAN FAMILY THERAPY

The strongest impulse toward the evolution of Italian family therapy came from professionals who ventured directly to the United States to study whatever new ideas might have burgeoned in the field. The first was Mara Selvini Palazzoli, a psychoanalyst in her late forties, already well known for her research into nervous anorexia (Selvini Palazzoli, 1974), but still sufficiently restless. Having taken 2 years of voluntary sabbatical away from her patients, she was one of the first to embark on a trip to the United States with the view to bringing her studies up to date (Selvini Palazzoli et al., 1975). There she met the new ideas of the fledgling American family therapy (she was present at the Philadelphia meeting where Murray Bowen disclosed to the fellow therapists his own struggle with his own family of origin), and also two younger Italian colleagues, Luigi Boscolo and Gianfranco Cecchin, who had already spent 7 years there studying, first psychiatry and later psychoanalysis.

1. It is interesting, moreover, that in the United States political criticism is being discovered at the present time, mostly stimulated by feminism and "political correctness."

Again, it was Mara Selvini Palazzoli who, together with her colleague Pierfrancesco Galli, organized the first Italian symposium on family therapy in Veltri sul Mare, in 1967. It is interesting that the two main guest speakers covered exactly the two areas of great importance for Italian psychiatry of the time: Nathan Ackerman was the chief exponent of psychoanalytic family therapy in the United States (Ackerman, 1958), and Ronald Laing, the antipsychiatrist who had addressed his sharpest criticism to the family as an institution, as well as its dynamics (Laing, 1969). Besides, one finds among the members of the conference nearly all the young critical psychiatrists who are in the process of modernizing the institutions of the time, from Franco Basaglia to Giovanni Jervis.

In 1967, Selvini Palazzoli, Boscolo, and Cecchin, together with Giuliana Prata and four other colleagues, founded in Milan the Centro per lo Studio della Famiglia, with a view to applying all common psychoanalytical knowledge to the treatment of whole families. In any case, all therapists who at that time began working with family therapy were psychoanalysts. Among them one can count Italo Carta, who became acquainted with family therapy as an intern in Lausanne, together with Ciompi and Muller, and began to practice family therapy at the University of Milan in 1970. He continued for the next 20 years, training a number of therapists of psychiatric extraction, without founding an organized school of his own, however.

Luigi Cancrini was a psychoanalyst too. Having come to the end of his analysis under Ignacio Matte Blanco (and being, as we have already noted, rather critical of orthodox psychoanalytical attitudes), in 1970 he formed in his turn a working group in Rome, within a research project on drug addiction financed by the Agnelli foundation and developed by Rome University. Patrizia Angrisani, Maria Grazia Cancrini, Maurizio Coletti, Marisa Malagoli Togliatti, Maurizio Andolfi, and Gianni Fioravanti were members of his group, whereas Gaspare Vella followed their work from a distance and Luigi Onnis joined somewhat later. The various schools of Roman family therapy grew out of this group and its subsequent splits. From the very beginning, however, the Roman therapists placed the psychoanalytical concepts side by side with those of systemic and structural family theory.

In 1971, feeling dissatisfied with the results of psychoanalytical family therapies, Selvini Palazzoli, Boscolo, Cecchin, and Prata chose to abandon their own psychoanalytical references to embrace the strategic-systemic theory propounded by the Mental Research Institute of Palo Alto (Watzlawick et al., 1967, 1974). Paul Watzlawick assumed the role of supervisor during the first weeks of this new work mode.

In a way, the origins and personal trajectories of the founders exerted a profound influence on what became the course of the Milanese and Roman schools, at least during the 1970s. The Milanese therapists were private practitioners with interests that were predominantly epistemological and theoretical; they were aware of their choices regarding a type of research that was both discreet and secluded. As the group expressed it:

> For various reasons relevant to the position of Italian psychiatry, on which it would however be pointless to linger, a Center totally independent from grants and public institutions was opted for. The incidence of pressure likely to disturb a not autonomous team is by no means unknown: establishing of deadlines for the publication of data; imposition from outside as to the acceptance of new members; exploitation regarding matters extraneous to research, etc. (Selvini Palazzoli et al., 1975, p. 17)

The Roman therapists, instead, were connected with the various universities (Cancrini ad Malagoli Togliatti with the faculty of psychology, Vella with psychiatry, and Andolfi with child neuropsychiatry, then psychology), with a very strong politic and social interest. This is Luigi Cancrini's version of such a commitment:

> As we were saying, the intervention into the small system was an exercise analogous to the one which was developing politically in the larger social systems and we believed we would be able to detect important consonances. Even then, we felt that a correct psychotherapeutic intervention would be a liberating one, influenced as we were by reading Laing, for example, or the better known systemics, and certainly Basaglia's lesson. (Criconia & Scamperle, 1986, p. 5)

As a matter of fact, still in the 1970s, the strong Laingian mortgage did not mitigate within the group, as is shown in Cancrini's essay (1977), in which mental illness is read in terms of "mystification," and political criticism toward the power structures is penetrating. These, however, are views that tended to pale during the 1980s.

On the other hand, the interest in the application of family therapy within psychiatric services stayed to the fore. The Cancrini group, which had coalesced both with the university and the social groups, was indeed the first to enact training initiatives, which would address themselves mostly to professionals working for state agencies.

> We ourselves have always been a group half-way between those centered closely upon family therapy and its techniques and those which instead theorized "the community" and the non use of techniques. . . . This intermediate position between what was then called "the community" and the family therapy techniques has naturally lead [sic] to a priority interest in the development of a training activity within the public services or in any case in collaboration with them. (Criconia & Scamperle, 1986, p. 5)

The epistemological orientation of the two groups was influenced by this different origin as well. The Milan therapists tended toward an ever-growing theoretical rigor, and ended up by earning for themselves the definition of systemic purists, whereas those of the Roman school turned out more eclectic and pragmatic. The sometimes polemical comparison between the two tendencies was to shape the debate on Italian family therapy for years (Angelo, de Bernart, & Giacometti, 1987).

The second half of the 1970s was crucial for family therapy in Italy. Between 1974 and 1978 events occurred that transformed a more or less isolated series of schools into a real movement. In 1973, Cancrini's Roman group put together the Centro Studi di Terapia Familiare e Relazionale, which in turn, in 1974, inaugurated the first Italian program for the education of family therapists. In 1975 the Milan group published *Paradosso e controparadosso* (*Paradox and Counterparadox*, Selvini Palazzoli et al., 1978), the first comprehensive illustration of its own therapeutic model. More or less simultaneously, two more groups of family therapists were born, formed respectively by Maurizio Andolfi and Gaspare Vella.

After some years in the United States, where he studied first with Zwelring in New York, then with Minuchin in Philadelphia, and finally with Whitaker in Atlanta (Bertrando & Toffanetti, 2001), Andolfi founded, at the beginning of 1975 the Centro Studi sulla Comunicazione dei Sistemi, which was to become the Istituto di Terapia Familiare in Rome, where he was joined by Carmine Saccu, Claudio Angelo, Marcella de Nichilo, Paolo Menghi, and Anna Maria Nicolò, as well as Rodolfo de Bernart, who went on to found his own Istituto di Terapia Familiare in Florence.

> The unusual amount of attention devoted to the therapist, the supervisor and the patient . . . has been one of the unusual aspects of (our) group. We had in fact noticed that true resistance came not so much from the family, but rather from the therapist who, very often, represented a brake in the therapeutic process. With reference to this, we have actually coined an expression that has become widespread in the course of the years, that of "working on the professional handicap of therapists," convinced as we were that at the beginning of his career, a therapist was basically handicapped as well as insecure. (Criconia & Scamperle, 1986, p. 2)

Indeed, because of so strong an accent on the person of the therapist, the Istituto di Terapia Familiare was to become the center that placed the greatest stress on the structuring of the training, which in turn envisages three training levels, that is, introductory courses, basic training, and specialization schools, with a total of 10 years' training.

At the end of 1974, Gaspare Vella created the Centro per la Psicoterapia della Coppia e della Famiglia (which was to become the Istituto di

Psicoterapia Relazionale) together with Camillo Loriedo, Chiara Angolari, Sergio Lupoi, Luisa Martini, and other colleagues. To begin with, the aims of the center were above all studying family therapy theory and keeping up to date, as well as organizing conferences and reunions in which various charismatic therapists participate; among them Carl Whitaker stands out. The latter, together with Milton Erickson, came to represent the point of reference during the shaping of a model for the center (Vella, Loriedo, & Schepisi, 1995).

> The belief that Whitaker's experiential orientation and Erickson's therapy are complementary with each other owing to a common philosophy founded on a positive view of humankind (symptomatic behavior not excluded) and of the evolutionary capacity of human systems, has led us to elaborate an approach that attends to the two aspects we consider essential. (Criconia & Scamperle, 1986, pp. 9–10)

The last of the great Italian family therapy centers, according to chronological order, is the Centro Interdisciplinare di Ricerca e di Intervento sui Sistemi Umani (CIRISU), founded in 1978 in connection with the University of Bari by Piero de Giacomo, Giampaolo Pierri, Antonietta Santoni Rugiu, and Marisella Buonsante. De Giacomo, who spent 1 year (1977–1978) in Minuchin's Philadelphia Child Guidance Clinic, founded the center mainly with the aim of perfecting, together with colleagues (also from other disciplines, such as physics and informatics), his "elementary pragmatic model" (De Giacomo, 1993), a highly formalized model that seeks to "create a 'scientific' foundation for relational psychotherapy to be used for purposes of teaching, the diagnostic of systems, putting into operation predetermined interventions, and the evaluation of results" (Criconia & Scamperle, 1986, p. 8).

Finally, in Milan, between 1977 and 1978, Boscolo and Cecchin began to organize their own training, alongside the continuing work of clinical research, as others had done earlier. In 1980, this decision would lead to the final break of the original Milan group. Boscolo and Cecchin went on to establish their Centro Milanese di Terapia della Famiglia, mainly devoted to training and clinical purposes; Selvini Palazzoli and Prata created the Nuovo Centro per lo Studio della Famiglia, devoted mostly to research into their developing new model of "family games." The Milan centers were to be the origin—owing above all to the first training cycles—of a second generation of "systemic purists," among them Valeria Ugazio, Umberta Telfener, Marco Bianciardi, Maurizio Viaro, and the members of the Bologna center, such as Laura Fruggeri, Maurizio Marzari, Anna Castellucci, and Massimo Mattein.

In 1997 Andolfi founded the first Italian journal devoted to family therapy, *Terapia Familiare*, which, in spite of having been born essentially as an organ of his institute, enjoyed a progressive growth both of readers and editorial boards. The latter ended up hosting exponents of all the most important schools and thus represented the principal arena for debate among Italian family therapists as well as a vehicle for the most recent contributions from abroad. A similar function was carried out at the same time by several volumes published by the Cancrini group and by the two national congresses on "La prospettiva Relazionale nei Servizi territoriali" promoted by the Vella and Loriedo center. Within the framework of these and other conferences a breach occurred between family therapists and the more orthodox wing of radical critical psychiatry, "Psichiatria democratica."

> The opposition had to do with one idea: at the time it was held that any technique at all was a way of adapting persons, families and people to social contradictions. Family therapy had only just appeared on the scene yet one could say that, at the very moment it reared its head, it was immediately branded as reactionary by Psichiatria Democratica. I remember short newspaper articles in which I was described as the reactionary North American who wished to recondition all families. In 1978, during an important conference in Florence, 1,500 people came along and there was picketing by Psichiatria Democratica which blocked all entrances and distributed leaflets undermining the conference. At the outset there was a first crisis in my own Institute in Via Reno, when my very students, after one year, picketed against the family therapy I myself had taught them, because it was not "in line" with the political statute of the time. Indeed a time of sheer folly. (Andolfi, personal communication)

As we reach the end of the decade, we notice that the family therapy movement had reached a remarkable numerical consistency and a fine level of conceptual exchange. Besides, systemic ideas—in a wide sense—had grown to be increasingly interesting for many psychiatric operators, in spite of opposition on the part of Psichiatria Democratica, owing to the altered work conditions that followed the psychiatric reform of 1978. Before dealing with the spreading of family therapy in Italian psychiatry and psychology, however, we must devote some space to the most important models of Italian family therapy.

ITALIAN MODELS OF FAMILY THERAPY

In Italy, between 1975 and 1985, family therapy produced its most startling results, thanks above all to the original work carried out by the Milan and Andolfi groups; other therapists, such as Cancrini and Vella, chose to work on integrative models.

When, at the beginning of the 1970s, the Milan group adopted the MRI model, its attention was focused mainly on the organization of the family. The team attempted to devise a systemic hypothesis on the way the family had organized itself in relationship to the presenting problem(s): The hypothesis corresponded to the "family game," or at least to some of it, as a key corresponds to a lock. The therapy aimed to eliminate the rigid configurations of dysfunctional behavior, leaving space for the possible emergence of more functional configurations. Such an aim was reached through the positive connotation of all kinds of behavior, symptomatic or not, found in the family (paradoxical reformulation) and by means of family rituals. The Milan therapists became famous both because of the dramatic quality and power of their "counterparadoxical" final interventions, and because of the great discipline and organization that informed their team work. Many others took the session divided into five parts and the monthly meetings as an example (Selvini Palazzoli et al., 1978).

Around 1975, the publication of the collected works of Bateson, *Steps to an Ecology of Mind* (Bateson, 1972), opened new horizons for the group. An attempt was made to infuse Bateson's complex cybernetic epistemology into clinical practice, to think in systemic mode in order to act likewise. If compared to the position adopted by the Mental Research Institute, Bateson's original writing appears to hark back to a systemic thought that is both purer and more complex. The distinction between map and territory, the logical categories of learning, the concept of mind as system, and system as mind, the notion of cybernetic epistemology, and the introduction of semantics assumed a central position. The application of these ideas in a clinical framework led to the development of a new method for collecting and elaborating information and for interventions on human systems, with the enunciation of three guidelines for the conductor of a session: hypothesizing, circularity, and neutrality, which ended up being the distinctive feature of the model (Selvini Palazzoli et al., 1980).

The concept of systemic hypothesis was especially important: The therapist worked on hypotheses that were now considered always tentative and revisable, setting aside the idea that it is possible to reach the "ultimate reality" of the family game. At the same time, the Milan therapist was now assisted in his work by a new and efficacious instrument: the circular questions, built directly on the Batesonian concept of "a difference that makes a difference," and so defined, in that the therapist poses questions to various members of the family in turn on the behavior of two or more other family members. Both family and therapist are able, on the basis of these questions, to constantly change their understanding according to information offered by the other. Circular questions provide news of differences, fresh links among ideas, meanings, and behavior, which might change the epistemology, that is, the sum of unconscious assumptions (Bateson, 1972) by the whole family. In this way the circular questions turned themselves into an intervention, perhaps the most important one for the systemic Milanese therapist (Boscolo et al., 1987; Penn, 1982, 1985; Tomm, 1985).

After the 1980 split, the two halves of the team developed two very different models. Selvini Palazzoli and Prata seek to "discover" possible, specific family organizations (games), related to specific syndromes, such as psychoses. Later, in 1983, Mara Selvini Palazzoli, Stefano Cirillo, Matteo Selvini, and Anna Maria Sorrentino formed a new foursome, in order to further the research into family typologies. The results are published in the volume *I giochi psicotici nella famiglia (family games)* (Selvini Palazzoli et al., 1988). In subsequent years, such ideas were developed in regard to drug addiction (Cirillo et al., 1995) and eating disorders (Selvini Palazzoli et al., 1998). Soon after the publication of the latter book, Mara Selvini Palazzoli died, 1999.

Boscolo and Cecchin followed a different course, considerably influenced by training. Families were now seen by one or two therapists, who often were trainees, whereas from behind the mirror the remaining trainees observed them together with two trainers. The interaction between trainers and trainees led to an alteration in the very nature of the hypotheses: Most trainees operated, as we have seen, in the public services. This determined that the therapist's hypothesis should include at least the patient, family, referring person, other professionals, and the whole organization, with its own rules, professionals of different professionalism, and variegated technical formulations: the "significant system," similar to Goolishian's "problem-determined system" (Anderson et al., 1988). Naturally, the significant system included the therapist as well, in his role of observer, together with his theories and prejudices. Milan therapists attempted now to understand the ways in which the patterns of ideas and meanings, which emerged at the same time as the complex net created by the significant system, contributed to the consensual birth of the observed clinical image.

Later, in the early 1980s, Boscolo and Cecchin began to travel widely, communicating as well as applying their method as consultants, and in workshops and conferences. Both in Europe and America several teams started experimenting with what is becoming known as the "Milan Approach." Personal exchanges with Humberto Maturana, Heinz von Foerster, and Ernst von Glasersfeld began with a conference, "Philosophers meet Clinicians," organized in Calgary in 1984 by Karl Tomm, opening the way to the concepts of radical constructivism. Thus attention moved from the observed to the observing system, both conceived as "minds" equipped with the same level of organization: The patients observed the therapists just as the therapists observed the patients. As a result, in coherence with prospects that are both constructivist and second class as far as cybernetics, emphasis in the therapies goes from observed behavior to behavior, to ideas, to theories, and to the personal premises of the therapists. Greater attention was being paid to what used to happen during sessions: exchange of information, expressions of emotion or feeling between therapists and patients, that is, to the therapeutic process rather than the final intervention (Boscolo et al., 1987).

The various Roman schools of family therapy were displaying, in the same period, less assertiveness than the Milanese. If it is true that the latter affirm to the very end their own absolute originality. The Romans were aware of their indebtedness to the masters. If Vella and Loriedo point above all to an integration between Minuchin's structural theories and Milton Erickson's paradoxical praxis (Loriedo was becoming *inter alia* one of the greatest Italian experts in hypnosis), Cancrini was operating increasingly on a level of eclecticism founded upon an idea not dissimilar from the one that informs research on common factors in psychotherapy. Basically, for Cancrini only one approach exists, whose all known techniques are nothing but specific applications. To adhere to a theoretical purism, then, is mere illusion. Moreover, this position is particularly suited to the founder of a school whose task had always been the training of students who originated from a wide range of professions, and were active in the public sector, although Cancrini was to acquire renown through a series of inquiries into specific problems, which range from learning problems (Cancrini, 1974), to drug addiction (Cancrini, 1982), to psychiatric rehabilitation (Cancrini, 1999).

> It could well be that Maurizio Andolfi is the most creative of all Roman therapists. At the time of founding his school, Andolfi had been under the powerful influence of, first, Salvador Minuchin and, later, Carl Whitaker. These two therapists underlie his therapeutic conceptions, as does the work of Karen Horney (indeed, during his spell in the States, Andolfi undergoes a Horneian oriented analysis).
>
> To me, a structural approach means no structural approach, it means Minuchin. I do not consider Minuchin a great trainer (he was so worried that someone might not be in agreement with him, that in the end it was no longer possible to be creative), but certainly a great clinician. I recall that in therapy he showed such compassion, was so well disposed towards people, so prepared to be questioned, to fail without feeling shame of any kind. To me, he gave a great deal of what I, not unlike an artisan, was building on my own: a study of the family through the attitudes of a child and, above all, the ability to understand the family world through infantile symptoms.
>
> Years later, Whitaker came to represent for me another cornerstone of family therapy. For years there was an association between us, I went to see him at home, canooed with him, saw eight families a day and for years we held seminars together around the world. Minuchin had no

> conception of what a psychotic human being meant, was in terror of everything not rational or controllable, or of anything that in some way could not be reorganized in spatial or operative terms. Whitaker knew how to enter the irrational and the symbolical in a truly fantastic, unimaginable way. And then there was the generational dimension. Whitaker's way of working was to observe three to four generations, and thus extend the story. This is a way of normalizing the pathology which, once placed on a relative, historical level is no longer so fundamental. (Andolfi, personal communication)

In the early 1980s, Andolfi formalized his own model in a book written together with his most faithful colleagues (Andolfi et al., 1982). In many ways, his style was the opposite of the one adopted by the Milan therapists: If the latter were quiet, apparently detached, according to Andolfi the therapist was, at the time, a protagonist who assumed a central place at the heart of the family so as to be able to remove from the patient his own central, yet problematical position. Hence the use of very strong verbal expressions, of objects and games (remember that Andolfi comes from the infantile brand of psychiatry) that are brought to therapy as if they were metaphors rendered concrete. In the years when, after the enforcing of the law so strongly desired by Basaglia, the psychiatric hospitals opened their doors, and for the first time psychotic patients circulated freely in the streets, this confrontational and vigorous way offered by his brand of therapy seemed apt. With the passing of time, however, it became attenuated:

> Now more than ever it is a matter of collaboration, of co-therapy with the patient. If a child is undergoing therapy, almost always, after a few sessions, I call him, I draw him close and establish a physical contact. Then we talk about the family. In this way a truly different dialogue is created, in which one inside, and the other outside the family try to exchange ideas on how the family may be helped to proceed. (Andolfi, personal communication)

What has survived of Andolfi's position is the idea of looking for an area of competence even in the most disturbed kind of behavior without attempting to connotate positively, and more or less provocatively, everything done by all members of the family, nor going off in search of unique outcomes according to the style of narrative therapists (White & Epston, 1991).

> Instead it is a matter of recognizing that the apparent instances of incompetence displayed by the patients are in fact proper manifestations of competence. It is a question, therefore, of a ceaseless work of redefinition of how the problem was described and lived, both by the patient and

> his family, so much so that today, when in the course of training I perceive that a therapist is in difficulty, I summon the patient in order to help the therapist. In the field of psychotherapy, this corresponds to when, acting as supervisor, I employ the resources, which I feel the patient is activating in order to help the therapist who ought to be helping him. (Andolfi, personal communication)

PROLIFERATION OF FAMILY THERAPY IN ITALY

After decades of a stagnation that was more or less accepted by psychiatry and society at large, the 180 law of 1978 produced dramatic changes in the realm of psychiatric assistance in Italy almost instantly. Such law, which represented simultaneously the highest point in social critical psychiatry as well as the beginning of its decline (especially in the wider public opinion), was closely intertwined with the destiny of family as well as relational therapy in general (Fruggeri et al., 1995).

The 1978 law, which is doubtless the most quoted and controversial point in the whole of Italian psychiatry, was in fact rendered necessary by a series of contingencies. Although the birth of democratic psychiatry in 1973 gave a crucial impulse to social psychiatry, it had only a marginal effect on Italian psychiatry on the whole. The law that governed psychiatry was still the royal law of 1904 and the various proposals to reform had been bogged down in indifference except for the modification of a few norms in 1968, following a sentence promulgated by the Supreme Court. The precipitous passing of the 1978 law had derived above all from a desire to thwart a referendum, which would repeal the 1904 law. Thus, Italian psychiatry became a community psychiatry according to a norm of law.

At the same time, most psychiatric operators realized that they were dramatically short of the theoretical and operative instruments they needed in order to face the new need for a psychiatric territorial assistance for the public. A paradigm was needed that could accompany the biological one (at the time truly negligible in basic psychiatry) and the psychoanalytic one (often predominant), but a paradigm that could at the same time guarantee greater elasticity and versatility. On the whole, the various relational models seemed to offer one of the more likely answers, at least in intention, if the theoretical and methodological void, often present in the services, was to be filled. Family therapies, generally considered more "social" and manageable than psychoanalytic ones, enjoyed a spell of good fortune. Years later Luigi Boscolo would narrate: "So many psychiatric professionals would come to us, in Milan, and said: we have brought psychiatry to the families, but now we don't know how to work with them; you must teach us how to treat them" (personal communication).

Therefore, the 1980s engendered a strong polarization in the schools, favored also by an uncertain legislative situation. This phenomenon led on the one hand to considerable vitality, witnessed by the emergence of a series of new magazines that little by little joined *Terapia Familiare*: *Ecologia della mente, Attraverso lo specchio, Psicobiettivo,* and *Connessioni*; and, on the other, to an ever-growing number of conferences and seminars where, also with practical workshops, the exponents of various orientations held discussions. In 1981, after 5 years of activity, for the first time an issue of Terapia Familiare was seen to contain only Italian contributions.

The progressive pulverization and filiation of the great, principal schools with a strong tendency toward "nominalism," however, was the other face of proliferation. During the 1980s, comparisons between schools were often marked by an emphasis on differences (purism against eclecticism, centrality of technique against centrality of the person, setting against environment, system against individual, and so on). An examination of the first decade of *Terapia Familiare* (Angelo et al., 1987) discloses in this respect the tendency to lay stress on discrimination rather than contact.

The tendency to set up new schools, moreover, did not lessen with the passing of time. On the contrary, in the early 1990s two notable events took place: Mara Selvini Palazzoli's new group presented a new kind of training for the model of psychotic family games, thus interrupting the voluntary didactic exile of the group; Maurizio Andolfi left the Istituto di Terapia Familiare to Carmine Saccu, and went on to found the Accademia di Psicoterapia della Famiglia, not relinquishing however his editorship of *Terapia Familiare*.

After the first half of the 1980s, family therapy was embraced by more and more professionals. Social workers, who had not, as had been the case in the United States, had a great deal to do with the emergence of the movement, were increasingly involved in systemic intervention courses; also official psychiatry started to show interest toward the systemic and family dimension. This was owing not only to the contribution of the various family therapy institutes attached to universities, but also to the discovery of family expressed emotion research (Leff & Vaughn, 1985).

In Italy, such research was introduced by the Associazione Ricerche sulla Schizofrenia (ARS: Association for the Research on Schizophrenia), affiliated to the Milan University, under the direction of Carlo Lorenzo Cazzullo (Bertrando et al., 1992; Maffei et al., 1986). The international workshop "Schizofrenia e Famiglia: Modelli a Confronto" (Schizophrenia and the Family: a Comparison of Models), organized by ARS in 1987, was a national event, the first to broadcast the idea of expressed emotionality and compare the main systemic orientations with the methods of family treatment addressed to chronic psychiatric patients, employed by a new brand of family therapists, who referred to themselves as "psychoeducational" or, more generically, "psychosocial" (Leff et al., 1982).

The first model of a psychoeducational nature to find application in Italy was perfected by the ARS research group coordinated by Massimo Clerici and addressed to families with schizophrenic members (Clerici et al., 1995). Soon afterward other groups were born, such as the one in Aquila University, directed by Massimo Casacchia and coordinated by Rita Roncone. In the early 1990s, behavioral family therapy, in its psychoeducational version, also reached Italy through a series of seminars conducted by Ian Falloon for the personnel of psychiatric services.

Although psychoeducation in Italy was met with a certain favor in Italy, it was also strongly criticized by the supporters of a different model of integrated intervention on psychoses. For example, the group of Verona University, led by Orazio Siciliani, proposed instead a model founded mainly on the Milan systemic therapy as well as on object relations psychology (Siani, Siciliani, & Burti, 1991).

The most positive aspect of this set of events resides, however, in the fact that family therapy (or at any rate an intervention on systems, whether they be familial or not) in its various meanings turned in the 1980s into an asset of Italian psychiatric assistance, somehow closing the circle that had opened in the 1960s: from community psychiatry through elaboration in specialized family therapy centers back to community psychiatry. Toward the mid-1980s Gianfranco Cecchin observed: "At this point Italy is nothing but a proliferation of one way mirrors, videotapes and telecameras!" (Cecchin, personal communication).

INSTITUTIONAL CONSOLIDATION

Toward the mid-1980s the rigid subdivision between opposite schools revealed its less attractive aspects, and was followed by the emergence of unitary initiatives by the various schools. As early as 1975, Andolfi had founded a Società Italiana di Terapia Familiare (Italian Family Therapy Association), which had not, however, managed to set itself up as hyphen for all Italian family therapists. Ten years later, the representatives of the six principal schools (Andolfi, Boscolo, Cancrini, Cecchin, de Giacomo, and Vella) founded at last the Società Italiana di Psicologia e Psicoterapia Relazionale (SIPPR: Italian Association for Relational Psychology and Psychotherapy), whose first president was Gaspare Vella. The aims of SIPPR, soon after the foundation, are synthesised as follows:

> Essentially, there are three objectives, a cultural one, concerned with putting in touch with one another the schools which are exerting themselves towards the same aim, i.e., to operate a relational training; also a political one, in the sense of giving political power to this society; for example, it could become the driving group of a possible school of official training; lastly that of giving our students the sense of a more national participation in this movement. (Criconia & Scamperle, 1986, p. 8)

More or less at the same time, trainers and former students of the Milan center founded the Società Italiana di Ricerca e Terapia Sistemica (SIRTS: Italian Association for Systemic Therapy and Research). One must not wonder at such association-oriented activity: On the whole, the situation in Italian psychotherapy was coming to the end of the pioneer era, and the movement aspired to some legal control of psychotherapeutic activity, as was the case in the United States 20 years before. In 1989 the law was at last enforced, with the consequent legal acknowledgment of the schools of psychotherapy, which led, if not to ratification, at least to a greater homogeneity between programs of all schools of psychotherapy, those of family therapy included.

It is not mere chance that at this time the first texts that went beyond the definition of "school," in favor of a greater ecumenism begin to appear. The first important example is *Dall'individuo al sistema* (*From Individuals to Systems*), the "manual of relational psychopathology" edited by Marisa Malagoli Togliatti and Umberta Telfener (1991): an initiative, this, which involved the representatives of various schools and adopts for the first time the institutional format of a manual. In 1995, an Italian translation of the weighty *Handbook of Family Therapy* by Alan Gurman and David Kniskern (1991) was published, complete with an appendix that listed the main Italian schools of family therapy, with the details of their training methods. At this point, one might say, Italian family therapy had reached a level of institutional stability and was at last recognized. What lacked stability, however, was the economic and social context, which underwent tumultuous changes and influenced even family therapists heavily.

CHALLENGES AT THE END OF THE MILLENNIUM

During the 1990s, Italian family therapy found itself facing a period of profound changes, as happened to family therapies the world over (Bertrando & Toffanetti, 2001). During the decade, it became increasingly clear that systemic models, in all their different declensions, no longer represented "the new" in the field of psychological and psychiatric theories. Now novelty lay elsewhere. Two main areas of change were discernible: one theoretical, accompanied by the birth of new models of family therapy, different from those linked with the main body of Italian schools; one practical, with the emergence of a new way to practice a psychiatry that for decades had been the high point of reference for Italian family therapists.

If we were to look into the theory, we would observe a growth in the influence of narrative therapies (especially in the rest of the world), born mainly out of an impulse by the Australians White and Epston (1991; White, 1995), which soon spread to the rest of the world, but especially to the United States. Moreover, the postmodern vision of therapy led to the emergence of different models, brought together by the intolerance toward the traditional vision of family therapy., among them, solution-focused therapy (de Shazer, 1991) and conversational therapy (Andersen, 1991; Anderson & Goolishian, 1992). The loss of centrality for the family as such for many models is among the effects of this renewal (Bertrando, 2000).

Psychiatry too, had developed its own novelties, which consisted mostly in a progressive affirmation of psychoeducation. If until 1990 taking care of families within the state psychiatric services had been the almost exclusive task of the family therapists trained by one of the main schools, now this duty fell more and more to those who were prepared to adhere to one of the principal psychoeducational models (Bertrando et al., 1995). This choice was encouraged by a prevailing biological prospect in the realm of psychiatry, even in Italy. All forms of psychological treatment, especially in serious psychiatric pathologies such as schizophrenia or mood disorders, tended to be abandoned or relegated to second place.

Rather than dwindling, the application for training in the various schools was increasing, mostly because of the law, which compelled all psychologists to obtain a psychotherapeutic specialization in order to be able to practice. This, however, led to a significant difference in the population of would-be trainees in family therapy. In the heroic years, experienced psychiatrists and psychologists, usually already in possession of training, mostly of the psychoanalytical kind, poured into family therapy schools. In the 1990s, most students had recent degrees in psychology (psychiatrists tended to vanish from the schools, seduced as they were by the new biological psychiatry), requiring a basic, generic psychotherapy training that would enable them to find a way into a competitive market where choosing the format of one's favorite type of work was increasingly difficult. As a result, the new therapists trained in family therapy ended up being individual therapists, "experts" in psychoeducation, or even educators in therapeutic community.

As usual, the response of Italian family therapy was both vigorous and creative. On a theoretical level, Italian family therapists did not show excessive enthusiasm for the prevailing narrative and postmodern tendencies, insisting above all on the usefulness and centrality of the systemic vision, in its widest meaning, for the understanding and meaning of complex and multiform human problems. On the one hand, therapists who had become part of the academic world proposed a view of the family (Fruggeri, 1997) or psychopathology (Ugazio, 1998) characterized by the systemic model, whereas yet others opened the area of the individual therapies to the systemic model (Boscolo & Bertrando, 1996), an evolution that was made possible by new systemic conceptions that no longer confined the "system" to the nuclear family alone.

Meanwhile, new spaces were opening for the work of family therapists. First, couple therapy, which up to then had hardly enjoyed great fortune in Italy, because in our country there was no solid tradition either of couple consultation or of marital and premarital therapy, as there was in the United States (Broderick & Schrader, 1991), was the object of growing interest. Family consultation, which used to be underestimated because of the excessive weight of the therapy, gained some importance. Last, if it is true that adult psychiatry tended to lean less on family therapy, it must be said that child psychiatry relied on it more and more.

In the 1990s, Italian family therapy accomplished also its evolution toward a new generation of therapists; we may trust that the characteristics that have always distinguished our work in the family context shall endure.

DISTINCTIVE CHARACTERISTICS OF ITALIAN FAMILY THERAPY

Having reached this point, it is perhaps possible to attempt a synthetic conclusion as to the contribution that Italian family therapy has been able to offer on the one hand to the family therapy movement on the whole, and on the other to the body of mental health professions. At least five examples come to mind that, if not absolutely specific to Italian family therapy, are at least remarkable and give it a unique character.

Creativity

Although the initial stimuli toward the adoption and use of family therapy have come to us, as was inevitable, from the great American models, none of the major Italian family therapists has lain on principles directly dictated by charismatic transatlantic personalities. Rather, they created original syntheses for themselves, elaborating anew the known references with conceptual force and creativity, so much so that certain models (or clinical examples) of some of our therapists have been exported successfully to other countries.

Complexity

In comparison with such models as strategic or behavioral therapy, at least in some versions, Italian family therapies tend to flee from magical or simplistic solutions. At all times there is an awareness of the difficulties inherent in the therapeutic task and the seriousness of many problems. This process is favored by the fact that, unlike what took place in the United States from the end of the 1970s on, our family therapists have not given up the serious psychiatric pathologies, such as schizophrenia, mood or personality disorders. The review of the first decade of *Terapia Familiare* (Angelo et al., 1987) proves, for example, that the debate on psychoses remained beyond the mid-1980s. Such a position favors the awareness of what Roy Schafer (1990) calls the "tragic" in therapy: the fact that human existence places everybody before irremediable dilemmas and that a "well conducted" therapy is not sufficient to remove obstacles and restore a happiness devoid of problems, as some ultraoptimistic therapists, especially in the United States, seem to believe.

Multidisciplinary Approach

The fact that family therapy in Italy has not decisively broken with the psychiatric environment leads all Italian family therapists to prefer a multidisciplinary logic. Even if one considers family therapy an elective treatment, it is never conceived as sole treatment; rather, the tendency to hold a dialogue with other health or allied professions (psychiatry, medicine, individual therapy, schools, tribunals, etc.) is always stressed. This is an attitude that saved Italian family therapy from the danger of becoming marginal or introverted. Contributions such as that offered by the Cancrini group in Rome or by the Bologna and Verona groups show, on the contrary, that the interchange between family therapists and colleagues of other orientations has remained both vivacious and varied.

Roots in the Community

In a parallel way, Italian family therapy has assumed a dimension that is largely public (Fruggeri et al., 1995), not unlike its British, German, or French counterpart, but certainly dissimilar from the American one. In Italy, the use of family therapies, or in any case of contextual approaches that employ many of the theories, if not the techniques, based on family systems vision, is not limited to an elite of patients as a result, but involves instead a large public of users (Siani, Siciliani, & Burti, 1991).

Therapeutic Philosophy

Italian therapeutic thought has been criticized often for an excess of ideology. Yet, to be fair to Italian therapists, it is as well to recall that Italian models, indeed because they are more problematic, are generally well founded, and avoid some misunderstood or misrepresented influence of philosophical thoughts. From that point of view, the adoption of constructivism and social constructionism on the part of the systemic American therapists, who often find a solution to philosophical problems that have been debated for millennia with only a few lines, is exemplary.

CONCLUSION

To conclude, Italian family therapy today is a mature and widespread profession, not the least inferior to other forms of psychotherapy. As a matter of fact, it shows deep roots and an ability to exchange ideas with similar professions; however, without being less vital from the theoretical or clinical point of view. Only the dedication of those who will decide to undertake this activity in the future will be able to determine the margins of further extension and refine the different models that are gathered under the definition of (Italian) family therapy.

REFERENCES

Ackerman, N. (1958). *The psychodynamics of family life*. New York: Basic Books.

Andersen, T. (1991). *The reflecting team. Dialogues and dialogues about the dialogues*. New York: Norton.

Anderson, H., & Goolishian, H. (1992). The client is the expert. A not-knowing approach to therapy. In S. McNamee & K. Gergen (Eds.), *Therapy as social construction*. London: Sage.

Anderson, H., Goolishian H., & Winderman, L. (1988). Problem-determined systems. Towards transformation in family therapy. *Journal of Strategic and Systemic Therapies, 5*, 1–13.

Andolfi, M., Angelo, C., Menghi, P., & Nicolò-Corigliano, A. M. (1982). *La familgia rigida*. Milano: Feltrinelli.

Angelo, C., de Bernart, R., & Giacometti, K. (1987). "Terapia Familiare" 1977–1986. Bibliografia ragionata. *Terapia Familiare*, 24.

Bateson, G. (1972). *Steps to an ecology of mind*. New York: Ballantine.

Bertrando, P. (2000). Text and context. Narrative, postmodernism, and cybernetics. *Journal of Family Therapy*, 22(1), 83–103.

Bertrando, P., Beltz, J., Bressi, C., Clerici, M., Invernizzi, G., & Cazzullo, C. L. (1992). Expressed emotion and schizophrenia in Italy. A study of an Italian urban population. *British Journal of Psychiatry, 161*, 223–229.

Bertrando, P., Cazzullo, C. L., & Clerici, M. (1995). *Terapie familiari e psicoeducazione*. Milano: Franco Angeli.

Bertrando, P., & Toffanetti, D. (2001). *Storia della terapia familiare*. Milano: Cortina.

Boscolo, L., & Bertrando, P. (1993). *The times of time. A new perspective for systemic therapy and consultation*. New York: Norton.

Boscolo, L., & Bertrando, P. (1996). *Systemic therapy with individuals*. London: Karnac Books.

Boscolo, L., Cecchin, G., Hoffman, L., & Penn, P. (1987). *Milan systemic family therapy*. New York: Basic Books.

Broderick, C. B., & Schrader, S. S. (1991). History of marital and family therapy. In A. S. Gurman & D. P. Kniskern (Eds.), *Handbook of family therapy*. New York: Brunner/Mazel.

Cancrini, L. (1974). *Bambini "diversi" a scuola*. Torino: Boringhieri.

Cancrini, L. (Ed.). (1977). Schizofrenia: Una definizione ancora utile? In: *Verso una teoria della schizofrenia*. Torino: Boringhieri.

Cancrini, L. (1982). *Quei temerari sulle macchine volanti*. Roma: La Nuova Italia Scientifica.

Cancrini, L. (1987) *Psicoterapia: Grammatica e sintassi*. Roma: La Nuova Italia Scientifica.

Cancrini, L. (1999). *La luna nel pozzo*. Milano: Cortina.

Canosa, R. (1979). *Storia del manicomio in Italia dall'unità a oggi*. Milano: Feltrinelli.

Cirillo, S., Cambiaso, G., Berrini, R., & Mazza, R. (1995). *La famiglia del tossicodipendente*. Milano: Cortina.

Clerici, M., Bertrando, P., & Cazzullo, C. L. (1995). Un modello di intervento multimodale per familiari di schizofrenici. In P. Bertrando, C. L. Cazzullo, & M. Clerici (Eds.), *Terapie familiari e psicoeducazione*. Miano: Franco Angeli

Criconia, M., & Scamperle, S. (1986). Intervista a Maurizio Andolfi, Luigi Cancrini, Gianfranco Cecchin Piero de Gicomo, Gaspare Vella. *Psicobiettivo, 3–4*, 2–10.

De Giacomo, P. (1993). *Finite systems and infinite interaction*. New York: Bramble Books.

de Shazer, S. (1991). *Putting difference to work*. New York: Norton.

Fruggeri, L. (1997). *Famiglie*. Roma: La Nuova Italia Scientifica.

Fruggeri, L., Marzari, M., Matteini, M., & Castellucci, A. (1995). Servizi pubblici e terapia sistemica: teorie e tecniche nell'incontro con le famiglie. In A. S. Gurman, & D. P. Kniskern (Eds.), *Manuale di terapia della famiglia*, Italian edition edited by P. Bertrando. Torino: Bollati Boringhieri.

Laing, R. (1969). *The politics of the family*. New York: Ballantine Books.

Leff, J. P., Kuipers, L., Berkowitz, R., & Sturgeon, D. (1982). A controlled trial of family intervention in families of schiophrenic patients: A two-year follow-up. *British Journal of Psychiatry, 146*, 594–600.

Leff, J. P., & Vaughn, C. (1985). *Expressed emotion in families*. New York: Guilford.

Maffei, C., Bertrando, P., Cereda, G., Bressi, C., Ciussani, S., Da Ponte, C., & Cazzullo, C. L. (1986). Expressed emotion (EE): Rassegna storica e prospettive teoriche. *Rivista Sperimentale di Freniatria, 110*(1), 3–19.

Penn, P. (1982). Circular questioning. *Family Process, 21,* 267–280.

Penn, P. (1985). Feed-forward: Future questions, future maps. *Family Process, 24,* 299–310.

Ruesch, J., & Bateson, G. (1951). *Communication. The social matrix of psychiatry*. New York: Norton.

Schafer, R. (1990). *A new language for psychanalysis*. New Haven, CT: Yale University Press.

Selvini Palazzoli, M. (1974). *Self starvation*. London: Human Context Books.

Selvini Palazzoli, M., Boscolo, L., Cecchin, G., & Prata, G. (1975). *Paradosso e controparadosso*. Milano: Feltrinelli.

Selvini Palazzoli, M., Boscolo, L., Cecchin, G., & Prata, G. (1978). *Paradox and counterparadox*. Mahwah, NJ: Aronson.

Selvini Palazzoli, M., Boscolo, L., Cecchin, G., & Prata, G. (1980). Hypothesizing-circularity-neutrality. Three guidelines for the conductor of the session. *Family Process, 13,* 429–442.

Selvini Palazzoli, M., Cirillo, S., Selvini, M., & Sorrentino, A. M. (1988). *Family games*. New York: Norton.

Selvini Palazzoli, M., Cirillo, S., Selvini, M., & Sorrentino, A. M. (1998). *Ragazze anoressiche e bulimiche*. Milano: Cortina.

Siani, R., Siciliani, O., & Burti, L. (1991). *Strategie di psicoterapia e riabilitazione*. Milano: Feltrinelli.

Tomm, K. (1985). Circular interviewing: A multifaceted clinical tool. In D. Campbell & R. Draper (Eds.), *Applications of systemic family therapy. The Milan approach*. London: Grune & Stratton.

Ugazio, V. (1998). *Storie permesse e storie proibite*. Torino: Bollati Boringhieri.

Vella, G., Loriedo, C., & Schepisi, L. (1995). Istituto Italiano per la psicoterapia relazionale. In A. S. Gurman & D. P. Kniskern (Eds.), *Manuale di terapia della famiglia*. Italian Edition edited by P. Bertrando. Torino: Bollati Boringhieri.

Warner, R. (1985). *Schizophrenia and healing*. New York: Norton.

Watzlawick, P., Beavin, J. H., & Jackson, D. D. (1967). *Pragmatics of human communication*. New York: Norton.

Watzlawick, P., Weakland, J., & Fisch, R. (1974). *Change: Principles of problem formation and problem resolution*. New York: Norton.

White, M. (1995). *Re-authoring lives. Interviews and essays*. Adelaide: Dulwich Centre Publications.

White, M., & Epston, D. (1991). *Narrative means to therapeutic ends*. New York: Norton.

CHAPTER 8

Family Therapy and Family Life Cycle in Russia

ANNA VARGA

From the very beginning, the field of psychology has existed in the form of an academic discipline and is very psychodiagnostic in nature. In the mid-1980s, Russian psychologists timidly began to explore psychology in clinical practices. Incidentally, some family doctors in the past used different forms of hypnotherapy and rational therapy on their patients. In one sense, there is not a collective focus on the movement of psychology in Russia. Knowledge in psychology was primarily derived from books and also from the rare visits of world-renowned psychotherapists such as Carl Rogers, Virginia Satir, Victor Frankl, and others, who gave lectures and held workshops in Russia around the mid-1980s. Those visits opened new horizons and made great impressions and ultimately encouraged professionals to try different ideas in the new domain of the knowledge and practice of mental health.

The emergence of systemic family therapy began in Russia during the last two decades like other schools of psychology. As a result of the need to work in a broader context, primarily with different families, certain centers were started in the late 1970s and early 1980s. The Center for Psychological Assistance was one of the earliest centers to offer therapeutic help to families in Moscow. Inaugurated in 1981 in the Department of Psychology at Moscow State University, the center was initially directed by Vladimir Stolin, a veteran psychologist. Therapy for families was provided free of charge and the center's personnel were basically composed of the staff from the department. Nine of us pioneered the work with much enthusiasm, anticipation, and a hunger to learn.

At that time, we were aware of the fact that we lacked essential knowledge and skills, but we did our best to acquire them. The center received families 4 days a week, and all the sessions were recorded on tape. On the fifth day, the clinical staff listened to the case recordings and discussed them as a way of self-learning. We were pioneers in learning to cosupervise each other on family cases. We also listened to books and discussions, analyzed them, and eventually applied those ideas to the families with whom we worked. Unfortunately, during those days there were very few books on psychotherapy and family therapy in the Russian language. We compiled a list of books in English and German that were available in Moscow libraries that related to our work. The books were divided among those who could read the languages. We then provided detailed translated information to other team members. When I think back to that period, I realize that our work was difficult and it was hard to gauge the results of our work. The careful, step-by-step review of our work, the analysis of the recordings of the sessions, and our intense gathering of knowledge allowed us to work with those families to the best of our ability (Varga, 1998). This was a remarkable experience for all the members at the center. Most of the time we gained valuable experience in family therapy work that was unique in the Russian culture and we were also able to work with enthusiasm at a time of widespread social cynicism and political indifference in our country.

The Bekhterev Institute was a center in Leningrad that offered family therapy to families in need. Several well-known professionals, including V. K. Myager and E. G. Eidemiller, both psychiatrists, were some of the key people involved with the center. The Bekhterev Institute was a part of the state mental hospital system. The psychiatrists started to invite families of neurotic patients to join the therapy and offered them long-term therapeutic interventions. They were one of the first in Russia who work with such families. In subsequent years, family therapy developed fairly rapidly and became more popular.

Therapy with family was gradually recognized as a domain of psychological practice. About this time, quite a few family and marriage clinics began to open in a few obstetric clinics, and psychologists were invited to work with families there. These clinics are rather widespread today in most major cities, and many mental health specialists are able to find work in such settings.

In addition, psychologists and doctors began to understand that children with developmental problems or emotional disorders can be helped more effectively when their families are also involved in therapy. Child therapists working in psychiatric hospitals started trying to get parents involved in consultations. School and kindergarten psychologists also tried to invite parents to be involved in therapy with children (Varga, 2000). Overall, across the board mental health specialists felt the need to utilize a more systemic approach to their area of clinical work.

At the same time, programs for training family therapists in conformity with international standards were beginning to emerge. Hannah Weiner, my teacher and adviser, gave the first training course in systemic family therapy in Russia in the late 1980s. She worked for more than 8 years in Moscow and taught systemic family therapy to psychologists basically free of charge. She was also instrumental in inviting such excellent masters as Gianfranco Cecchin, one of the founders of the Milan School, Florence Kaslow, the founder and first president of the International Family Therapy Association (IFTA), and others to give lectures and demonstrate their work with different families.

During the *perestroika*, many well-known family therapists took on the task to train Russian psychologists in family therapy. One of the most popular methods in those days was psychodrama work with families. Later on, it appeared that the trainers were also doing training beyond Moscow, moving to other provinces such as St. Petersburg, Izhevsk (Ural Region), Novosibirsk, Samara, and Nizhny Novgorod. Working with families was readily welcomed by psychologists and specialists of all persuasions. They ultimately became strong advocates for family treatment. This provided a swift and loose transition from individual psychology to systemic therapy.

Family therapy for the last 10 to 12 years has gained popularity in Russia. In my opinion, it is the most rapidly growing domain of psychological practice in the country today. The last project to be implemented (in the summer of 2000) was a 3-year course in systemic family therapy for doctors and psychologists working in children's psychiatric hospitals. Different courses were conducted by Tobias von der Rekke, the Director of the Munich Institute for Family Therapy. Two long-term training projects in family therapy are being implemented in Moscow: a course on M. Bowen's theory given by Catherine Baker and Peter Titelman of Georgetown University and a 5-year course in systemic family therapy given by Gerda Klammer and Joachim Hinsch in the framework of the Moscow Project of the EAP (European Association of Psychotherapists).

The Moscow Institute of Practical Psychology and Psychoanalysis also offers ongoing training in systemic family therapy. This is a 3-year program, which includes 200 hours of supervised practice behind a one-way mirror. Growing professionalism in this domain has led to the creation of the first association of family therapists in Moscow, called The Society of Family Consultants and Therapists. It was registered in November 1998. This organization's purpose is to coordinate the effort to retrain family consultants and therapists. Furthermore, the Society provides its members access to professional contacts and support, consultation for complicated cases, and the exchange of professional networking experiences. Specifically, the bylaws of the Society of Family Consultants and Therapists encourage its members to:

- Inculcate and develop international professional standards among the community of family consultants and therapists in Russia
- Increase the public awareness of the profession
- Create a system for the exchange and diffusion of professional scientific and practical information
- Make the achievements of family consulting and therapy accessible to the layman
- Define the bases and criteria for certifying and licensing professional activity (Budinaite, 1999, pp. 109–116).

In one sense, the development of family therapy in Russia has come a long way because of numerous complex factors. But the encouraging news is that family therapy is gaining popularity and that local therapists are motivated to learn how to help families at all costs. In terms of formal systemic training, we still have quite a way to go because of the large population, extensive needs of families, and lack of trained therapists.

FAMILY LIFE CYCLE

The life cycle of the Russian family differs considerably from that of its American counterpart. The differences primarily result from the economic, cultural, and mental circumstances of an average Russian citizen. One of the principal differences lies in the fact that there are very few nuclear families living in Russia today. According to the General Census of Russian Population, only 124 of 1,000 couples live away from their family of origin, and the probability of the young family living separately from their family in the first year of marriage is less than 10% (Volkov, 1986). This is owing to the fact that the majority of Russian people lack the financial resources to buy an apartment or house of their own.

On the other hand, living in a big family is considered a societal norm and has been accepted for generations. Thus, family ties are greatly valued in Russian culture. One can address an elderly woman anywhere as "grandmother." This is considered proper and polite. We often hear strangers on the street say, "Could you help me, my son?" or "Thank you, my daughter."

Russian politicians also often used the concept of family ties in political oratory. In Soviet times, the official way of addressing people was to use either "citizen" or "comrade." We are all citizens of the state, and many are also members of a unique party, comrades. During the Stalin years, everyone easily became a suspect and potential enemy of the people. When the Soviet

Union entered World War II, Stalin addressed the people, summoning them to defend their country; he began his speech with the words "Brothers and sisters!" This made an enormous impression at the time and resulted in a burst of patriotism.

Let us consider the life cycle of the Russian family in more detail.

1. The *first stage* of the life cycle is the family with grown-up children. Generally, from childhood, the young man (or woman) is an important element of the family system—a carrier of the family norms and rules, and most important of all is a child to his parents. In most cases, he does not have clear goals of what he wants to achieve, and he may have difficulty developing a sense of personal responsibility for his life. He finds it hard to test the rules of life, standards and norms that he got from his parents, and is frequently unable to develop his own rules. A self-reliant person is rare according to the General Census of Russian population—only 17% of young men and 15% of young women (below age 30) live independently from their parents (Gerasimova, 1998). It is indeed very common for adults to stay in their parent's house until their thirties or forties.
2. During the *second stage* of the family life cycle, the young man (or woman) meets his future marriage partner, marries, and moves in to live with their parents. A very difficult task lies before the young couple: They have to form a small family within a large one. The young couple must not only agree with each other on the manner in which they live together, but they must also agree with the parents' rules. The patriarchal solution to this problem is to have the young husband or wife take on the roles of two children. He or she is invited to call the parents "mom" and "dad." In this case, the young couple takes on the role of a brother or sister to other siblings. Not every young couple is willing to follow such family traditions. In a lot of cases when the tradition is not followed, it creates a lot of conflict until both parties are able to work out the differences. For example, a member of the couple may want to be husband or wife first and son or daughter second. The resulting conflict is familiar to everyone and often takes on the form of a falling-out between the mother-in-law and son-in-law or daughter-in-law. In reality, it stems from the couple's conflicting role priorities.

   The new subsystem often desires separation, whereas the old system wants to preserve the traditional family values by staying together in one household. In this way, a paradoxical situation arises: The couple is married and being treated like children. When a young couple is out of the parental home—say at their friends', or on a trip together—they feel they are really married. They are closer to each other, more responsible, more caring. When they are at home with their parents, their marriage status appears to be voided, because they now have to be children again.

This is a situation that is agonizing for everyone. For example, in one family, the husband's mother kept her things in her son's room where the young man had lived from his childhood. When he got married, she did not change her ways. In any case, there was no place to put a new wardrobe. The mother came into the newlyweds' room at any time of the day or night in order to get her things. It is surprising that the young couple was able to keep their marriage from falling apart, although conflicts in family relations do not always accompany an intrusion into the life of the young couple.

3. The *third stage* of the family cycle is marked by the birth of a child by the couple. This is also a time of crisis for the whole family. It is once again necessary to agree on who does what and divide the different responsibilities between the two generations. In families with unclear boundaries between the subsystems, family roles often are poorly defined. In some Russian families, it is unclear what the function of the grandmother or mother should be in relation to the child. When this role is confused, the child becomes more of the son of the grandmother than the mother. The child's own parents in this case are like the elder brother and sister. When the mother and father have gone to work and the grandmother spends a lot of time with the child, this maternal role often creates conflicts within the family subsystems. Marina Arutyunyan told me of a family who illustrates such family dynamics. The family turned to her for help, complaining of the misbehavior of an 11-year-old girl, who they claimed was acting aggressively toward her grandmother. The family was composed of three women: the grandmother, the mother, and the child. The grandmother and mother had a long history of relational conflict. Once the girl locked her grandmother out on the balcony during winter and did not allow her back in for a long time. After this episode, the family decided to turn to a therapist. When the mother related how her daughter offended the grandmother, the child felt triumphant. The daughter did what the mother could not permit herself to do. This form of rebellion with the established rules appears to be common in family relations in Russia.
4. The *fourth stage* is the appearance of a second child in the family. During this stage, the family has to deal with the children's jealousy toward each other. In Russian families, jealousy between siblings often causes stress between the adults. For example, the mother entrusted her first child to the grandmother and he or she became a substitute child for the grandmother who brought him or her up. The child tends to choose to side with the grandmother when there is a disagreement between the adults. This situation often becomes worse when the second child is born. The second child generally is on the mother's side. The children's natural jealousy toward each other is intensified and used by the adults as well. Two

children become the "mouthpieces" of two "hostile" women. This situation results in constant conflicts between the children and is also a projection of the mutual rejection of the two women. In this case the conflict among the siblings is less severe compared to the adults.

5. During the *fifth stage*, the aging parents begin to experience increasing physical ailments. Here, the family experiences another crisis. The aged parents become more helpless and dependent on the middle generation. In one sense, they take the place of small children in the family, although they are more often met with annoyance and irritation rather than with love. The aged parents would feel unwanted despite the fact that until then they were accustomed to being in control and making decisions for others. During this stage, the family must once again agree to renegotiate their roles, a process that is agonizing for everyone. In Russian culture, there exists a stereotype of a "good son or daughter": This is someone who fetches his parents a glass of water when they are old. Elderly people without relatives are to be pitied, because "no one will fetch them a glass of water." It is unimaginable for the elderly to live in isolation or independence. It is considered a disgrace to let one's aged parents die outside of the home or to put them in an old people's home. It is seen as being a particular merit and responsibility to take care of an elderly person at home during their illness and not to put him or her in a hospital. This period in the life of senior family members frequently coincides with the adolescence of the children. The grandparents and adolescents may form alliances against the middle generation. For example, the grandparents may help the adolescents to conceal their absences and failures in school. At the same time, the middle generation has a good way of keeping the adolescents in check. The grandparents must be cared for and tended to. This duty can be assigned to adolescents who are attached to the home and taken off the street.
6. The *sixth* and final stage is a repeat of the first life cycle stage. The elderly parents in this stage have died and the family has grown-up children. At this stage, the family is as small as any Russian family can get. Many of the stages of the life cycle of the American family are present in the life cycle of the Russian urban family, for example, courting, divorce, the birth of children, the stages of their psychological development, etc. However, they are present in a modified form in the context of a large, three-generation family. The principal features of the Russian family are the following: (a) As a rule, the family is not a traditional nuclear family but rather is composed of three generations. (b) The material and moral dependence of the family members on one another is very great. (3) The merging and intertwining of family roles and the indistinct division of functions in the family is frequently observed. People constantly have to come to an agreement in spite of their personal differences. Role substi-

tution is very common in Russian families; as a result, each member could functionally replace any other member at any given time. For example, a grandmother brings up a child in a family and therefore takes on the role of a maternal parent. In many families, the grandmother also manages the family budget and therefore functions as the head of the family. This arrangement often renders the daughter-in-law powerless, especially when the son sides with his mother. (d) Individualism and sovereignty are practically nonexistent in a traditional Russian family. The young generation is much more tightly and rigidly bound to the preceding generation than in the West. Traditionalism is extremely prevalent and openly practiced. Every family member is in daily contact with a large number of relatives. He or she participates in various difficult relationships and simultaneously performs many social roles that are frequently hard to reconcile. In the very early years, the child must understand the social strata, negotiations, and art of dialogue with the different adults in the household. Given such a family organization, the question of power is frequently the principal issue. It is seen in every interaction, such as when the father forbids the child to do something, whereas the mother allows it. All of this takes place in the child's presence, and the hidden message is, "The child listens to me and not you; therefore, I am in charge."

POLITICAL EFFECTS ON THE FAMILY

Cultural factors are also responsible for the fact that the struggle for power is becoming the main theme in Russia. Families see their social environment as being something hostile, dangerous, and unpredictable. The laws, politics, and financial and fiscal policies have always been considered by practically all levels of society to be illogical and extortionate. It is often the people's interests that hinder them from implementing their goals. The last decade has also been marked by rapid changes in the social environment in the country because of the lack of political stability. The "rules of the game" are constantly changing, whereas the government's disregard for the people's goals and interests stays the same.

The ubiquity of informers, the promotion of treachery, and the systematic destruction of family ties during the Soviet period resulted in the appearance of a certain type of mentality, which is characterized above all by a high degree of anxiety, suspicion, and the desire to conceal one's weaknesses. The characteristics of the interior policy in relation to family consisted of the fact that the value of the family would always be reduced. For instance, during Stalin's reign betraying one member of the family to another was encouraged. There existed the article in the Criminal Code of the Soviet Union where "noninforming" of the anti-Soviet view by somebody—husband, wife, or children—was equal to the crime. Such a measure led to a weakening of family ties (Solzhenitsyn, 1989).

In the Soviet Union, everything was done to prevent people from controlling their own lives. Families did not own anything and there were no private properties. All the people's property belonged to the government and an individual could be stripped of it at any moment. Family ties often were depreciated and broken. Obviously, the devotion to the State was of greater importance. My uncle committed suicide in 1937 after being excluded from the Communist Party. People were frequently arrested after being excluded from the Party, but many did not know this and neither did my uncle. Before his death, he told his wife, whom he greatly loved, "I can't live without the Party."

For a family wage earner, the salary was extremely low and women had hardly any maternity leave. This made it impossible for one spouse to support a family and required both husband and wife to work, which resulted in children being brought up in daycare centers and kindergartens. Informants were encouraged even within the family: husbands against wives, and wives against husbands. In this way, the people could not control anything in their lives, could not trust anyone, and lived in an ever-suspicious social environment. This situation was more or less the same during the whole period of Soviet rule, and several generations grew up in such conditions.

The hostility and unpredictability of the social environment made every person anxious, and the government's domestic social policy did not allow people to make decisions for themselves, thus creating very mechanical and predictable social and family environments. The need for control, which allowed individuals to relieve their anxiety, did not disappear. The sphere of life that gave the freedom to meet this need was interaction in the broadest sense. With the help of interaction, one could try to control others and raise one's status by debasing others. The family was ideally suited for this; it offered worthy and ever-present partners for this cruel game. The struggle for power in the dysfunctional Russian family was the common rule. The simplest way to raise one's status and obtain temporary satisfaction was to discredit the partner's actions. One such example was in a family consisting of grandmother, mother, father, and two girls. The eldest was 19 and the youngest ten. The grandmother was an active woman and when the eldest girl was growing up, she spent a lot of time helping the girl with her homework, which enabled her to be a good student. The mother, on the other hand, told the grandmother that she did not spend enough time helping the youngest girl with her homework, resulting in her receiving poor grades. When the second girl went to school, the grandmother told the mother, "Now you'll help the child with her homework yourself. Let's see how you manage." The youngest girl, who was very attached to both her mother and grandmother, found herself in a situation of conflicting loyalties. If she were a good student, the grandmother would lose; if she were a poor student, the mother would lose. The girl stopped learning altogether: She did not do her homework and skipped school. Each time the mother helped her with her homework, the girl became panic-stricken. The peculiar life cycle of the Russian family and the struggle for power at different levels are some of the family dysfunctions with which the family therapist has to deal in Russia.

CONCLUSION

I have reiterated the historical development of family therapy in Russia as clearly as I can. Being a first-generation Russian family therapist and being involved with some of the earliest efforts, it has indeed been a daunting task to gather the "facts" with minimal written records. Most of the information I researched is from oral tradition. Even today, little has been written on family therapy. My desire is to see this trend revised. My hope is that in the future, there will be more written texts and research information on family therapy with Russian families, so that the information can be passed to another generation.

Last, but not least, we are hard pressed for a culturally sensitive family therapy approach for Russian families. Because most if not all family therapy approaches are either from Europe or North America, the question of relevance has seldom been addressed. I think as family therapy matures in Russia, we are more able to dialogue and research approaches that are relevant, efficient, and effective for families in Russia.

REFERENCES

Budinaite, G. (1999). The founding of The Society of Family Consultants and Therapists. *Journal of Family Psychology and Family Therapy, 2*, 109–116 (in Russian).

Gerasimova, I. A. (1998). *The structure of the family.* Moscow: Statistica (in Russian).

Solzhenitsyn, A. (1989). *Archipelago "gulag."* Moscow: Sovetski Pisatel-Novy Mir (in Russian).

Varga, A. (1998). Characteristics of systemic family psychotherapy in the Russian cultural environment. *Journal of Russian and Eastern European Psychology, 36*(1), 32–50.

Varga, A. (2000). *An introduction to systemic family therapy.* Nizhny Novgorod: Nizhegorodsky Gymanitarny Center (in Russian).

Volkov, A. (1986). *The family as an object of demography*. Moscow: Mysl (in Russian).

CHAPTER 9

Family Therapy in France

A Brief Overview

JEAN FRANÇOIS LE GOFF

In France, therapists, for the most part, are influenced by the psychoanalytical orientation, and the development of family therapy has been more difficult than in other European countries. After approximately 20 years family therapy is beginning to be recognized and developed.

DIFFICULT BEGINNINGS

At the end of the 1960s the French context was marked by the major influence of psychoanalysis. Freud himself had attached much importance to the development of psychoanalysis in France, the country where he had been a student. But French psychiatrists have long been hostile or cool toward the notion of infant sexuality. It was also a clear rejection of what had come from German-speaking countries during the first half of this century.

From the 1950s onward, psychoanalysis played an innovative role in French psychotherapy institutions, whereas it had almost disappeared in German-speaking countries following the emigration of psychoanalysts fleeing Nazism. It has since been the origin of institutional psychotherapy, the "psychiatric de secteur" and child psychiatry.

But this influence was made at the cost of splits and controversy: The majority of French psychoanalysts influenced by the nonconformist works of Jacques Lacan found themselves in disagreement with the international psychoanalytical movement. One of the first papers published by Lacan in 1938 dealt with the family. Despite different vocabulary and conclusions, there are notable similarities with the early works of Theodore Lidz on families of schizophrenics. Other pioneers of psychoanalysis in France who were interested in the family included Laforgue, an intimate friend of Freud and author of an article on "family neurosis" (1936). After 20 years of development French psychoanalysts are still divided, but these splits are receding under the perceived threat of the neurosciences. However, France is still, with Argentina, the country where there are the largest number of psychoanalysts per capita.

This preponderance of psychoanalysis did not create a favorable context for family therapy. By the end of the 1960s, the Italians, such as Mara Selvini; the Dutch, such as Amy Van Heusden, organizer of the first training program for family therapy in Europe in 1967; and such Swiss as Luc Kaufman, who eventually directed the Center for the Study of the Family in Lausanne; had visited the main centers for family therapy in the United States. Ronald Laing and Helm Stierlin made original contributions.

Nevertheless, French therapists ignored the developments of family therapy and kept their distance. The French tradition of separating the patient and his or her family, which came from the origin of psychiatry, was reinforced by the application of analytical principles in the institutional domain. For the majority of psychiatrists, contact with the families had to remain minimal—or there even had to be no contact—in order to protect the difficult work of self-sufficiency of the patient. Thus, before the end of the 1970s, it was difficult to find teams practicing family therapy, and the possibilities of finding family therapy training in France were nonexistent.

However, after a trip to the United States in 1966, Jacques Hochman, published in *Psychiatric Information* two well-informed articles on the research of Gregory Bateson and Jay Haley. His own elaboration such as the "Postulat fusionnel" (1969) and the "Psychiatrie des ensembles" (1967), a very original view of systemic theory, opened up an original line of thought. But several years later, Hochman explained that he had not wished to become an expert or a leader in this field, despite numerous invitations and pressures.

The social and political events of May 1968 caused the cancellation of a meeting with Ivan Boszormenyi-Nagy, one of the pioneers of family therapy. It was 20 years later, in 1988, that he was reinvited to France.

It was particularly with the publication of the first works of Selvini and her team (*Paradox and Counterparadox* was translated into French in 1978) that systemic family therapy began to arouse interest. This original work was attractive because of its concrete proposals and radical differences with psychoanalytical psychotherapies. It should be noted that Mara Selvini occupies a position between the pioneers and the following generations. She was one of the first Europeans to be interested in American approaches beginning in 1967. A family therapist of the "second generation," her celebrity and influence rapidly exceeded those of many pioneers. But with her, family therapy sometimes seemed to become a fight against family—considered as resistant to changes, and against psychoanalysis, which she considered a "waste of time." This attitude would come to weigh heavily in the introduction of family therapy in France by placing ideological debates and techniques at the forefront, before clinical and therapeutic aspects.

Systemic family therapy seems opposite psychoanalysis by aiming to become a rigorous and modern alternative through proposing brief and efficient therapy in contrast to an endless process based in intrapsychic exploration. For some therapists it was also an opportunity to detach themselves from analytical theory that was becoming dogmatic. It was around this dynamic idea of therapy that the works of Bateson and Paul Watzlawick, the strategies of Haley regrouped as the "school of Palo Alto," and also the creative work of Milton Erickson were discovered. However, debates had too often focused on epistemological questions at the expense of clinical elements: "Systemic circular causality" against "analytic linear causality" became new dogma. Too often practice was limited to experimentation of techniques already abandoned by their inventor. In those early activities, there was a regrettable ignorance of work of pioneers of family therapy. Family therapy seemed to be born from second- or third-generation Belgian or Italian therapists who then introduced it into France.

However, during the same period, several creative psychoanalysts began to elaborate on the ideas of W. R. Bion regarding group and process of thought—a model of analytic family therapy.

Currently in France family therapists have notably as much interest in transgenerational notions as in psychoanalytical and systemic therapies. After a controversial start, family therapy no longer encounters the same heated feelings, rejections, or enthusiasms as it did a decade ago. It has neither flourished (where "one can finally heal psychosis, the family therapist will replace the individual therapist"), nor has it disappeared (where "this is only a mode"). Family therapy exists and seeks to link in with other forms of therapy.

However, all too often, real recognition is late in coming; for example, in the recent general conference organized in Paris by the French Psychiatry Federation and UNAFAM (The National Union of Families and Friends of Mental Invalids), with regard to the choice of family therapy, advice is rather limited. Family therapy is suggested as a complement to neuroleptic treatments with psychotherapy, as a means of information for the family. One is very, very far from the optimistic hopes of family therapy pioneers and their numerous discoveries.

FAMILY THERAPY IN FRANCE TODAY

Family therapies have evolved considerably and few hold to one precise model. Each therapist seeks his style through training, holding family and team discussions. One can, however, distinguish three main but flexible trends.

Systemic Family Therapy

This is the most widely known and practiced of the therapies. The systemic certainties of the 1980s have given way to varied creative and evolving practices. The sphere of influence of Mara Selvini and strategic-structural therapists have diminished under the trigenerational elaborations of Maurizio Andolfi (Rome, Italy) and also under the concepts of resonance and singularity developed by Mony Elkaim (Brussels, Belgium), the well-known organizer of simulated families and seminars.

However, without doubt, Bateson's epistemology and second order cybernetics have provided the framework in which the majority of systemic therapies are found. But notions such as family myths, secrets, and affiliations are subject to specifics: The last theoretical developments of family therapy are the most often misunderstood. Thus postmodernism, founded on philosophical bases such as those of Lyotard, Foucault, and Derrida—all French authors, holds no influence. The debate between postmodernism and modernism is ignored by French family therapists. Narrative therapy and feminist therapy are almost unknown. Problems of ethnicity have found an original platform but are challenged, in an ethnopsychoanalytical model.

Analytic Family Therapy

Many family therapists acknowledge that the analytic family therapy trend is far from marginal. Elaborated at the end of the 1970s, it has developed without referring to the works of the pioneers of family therapy, who were influenced by psychoanalysis and the theory of object relationships. Using the works of Bion and Kaés on the group and process of thought, ideas have evolved from the notion of the family unconscious to the family psychic process, based on interfanstamatization. Therapeutic work, as opposed to systemic therapy which is most often used with cotherapists, is centered on transference and countertransference, in continuity with analytical individual cures. This sophisticated trend avoids both obscurity and simplification. Emphasis on pathogenic family secrets marks a return to a simple etiology.

Transgenerational and Contextual Family Therapies

Around the middle 1980s, several family therapists chose to reject the strategic and structural orientation of systemic therapies in France and the elaborations of analytical family therapy in favor of interest in the work of Boszormenyi-Nagy on relational ethics and loyalties (Boszormenyi-Nagy, 1987). This work has since been developed through seminars and training for contextual therapy under Boszormenyi-Nagy.

All three of these trends are in permanent evolution. Systemic family therapists are integrating analytical notions more and more, whereby certain analytical therapists no longer refuse to think in terms of system. However, the clash between these two currents remains problematic. It is the intergenerational notion that seems to provide a common and fruitful thinking pool.

WHERE IS FAMILY THERAPY PRACTICED?

Family therapists work mainly in three sectors: public psychiatric practice, liberal practice, and through associations.

Public Psychiatric Practice

In France public psychiatry is organized in the psychiatric sector. A multicompetence team managed by a psychiatrist is in charge of mental health (care and prevention) for 70,000 residents. In most teams psychoanalysis is the predominant influence. Out of 800 teams, 121 practice systemic family therapy, 38 analytic family therapy, and 29 contextual family therapy. Eighty-four of these teams benefit from regular supervision, mostly monthly. In 57 sectors, units of family therapy have been created for common use across several sectors; these include psychiatrists, psychiatric nurses, psychologists, and social workers. The health administration does not recognize specific qualifications, and the possibility of practicing depends on the interests and convictions of the head of service (Le Goff, 1997a). In other teams, some members have followed an initiation or a training in systemic therapy but do not practice it if it would be in opposition to other team members, opposition to the head psychiatrist, or if they are lacking in experience.

Schizophrenia is the diagnosis most often cited by team members dealing with adult patients. For the child psychiatrist, the main issues are family violence, sexual abuse, and adolescent problems.

Private Sector Practice

Family therapy practice and cotherapy by psychiatrists and psychologists in the private sector are restricted by the absence of refunds under Social Security (state insurance). Meetings between parents, child, or adult patient and therapist are seen as part of a consultation and cannot be given supplementary billing under Social Security, unless the people make their own financial arrangements and meet independently. The care form must be drawn up under the patient's name. The consultations are contractual and not based on an hourly basis. Family therapy is not listed in the "General Nomenclature of Professional Acts"; all changes are made at a price-costing. Because family therapy tariffs are not set, risks may be made by potentially quoting discounts for psychotherapeutic treatments. As a result of this economic constraint, family therapy is rarely an exclusive practice. It is only one therapeutic practice among others (consultation, analytic, psychotherapy).

The Association Area

This area is heterogeneous and includes child protection agencies. Systemic interventions are practiced by social workers, who rarely use family therapy in the strictest sense. Some associations have created family therapy consultations, mostly centered on a type of precise problem: toxicomany (Monceau Center) or sexual abuse (Center of Buttes-Chaumont).

TRAINING AND PROFESSIONALIZATION

The development of family therapy in France coincided with the application of a law favoring the financing of postgraduate training for salaried earners. Some associations have proposed often differing training that has not always allowed for the practice of family therapy. There is very little university training and the three or four programs that exist do not provide nationally recognized diplomas.

Is it necessary, therefore, to create a diploma for family therapy that is recognized by the health and social authorities? Answers are not coherent on this matter. Some associations propose training of up to 6 years, which places the therapist in a position of the perpetual student, blocking his or her creativity and autonomy. Nevertheless, the necessity of official recognition seems necessary for some therapists working over a number of years as, for example, psychiatric nurses. Being neither psychiatrist or psychologist, they cannot find autonomy and recognition of their work in the current professional framework.

The ideal would be an accreditation providing simple and clear process: through accrediting therapists following training on family therapy for a duration limited to 2 years; having completed a general training in another health or social field with regular participation in seminars and work groups; and accreditation through an assessment of regular activity and research in centers of family therapy.

ORGANIZATION FOR FAMILY THERAPY

Between local associations the competition is tight in the extreme. For example, at 2-month intervals three associations organized three conferences on the same themes (ethnopsychiatry and family therapy) with the same invited people. This behavior discredits such associations and disperses family therapists, and thus stops the possibility of dialogue.

Efforts to create a national association regrouping family therapists without sectarianism is laudable, but not always successful. The Association of Systemic and Family Therapists (ATSF) is the oldest association in France, creating a federation over local associations. It is a flexible network having few activities outside of national congresses. These conferences gather an important number of participants especially from the social sector, which is more interested in systemic interventions than family therapy.

Founded in 1995, the French Society of Family Therapy (SFTF) gathered family therapists on the basis of individual membership under precise criteria (training, practice, supervision, and so on) that qualify a certain standard of entry. It is comprised of 180 members, a small number in relation to the number of family therapists. It has several instruments: holding seminars, conferences, and an annual congress, and producing the review *Generations*.

Analytic family therapists were, until 1995, organized under a national association that has since broken down into several competitive groups.

JOURNALS

Several reviews in French are devoted to family therapy:

Family Therapy has been published in Geneva (Switzerland) since 1980. The board gathers together Swiss, Belgian, Canadian, and French authors. It is a review where attention is drawn toward the theory of systems, on first and second cybernetics. The majority of articles published over the last 3 years have been written by Italian and Belgian authors.

Resonance is managed by Mony Elkaim (Belgian). Each issue is centered on an interview with a major therapist (Haley, Selvini, Minuchin, Whitaker), with articles on the most recent developments in family therapy. Of irregular publication (one or two numbers per year), it ended in 1997.

Générations, the review of the SFTF, has been published quarterly since 1995. Each issue is built around a theme: violence in the family, resources in family therapy, brothers and sisters, and so on. The international title is *Elsewhere*.

Dialogue can be added to these reviews. It covers clinical and sociological research on the couple and the family. It began as a bulletin in 1965 and has been a review since 1979. It is published quarterly and is supported by the French Association of Marriage Consultation Centers (AFCCC), an institute of training in marriage counseling and couple therapy. In France, marriage counseling was created at the end of the 1960s in the context of the struggle of women's rights and availability of contraception. It has not evolved globally, as in the United States, as far as family therapy has evolved. *Dialogue* is not a theoretical review and aims to be pluridisciplinary. Each issue is centered around a theme: "The couple and narcissism," "Our children serve for what purpose?" "The feeling of solitude," "Incest and family bonds." Articles are of a very high quality with a majority of analytical orientation. Since the end of the review of analytic family therapy *Gruppo*, many analytic family therapists have written in *Dialogue*.

PUBLISHING

Three book collections are devoted to family therapy. Globally fewer than 10 books on family therapy are published every year. The crisis of the French publishing industry is restraining the publication of original work and the translation of classics.

Among the most important books written and published in French are the two family therapy dictionaries: *Dictionnaire des therapies familiales, théories et pratiques* (1987) by Jacques Miernont, whose well-informed articles and wide coverage of the family therapy field are of high quality; and *Dictionnaire clinique des therapies familiales systémiques* (1987), under the direction of J-C Benoit, which appears to be much more heterogeneous.

PERSPECTIVES

European Perspectives and the Risk of Marginalization of French Family Therapists

In years to come, the growth of family therapy will leave the national scale to enter the European arena. For French family therapists, this could accentuate their marginality in relation to Italy, Belgium, Germany, and Great Britain, because there are no family therapists of international renown nor a recognized school of family therapists in France. (Even the analytic family therapists have had little contact with therapists in other counties with the exception of Italy.) Elkaim's book *Panorama of Family Therapies* (1995) is revealing: There is no mention of a French therapist in the main chapters. Some are quoted in the intermediate chapters, but without real studies of their work. This does not render justice to the creativity and seriousness of French family therapists. The French language is not recognized at the international level. Although Italy and Belgium produce trainers and supervisors, there is almost no exchange with Germany, Holland, and the Scandinavian countries. In years to come, a certain number of questions such as those regarding training and professional status will be answered through European administration, leaving French family therapists at risk of having lost their credence in these debates.

The European Family Therapy Association (EFTA) for which the headquarters is in Brussels, Belgium, has been created to intervene in this new situation. It gathers many therapists from approximately 20 countries. (In 1994 there were 120 Italians and only 15 British and 12 Germans.) Even if up to 200 French joined, their influence would be limited.

The End of Isolation

For approximately a decade, family therapists, little by little, have been leaving their isolation. Hostility, found as part of the analytic psychoanalytical circle, as well as the arrogant attitude of some systemic therapists, is no longer valid. The family therapist uses a method of care that is becoming more and more recognized. This recognition depends on the complementarity with other forms of therapies, such as individual therapies. Therefore, the risk of ideological defense is always possible. If one proposes an overview framework for all interventions, partners who become disconcerted, family therapists do not gain credit.

One of the key points for the family therapist in France is the articulation with psychoanalysis. This is where developments have taken place: Let us remember that in the early 1980s most family therapists were not in accord with psychoanalysis. However, today, a large majority of them request double practices, both family and individual, systemic and psychoanalytic. However, this position does not favor reconciliation between different trends in family therapy. It is, nevertheless, an integration at the intrapsychic and relational viewpoints that might be an original contribution to French family therapy.

The Development of Families

In France, as in other European countries, the family institution is probably the most changed social institution during the last 20 years or so. The current context is a history of fragmentation of the family group. During childhood, many children may know several families and also periods of life in a single-parent family. Adults can have successive partners with whom they have tried to construct a family.

This fragmentation induces a great diversity of family forms: one partner families, enlarged families, extended families, and others. The new family types are very different from that of the typical conjugal family of the 1950s and of the early years of family therapy.

In regard to the family, the government has modified its types of intervention and control. It no longer defends a family norm, the conjugal family is no longer the standard, and it recognizes the diversity of cohabitation, one-parent families, and in the near future, the possibility of a contract of "social union." On the other hand, the government has become increasingly interventionist through legal and social work, to control relationships between adults and children, between men and women. Family therapists are increasingly being requested as a source of expertise or therapy.

Some notable changes have occurred within families. The idea of family therapy is no longer seen as a source of blame but often considered as a chance of reconciliation. The "rigid rule" or "absence of rules" that fascinated early family therapists are now of minor importance as compared to the fragmentation of bonds and the will to restore them. This absence of hostility toward family therapy has allowed an increase in demand, without the suggestion of a medical or social worker. In our consultations, we receive families that have already made a first, failed family therapy attempt that has not necessarily given rise to a rejection of family therapy. This situation favors orientation toward resources and often fruitful transgenerational conceptions of family bonds when dealing with fragmentation and solitude.

REFERENCES

Benoit, J-C. (1987). *Dictionnaire clinique des therapies familiales systémiques*. Paris: ESF.

Boszormenyi-Nagy, I. (1987). *Foundations of contextual therapy*. New York: Brunner/Mazel.

Elkaim, M. (1995). *Panorama des therapies familiales*. Paris: le Seuil.

Hochman, J. (1967). La psychotherapie familiale, une arme nouvelle pour le sociopsychiatre. *L'information psychiatrique, 38*, 17–22.

Hochman, J. (1969). Le postulat fusionnel. *L'information psychiatrique, 37*, 5–8.

Lacan J. (1938). La famille. *Encyclopédie française*. Paris: Larousse.

Laforgue, R. (1936). La nevrose familiale. *Revue Française de Psychanalyse*, *9*, 327–355.

Le Goff, J-F. (1997a). De la pathologie au Dialogue: un chemin vers les ressources en therapie familiale. *Générations*, *9*, 9–26.

Le Goff, J-F. (1997b). Une enquête sur les entretiens familiaux et les therapies familiales en psychiatrie de secteur. *Synapse*, *138*, 65–71.

Miermont, J. (1987). *Dictionnaire des therapies familiales, théories et pratiques*. Paris: Payot.

Ruffiot, A. (1981). *La thérapie familiale analytique*. Paris: Dunod.

Selvini, M., Boscolo, L., Cecchin, G. F., & Prata, G. (1978). *Paradox and counterparadox*. Montvale, NJ: Jason Aronson.

CHAPTER 10

Reflections on Forty Years of Family Therapy, Research, and Systemic Thinking in Greece

BASILIA (LIA) SOFTAS-NALL

In ancient Greek, the word "individual" was *idiotis,* which translated as "idiot."

The application of systemic thinking in Greece started in the early 1960s with the Vassilious. George Vassiliou, a psychiatrist, and Vasso Vassiliou, a clinical psychologist, were considered the "parents" of Greek systemic thinking. Both Vassilious were among the first students of Virginia Satir in 1956 to 1957 in Chicago. Under her supervision, they began to see families with important therapeutic gains. Through Satir they came in contact with the Mental Research Institute of Palo Alto, Don Jackson, Watzlawick, and Bateson's work (Sakkas, 1994a, 1994b; Vassiliou, 1990a). In 1963, the Vassilious developed a private center, the Athenian Institute of the Anthropos (AIA; Anthropos means the human being, both male and female in Greek), which under their directorship has offered systemic treatment and training for about 40 years. In addition, they have conducted research on the psychosocial changes of the Greek family and culture since the origins of the AIA. The Vassilious believe that in order to understand families they needed to understand the cultural context within which families functioned. George Vassiliou has been elected as an honorary member of the European Family Therapy Association (EFTA) and is president of various professional international organizations. Both George and Vasso Vassiliou participate as Honorary Founding Members of the two newly founded national family therapy organizations, the Greek Association of Systemic Therapy and the Greek Systemic Thinking and Family Therapy Association.

Charis Katakis, who completed her training at the AIA, started her own private center, the Laboratory for the Study of Human Relations. The laboratory was founded in 1982 to 1983 in collaboration with a number of her former trainees. It is located in Athens with affiliated centers and work groups in other Greek cities. The laboratory offers individual, group, and family therapy, and conducts research and training on aspects of family life, social change, and its relevance to therapy. Katakis is the first President of the Greek Association of Systemic Therapy, which was founded in 1999.

For 20 years (1963 to 1983), the AIA was the primary center offering therapy and postgraduate training around family therapy, couple therapy, and seminars for the development of family life in Greece (Sakkas, 1994b). Many AIA graduates went on to apply their skills in the public and private sectors. Also, therapists who completed their family systems training outside of Greece (which was a common practice, especially for psychologists, because psychology was recognized as a profession in the late 1970s and became part of academia in the 1980s, separate from the field of philosophy) developed private centers or infiltrated the public sector. Actually, a mushrooming of family therapy/systemic therapy centers occurred in the past 15 years (Kaftantzis, 1997; Tomaras, 2000). In the 1980s a total of 11 centers were developed and in the 1990s approximately an additional 18. About seven are private centers and the rest are in the public sector (five within University psychiatric clinics, 14 in mental health centers, and five in substance abuse units). Even though family therapy and training are offered in other centers of Greece (i.e., in Crete, led by Paritsis; in Athens, led by Tseggos; and the Aeginitian team under the auspices of Stefanis and staffed by two senior family therapists, Tomaras and Pomini), the two centers, directed by the Vassilious and Katakis, have been around long enough to have a history. They have provided the field with conceptual frameworks, training, and research issues that make them unique; this chapter mostly focuses on their work. The author's training in systems started with the Vassilious in the late 1970s. After the completion of her doctorate in the United States, she collaborated and trained in the laboratory. Since 1992, she has been teaching Marriage and Family Therapy at the University of Northern Colorado; she continues her connection with family therapy in Greece (Softas-Nall, 1998; Softas-Nall & Tokumine, 1999). She is a founding member of the Greek Systemic Association and is committed to bridge family therapy and systems thinking across cultures and contexts.

GREECE IN CONTEXT AND THE GREEK FAMILY SYSTEM

At the end of World War II, a terrible civil war erupted in Greece. When it ended in 1950, the country was left even more devastated. In the 1950s

Greece began to industrialize and the population started migrating from small communities to large urban centers. People left their agricultural pursuits in the villages to go primarily to Athens. In 1981 almost 40% of the population was concentrated in Athens and Salonika (Georgas, 1993). The population of Athens increased from 1,800,000 in 1964 to over 3,000,000 in 1984, to over 4,000,000 in 2000 (the total population of Greece is about 11,000,000 compared to 10,259,900 in 1991). Many millions of Greeks live outside of the country; they are called the Diaspora Greeks, and large communities exist in Australia, Germany, and the United States (Softas-Nall, 2000). "In the context of Greek Systemic thought, family dynamics and family interactional patterns of change were experienced and therefore conceptualized as phenomena inherently connected to the seismic shaking of the whole Greek society" (Katakis, 2000, p. 4). Processes that in other developed countries lasted for 150 years were condensed in record time in Greece, providing for the opportunity to witness a whole spectrum of cultural evolution and family transformation (Katakis, 1990a).

The characteristic Greek family type was extended. It was probably functional in agricultural societies because many hands were needed for the cultivation of the land. In traditional Greece the extended family was also characteristic of fishermen and merchants (Georgas, 1993). Research in the 1960s and early 1970s focused on the significance of the in-group as a determinant of values and attitudes in Greece (Triandis & Vassiliou, 1972). The Greek in-group was composed of members of the extended family, including relatives, in-laws, and friends "who show concern for me," and "will come to our aid in time of need." The appropriate behaviors toward members of the in-group was *philotimo* (Vassiliou & Vassiliou, 1973), loosely translated to mean that "one sacrifices for the in-group members to be correct in fulfilling obligations." Twelve years ago, Georgas (1989), a Professor at the University of Athens and a leading authority in the social psychology of the Greek family, was writing about the diminishing impact of the in-group in Athens. Collectivist values were being gradually replaced by individualistic values (Georgas, 1989, 1991). Recently, he presented an ecosocial model of the impact of family on the psychosocial differentiation of the individual under a contextual approach and discussed family bonds to family structure and functions across different cultures (Georgas, 1999, 2000). Comparing Northwestern European societies and Mediterranean societies, no systematic differences were found "in emotional closeness, frequency of meetings, or telephone contact with members of the nuclear family across the five cultures" (Georgas, 1999, p. 124). Differences were found in terms of the extended family. In Greek and Greek-Cypriot societies, the family functions extended to a larger kinship network in terms of frequency of meetings and contact by phone (Georgas, 1999, 2000). Close relatives such as mothers, parents, in-laws, sisters, uncles, aunts, and grandparents lived in a nearby or the same apartment building with frequent contact and communication, both by phone and in person (Georgas, 1999). It seems that even though the impact of collective values was diminishing in Greece, in comparison to other Northwestern European societies, the extended family in Greece is still present in many ways.

THEORETICAL CONCEPTS AND RESEARCH ON THE GREEK FAMILY

Katakis (1984), in a major book entitled *The Three Identities of the Greek Family*, referred to three consecutive forms of family life: traditional-rural, industrial-nuclear, and informational-transitional. She believed that families coordinated their shared ties on the basis of three coexisting and conflicting self-referential conceptual systems she has come to call ecotheories. (In ancient Greek, the term *eco* means the household, the family, and home.) The model of the three ecotheories developed within a period of 20 years and is based on research findings and clinical experience. This model was an attempt toward an operational definition of the concept of ecotheory based on the concepts and principles derived from general systems theory (Katakis, 1989). "Each of the three ecotheories was viewed as a hierarchy of cognitive-emotional dynamic structures which express how the individual or a group of individuals belong to a particular form of family perceive different aspects of family life" (p. 19). The relevant conceptual categories such as purposes, values, roles, and norms represent the codes and rules by which family members transact. Elements from the three different ecotheories create inconsistencies and incompatibilities for family members who try to coordinate their actions and interactions on the basis of dissonant and confused underlying purposes, values, and role definitions. "These symptoms can be seen as manifestations of what Bowen has called undifferentiated ego-mass created by the universally changing patterns connected to family life" (Katakis, 1989, p. 21). This conceptual model has been applied also in therapy with Greek couples who live outside of Greece (Softas-Nall & Baldo, 2000).

Psychotherapy can be seen "as the process during which crucial consecutive reframing alters the subjective reality in ways which enables them to live more productively creating more harmonious interaction with the environment" (Katakis, 1989, p. 16). The concept of self-referential conceptual system (SRCS) describes the way a particular person, family, or any other social group perceives itself in relation to others and its total life situation (Katakis, 1990a). The SRCS aims to unify key concepts in order to describe the functioning and malfunctioning of purposeful, self-regulated biopsychosocial living systems. It deals with the way specific living systems create their own theory about themselves. These conceptions are subjective and emotionally loaded and largely determine choices, actions, and interactions. The SRCS of an individual is developed in the context of the SRCS of one's family. The SRCS of the particular family constitutes the subjective view of itself in relation to its greater context, the culture or suprasystem. "A particular entity's SRCS is viewed as a constellation of systematic representations which are hierarchically-ordered conceptual categories and meta-categories expressing the subjective evaluation of its self-defined identity and purpose (who am I, where am I going, and why)" (Katakis, 1990b, p. 91).

In the late 1970s in her quest of the three identities of the Greek family, Katakis interviewed a 75-year-old shepherd living in a mountainous rural village, his 45-year-old son who lived in a nearby town, and his grandson, a 25-year-old teacher who lived in Athens. One of the questions she asked all three was "Why do people marry and have families?" She received three different answers, which represent the core code of the three ecotheories in a condensed form . The old shepherd, representative of the traditional-rural form of life, answered, "This is the destination of man." His son, who had experienced urban life, answered, "People get married to have children, educate them, and make them useful members of society." The grandson swept away what they thought in one sentence by saying, "Marriage is neither important nor necessary, what counts is the relationship." The three ecotheories are presented in order to describe the context of family relations and functions, values, childrearing practices, and gender roles. A new ecotheory seems to be emerging that is also described.

First Ecotheory: Traditional Family and In-Group

The first ecotheory was in place until the 1960s and included the traditional family and the in-group. (See Table 10.1 for a summary of all ecotheories.) Within the in-group there was cooperation, emphasis on doing what the in-group expected, self-sacrifice, and being concerned for the in-group's well-being and collective interests. The traditional Greek in-group was the family, friends, and guests. The predominant value was *philotimo*, which means sense of honor. Philotimo was connected with acceptable behavior within the in-group that promoted interdependence, collectivity, and the interests of the in-group (Vassiliou & Vassiliou, 1973). The out-group was everybody else, and they were treated with suspicion and rudeness (Triandis & Vassiliou, 1972). The only and common goal of both individuals and the group to which they belonged was to find and secure a means to survive. The goals and expectations of individuals were the same as the in-group.

Childrearing included indulgence and protection with the goal of promoting the in-group's collective interests. The concept of responsible be-

TABLE 10.1. Summary of Ecotheories

Family Function	Traditional	Child-Centered Nuclear	Nuclear Transitional Copntemporary	Year 1990 and Beyond
Goal	Survive	Raise children	Have a relationship	Have companionship/ partners
Unit	In-group Extended family	Nuclear family	Couple	Individual/Couple
Values	Cooperation Self-sacrifice within in-group Interdependence Preserve harmonious relationships Suspiciousness and rudeness toward outgroup Conflict viewed as catastrophic	Interdependence Dependence Education of children for upward mobility of the family Parents live through their children	Emphasis on dialogue and communication In theory: Equality In practice: Conformity/ conflict Conflict between personal (professional) pursuits and family responsibilities	Family cohesion Self-awareness Self-direction Disagreement/ Conflict is positive and viewed as expression of individuality Acceptance of separation
Child-rearing	Children are indulged and protected Children have several "mothers"	Children are overprotected Dilemmas of adolescents—whether to stay at home or leave the family Prolonged adolescence	Raising children is the focus of conflict Grandparents also care for children	Children add to the relationship Choice of not having children Parenting is perceived as an enormous responsibility
Gender roles	Woman is the giver Man is the provider Clear roles	Woman as mother becomes anxious and as wife lonely Man is anxious about being an adequate provider	Ambivalence about roles Conflict between independence and close family relationship	Greater overlap between men and women

havior was meaningful only in relation to the common goals of the group. Within that framework, women worked very hard to contribute to the survival of the family and in-group. By nurturing others, women gained self-respect. While they were young they were seen more as a burden as compared to boys. In order for women to be eligible for marriage, the family would have to provide a dowry, which was an economic burden. It was after women became mothers that they gained the greater respect of the community. Having girls was disappointing; most mothers wanted to have boys. Having a boy meant social mobility, better living conditions, and continuation of the family. Even when the son migrated, he supported the family. The mother–son relationship was closer and more intimate than with their husbands (Triandis, Vassiliou, & Nassiakou, 1968). Sons supported their mothers after their fathers passed away. Studies showed that boys as compared to girls were breast fed for longer periods and gently weaned (Vassiliou, 1970). Women were perceived negatively until they became mothers and were idealized. Men obtained self-respect by being good providers and supporting their families, in particular their mothers.

Second Ecotheory: Nuclear Family

In the 1950s, after World War II, Greek families immigrated to Athens and abroad. Marriage and the creation of a family progressively shifted to focus on the child. The purpose of the family was to raise children. Two people united their lives with the purpose of fulfilling the goals of a third person. This child-centered perception of marriage and the family served the basic need of stabilizing the family during a period of major changes. Studies in the early 1970s in Athens showed that parents prepared children for a new world and social upward mobility by exaggerated efforts at educating them (Katakis, 1976). Anxiety over the child's school performance was evident because success in school was tied to social mobility. In addition to the practical dimension of educating children, parents sought psychological satisfaction through their children's achievements. Parents lived through their children; although they reported that they expected nothing from their children, they did. On one level, they pushed their children to achieve personal goals, and on a psychological level forged "chains" on their children. If the children left home, the parents felt they were left without a purpose in life. Divorce rates among parents whose children were at the end of adolescence increased. The problem was greater for mothers who felt deprived of all that fulfilled their lives to that time. In the new urban environment, wives felt isolated from their husbands without the in-group support (Doumanis, 1983). The men were trying to gain respect in a competitive environment and their in-group was getting smaller. Men felt vulnerable to disappointments and loneliness (Softas-Nall, 1991). Somatic symptoms increased for both women and men. Somatization disorder has a high reported frequency in Greece for men (American Psychiatric Association, 1994). Much of research at that time was related to changes in the family structure, stress, and somatic symptoms (Georgas, 1984; Georgas et al., 1984).

Third Ecotheory: Transition to Contemporary

Research in the beginning of the 1980s in Athens reflected the confusion, loneliness, and desperation expressed by children (Katakis, 1984, 1998). These children represented the generation that was raised during the 1970s, a period of dramatic social changes in Greece (such as urbanization, industrialization, and the return of democracy after 7 years of military dictatorship, 1967 to 1974, and the invasion of the Turks in Cyprus). These children appeared undecided as to whether they should behave as individuals or as members of a family (Katakis, 1978). The 12-year-olds who lived in Athens in the 1980s felt suffocated by the impasse they faced. Research material derived from projective techniques (e.g., Thematic Apperception Test analyzed by story sequence analysis) revealed that children seemed to doubt whether they would survive psychosocially. They felt that significant others were absorbed in their own struggle for psychological survival and were not available. Using kinetic family drawings (Burns & Kaufman, 1972), children drew pictures of themselves and their families that depicted spaces empty of life, were prison-like, or were in a passive position centered around the television. In contrast, the materials collected from 12-year-olds from the provinces in 1981 were very different from their peers in Athens. These children, who lived in the traditional agricultural milieu, expressed faith in the value of collective effort, interdependence, and cooperation. In an unpublished study conducted in 1979 by the author and Dallas and Halikiopoulou, children were asked to draw pictures separating a cat and a dog from fighting. The results were revealing as to how children perceived the resolution of conflict. The sample of children from the provinces used interdependent relational solutions such as raising the cat and the dog from the time they were young so they would become friends; if each actualized their expertise, such as the cat chasing mice and the dog chasing foxes away from children, they would get along; if their owner treated them equally, pet them, fed them, played with them, then they would get along. The sample of children from Athens used very different solutions. A small number of them also used relational interdependence solutions; however, the majority drew pictures in which separation, force, or violence were themes. For example, the cat and the dog would be separated by a wall or a fence; if they got close to each other the owner would throw rocks at them, use a bat, etc. The most desperate solution seemed to come from an 8-year-old boy who used a military tank to keep the dog and cat from fighting. The difference in solutions in the two contexts paralleled Katakis' findings and raised a lot of questions as to how children felt when searching for solutions to deal with conflict in their own lives.

In-depth qualitative research on motives, attitudes, and patterns of interaction of young couples before marriage concluded that women were looking desperately for a way out from the impasses (Katakis, 1980). Women were trying to avoid being in the role of "queen of the house" as in the previous ecotheory, and they talked about independence, freedom, and meaningful relationships, although they doubted they would be able to experience them. The Greek women felt distrustful toward their partners because they felt they would be burdened with responsibilities they wanted to avoid. Women perceived having children as being tied to an older, traditional way of being that frightened them. They feared commitment and mistrusted intimate relationships and thus built a fence around themselves and distanced themselves from others. These women were very ambivalent in their relationships with men and they perceived their mothers' message to be contradictory. They were hearing their mothers say, "Don't go through what I went through. Get an education. Strive for a career. Don't depend on men, but I am your model and you should do what I did." Raising children became a point of antagonism and conflict for young couples. The big question for these young women with impressive academic records was whether they would be able to combine human relationships with a desire for a successful professional career. The traditional women derived their feelings of power and self-esteem by giving and nurturing others within their in-group (Doumanis, 1983). Women of the 1970s and 1980s did not want this kind of "giving," and yet had lost the feeling of power that was so intimately connected to self-denial (Katakis, 1984).

The same qualitative study with young couples showed that engaged couples wanted a relationship based on honesty and trust. In the traditional environment the man was the provider and breadwinner. In the transitional contemporary family ecotheory, the man was no longer the only provider. Men felt unsure of how to remain helpful to their families. The psychological distance between men and their families grew significantly. Growing up as boys, these men received messages from their mothers that "You need protection" and "You are capable of anything." There was competition between the mothers and wives for men's attention and they found no refuge in relationships with significant others. Both sexes talked about equality on a psychosocial level and they were searching for a new identity. In the 1980s the individualistic position they were expressing, while collective structures around them were crumbling, presented both a dead end and a new challenge. There was a need for family therapy and centers developed to offer such services.

FAMILY OF THE 1990S AND BEYOND

Recent qualitative studies conducted by the Laboratory of Human Relations give us information on what the fourth ecotheory might look like (Katakis,

1998). Katakis has not identified a fourth ecotheory; however, for purposes of explaining the new findings we are treating them as a new phase for Greek families. In the late 1980s and 1990s couples emphasized more what they gained from being in a relationship, and they seemed less willing to risk their relationship to advance their career. It is a very important finding that those current couples give priority to family cohesion. Through a developmental evolutionary process, they have rejected the child-centered model, recognized the enormous responsibility of the parental role, and many couples choose not to have children. The desire to create and cultivate satisfactory functional relationships was shown in an optimistic perspective. There was internal confusion for each member in the relationship, as shown in Thematic Aptitude Test (TAT) sequence analysis stories and, even though separation and divorce was not seen as the solution, the way to resolve problems remained vague or borrowed from traditional "recipes." Men appeared more ambivalent about remaining in or escaping relationships, and they expected women to take a dynamic position to keep them in the relationship. Young couples also saw marriage as a social necessity; however, they reported valuing the relationship as an important part of life. Many couples lived together and have children without getting married. Women felt they had more choices and they emphasized both the survival and growth of their relationship with their partner along with professional achievements. In general, it seemed that couples were more conscious of both the difficulties and the positive potential of relationships as compared to previous ecotheories. The criteria for the choice of a partner became more personal and internal and not social and economic, as in previous ecotheories. Commitment was seen in a more positive light as compared to the previous ecotheory. Having children was not viewed as interfering with a relationship. There was a greater overlap on the perceptions of women and men on values, identity, and life goals. There was a strong striving for equality between partners. As women were impacted by social changes and the feminist movement, their issues of empowerment and fear became clearer (Softas-Nall, Bardos, & Fakinos, 1993, 1995). As studies repeatedly indicated, the current Greek family and the three ecotheories with elements of a fourth one continue to coexist and be conflicting conceptual systems (Katakis, 1984). Elements of all ecotheories may coexist within a person and his or her family.

THERAPEUTIC TECHNIQUES AND PROCESSES

The Vassilious define the goal of therapy ". . . as the development of a creative attitude, an attitude which will enable people to detect and synthetically resolve their own contradictions and the contradictions in their family, in the groups in which they live and work and in their social context"

(Vassiliou & Vassiliou, 1983, p. 367). Both the Athenian Institute of the Anthropos and the Laboratory for the Study of Human Relations had as a goal the application of systemic thinking in Greece. The belief was that what was most important was conceptualizing and intervening within a systemic way of thinking rather than strictly doing family therapy. Their years of research and clinical experience with individuals and families in relation to psychosocial changes led them to the conclusion that family members are more open to participate and change in the context of a combination of group and family. "It is often more effective to start with one family member, not necessarily the most problematic one, who is most open or is most motivated" (Katakis, 1990a, p. 4). Reflecting on the evolving themes of conferences by the International Family Therapy Association (IFTA; organized in 1987 and had its first conference in 1989 in Dublin), Katakis (1991) commented on the "revolutionary spirit" of the conference and the frequent use of *systemic* rather than *family* therapy. She discussed that the term "family" therapy has

> become a confounded concept since it has been used to denote a mode, a method, or a form of psychotherapy and a way of thinking at the same time. . . . The core self-referential theme of the Dublin conference appeared to be that it is time to acknowledge that what is important is not the mode of treatment we use, but the systemic way of thinking, which can guide us in setting goals and choosing the appropriate approaches, methods, and techniques. After all, the systemic way of thinking is in the minds of individuals, both therapists and clients, and can be changed in different ways not just by seeing families together. Being eclectic in the context of the systemic frame of reference is to choose the modality and the methods and approaches on the basis of criteria derived from having understood the system's functioning, the situational limitations, and conditions inherent in the total situation as well as preferences and talents of the therapists themselves. (p. 9)

These reflections echo the conceptual beliefs of both Katakis and the Vassilious.

Both centers work with women's groups, children's groups, men's groups, and so on. At times family members of the same family belong to one of these groups and their work is also monitored in the context of their family processes.

> . . . family therapy has always been seen as one application of the systemic approach with its distinct theoretical and practical equipment which can be carried along in any kind of intervention and not only in family sessions. It is family therapy concepts and principles that are important and not seeing families together. Actually, in group therapy, where one member of the family decides to change, she or he becomes the vehicle

> for pervasive family change, whether we have ever seen the other members of the family or not. Whether, when, for how long, at what intervals, in what context we will see the family or part of it, depends on what we hear with a third ear and what we see with a third eye in the stories our clients tell us about themselves and their family relationships. Our integrative approach allows us to intervene in any way we sense will help them start re-storying their lives. Visits of other members of the family in the group have proven extremely beneficial, triggering change in a family as well as in other group members. In the context of the group, where the group becomes the reflecting team for the family, change is triggered both in the visiting family, the members of the groups, and their families. "The whole system moves ahead to alternative individual, family, and collective stories which untie the knots and free individuals and families from their love prisons." (Katakis, 2000, pp. 4–5)

It seems that these short-term visits by family members trigger changes at many different levels: individual, family, and group.

Letter writing has been a technique that has been employed in communicating with other family members. For example, in a men's group, one of the men, a librarian, was distraught because his 17-year-old son had left home, refused to finish his high school studies, and did not want to have anything to do with his father, let alone come to therapy with him. Each of the men in the group contributed a sentence that composed a letter that was given to the son through relatives who knew where he was. Parts of the letter said,

> I am writing this letter to you to tell you what I've wanted to say for a long time and I couldn't. I remember that when you first went to school and I did not hug you, I never caressed you. I would like to hold you in my arms for a long time . . . until you could feel how important and dear you are to me. I remember seeing you for short periods of time since I was busy at work, away from you. I did not share with you the joy of your first achievements in school . . . in life. . . . I was always absent, not present. I did not advise you or support you in your difficulties and problems. I was once again absent. Now that you are gone I understand for the first time how many things you struggled with pain to tell me with your 'rebellions.' For all the things I did not do, I ask you to try with me, to help me live the lost time as if you were a child and I was a young father. With love, your father. (Softas-Nall, 1991)

In this collaborative letter, men shared the pain and hopes of a man coming to grips with his lack of fathering and the loss of that for him and his son. This letter also captured their own losses and hopes as sons and fathers. The letter eventually reached the son, who still refused to talk to his father. He did notify his mother of his whereabouts, however, and the mother decided to enter couples therapy at that point.

In a country with a long history, where ancestors, loyalties, myths, and heroes are everyday concepts, genograms seem to speak to the heart of the Greek people. Vasso Vassiliou (personal communication, 2001) exuberantly described how they conduct intensive weekend systemic groups every summer in Mitilini, the islands of origin of her husband, and use genograms. One of the leading authorities in the teaching and construction of genograms in Greece is L. Stylianoudi, a forensic anthropologist with a background in systems (Softas-Nall & Stylianoudi, 1996). Monica McGoldrick, a leading authority in the United States in genograms (1999) was an invited speaker of the Laboratory in 2001; and her colleagues' book is being translated into Greek.

STAGES OF THERAPY

Therapy is conceptualized as a process of progressive reframing leading the individual to higher levels of self-organization (Katakis, 1989). These successive stages of the therapeutic process are described in detail along with interventions for each stage in Katakis' work (Katakis, 1989). Stage A, when the client enters therapy, is called "Nonsystematic View of Life"; Stage B1: "The Inner Void Stage"; B2: "The Internal Journey"; and Stage C: "A New Life Journey." "Therapeutic change can be defined as a process which aims at actualizing the human potential our minds possess and which can be activated through a creative personal and collective process of reconstructive reality" (Katakis, 1995). The characteristics of Stage A include the person feeling victimized, neglected, pressured, and so forth by outside causes. If they see themselves as responsible, they feel depressed (i.e., "I am a bad parent"). The focus at this stage is on changing interactional patterns between the person and usually significant others. The suggested therapist interventions are action-oriented with the goal of helping the client achieve his or her first basic reframing (i.e., role-playing, all forms of family approaches, such as strategic, structural, etc.). When strong resistance is anticipated therapeutic contacts made at the beginning of therapy help in overcoming it when it appears (Vassiliou & Katakis, 1980). During Stage B1, the person becomes aware of any consistent identity and has a frightening time acknowledging inner chaos without reassurance that it can be turned into order. The suggested interventions include reframing unproductive interpretations of feeling (i.e., a feeling of being "stuck," a feeling of being at a dead end) to be reframed to one being at crossroads. Techniques that trigger intense emotional reactions may lead to the acceptance of inner confusion.

Helpful metaphors seem to relate to setting out into the wilderness, or to climbing a high mountain without the necessary knowledge, skills, or equipment. The bittersweet taste toward the end of this stage is, "I don't know who I am, where I am going, and why." Stage B2: "The Internal Journey" is characterized by rich interconnections. "Having accepted the systemic frame of mind, the person begins the struggle to comprehend the feedback loops that have led to the present assumptions about inner and outer reality—a network of interdependent elements that constitute a dynamic integrated whole. By progressive reframing the person changes the old inner cognitive-emotional structures" (Katakis, 1989, p. 490) and replaces them with new elements of the self-referential conceptual system. When exploring decisions made early in life such as "I couldn't decide on anything because I thought if I were weak I would be loved and protected. If I were strong and independent I would be deserted" (p. 491), persons may feel relief but also wonder how they can actually be different. Deeply embedded beliefs and attributes are not easily changed. Any techniques that can promote self-differentiation and facilitate connections between the past and the present are recommended. Sculpting, psychodrama, early recollections, empty-chair technique, etc. activate the re-experiencing of painful feelings of the past and trigger cognitive-emotional restructuring. "Sessions with the whole family or with particular family members increase the intensity of affective response and help one to acknowledge the full implications of one's position in the family constellation" (p. 491). The breakthrough toward the end of this stage (if it is achieved during therapy) has to do with serious life decisions. Therapeutic "techniques" are not very helpful. This is when people take action to interrupt relationships that have been dysfunctional, give up nonrewarding jobs, take professional risks, or leave therapy. The next stage is the "New Life Journey," where one sets out to develop meaningful relationships and new professional activities.

In the book, *The Purple Liquid,* published in Greek (Katakis, 1995), the theoretical base of Greek systemic thinking is reviewed and case studies presented. It is a book that evolved by the assimilation of constructivistic and social constructivistic notions. It is noted that Greek systemic thinking was embedded in self-referential and social constructivistic notions from the beginning, 40 years ago.

Training

Perhaps the most unique aspect for the trainees undergoing systemic training in either the AIA or the Laboratory of Human Relations is their participation in the therapeutic groups. All trainees, apart from their participation in systems-oriented seminars, practica type experiences in facilities with one-way mirrors, and experiential learning, they are required to be *therapevomeni* (in loose translation: to be involved in the therapeutic process). The trainees (whose systems education program extends to about 4 or more years postgraduate) are not placed in special trainee groups but in groups of people who have asked for help (Katakis, 1991). "They [trainees] start to see that there is not a clear line between those who offer services [to be a therapist in ancient Greek means to offer services] and those who receive them. They begin to challenge ideas such as 'I'm well and you are problematic,' 'I know and you don't.'" (p. 184). Their perceptions change from seeing themselves in the role of the expert to often realizing that having chosen to become a therapist was an extension of their role in their family of origin. They wonder how and from where they will receive help for their own personal life. Their family of origin often will be asked to come in during the therapeutic process. Family sculpting and role-play are also techniques often utilized when trainees reach higher levels of complexity, clarity, and self-actualization, both in their professional and personal lives. They become more understanding of other people's struggles to overcome their "resistances" but experience relief when they give up patterns and roles that were not functional for them.

> . . . Since the early years, therapy of the trainees has been the central axis of our training. All of us as trainees join therapy groups together with clients for long periods of time, where we share our personal and family stories and experience, in vivo, the high cost of trying to live our lives following the dominant stories which were changing at an unprecedented pace all around us. Nevertheless, at the same time, we also experienced the exhilarating process of creating together "with blood, sweat and tears" (as Vasso Vassiliou used to say) new "truths" which were more compatible with the emerging alternative cultural narratives. (Katakis, 2000, p. 4)

Other centers offering training in Greece do not necessarily require trainees to undergo therapy. Within the university arena at least one course is taught in family therapy within a clinical psychology postgraduate degree offered at the University of Athens. At the present time, no degrees lead to a couple/family therapy degree (Georgas, 2001, personal communication).

PROFESSIONAL AFFILIATIONS

The Greek Systemic Association founded in 1999 has close ties to EFTA and currently is composed of 85 members who are psychologists, psychiatrists, and social workers. In order to become a member, one has to be licensed within his or her own profession and have completed systems training. The great majority of the members have completed their training at the Institute and the Laboratory. Members receive a newsletter and annual conferences are held. The Greek Systemic Thinking and Family Therapy Association was founded in 1998 by Tomaras and Pominis. The creation of professional organizations is creating an umbrella for a number of systems therapists who work in different settings with common goals. The International Family Therapy Association had its eighth World Congress in Family Therapy in 1996 in Athens.

CONCLUSION

The story of systems thinking in Greece can be seen as multigenerational, starting with the Vassilious and their trainees (including Katakis and her trainees and associates). Centers offering family therapy in Greece started in the early 1960s and significantly multiplied in the 1980s and 1990s. The identity of the Greek family changed dramatically from the 1960s to the 1990s. The work of the first two major centers were reviewed, including their research on the changes of the Greek family and psychosocial developments. Systemic thinking and family therapy were stressed as important and family members were not necessarily seen together. The further professionalization of family therapy and training is seen by the creation of the two Associations of Systemic Thinking and Family Therapy in 1990 and 1999. Greece has absorbed a large population from the Balkans (i.e., Albanians) and surrounding areas in the past 15 years that has created a new challenge in regard to diversity, intermarriage, and the continued transformation of the Greek family. It is expected that systemic thinking, which tends to emphasize cooperation, will be of help in the process of the new transformation.

ACKNOWLEDGMENTS

Many thanks to the following people who helped with interviews and materials: M. Charalambidou, M. Fakinos, J. Georgas, C. Katakis, E. Koutroumbis, M. Polemis, and V. Vassiliou.

REFERENCES

American Psychiatric Association. (1994). *Diagnostic and statistical manual of mental disorders* (3rd ed., rev.). Washington, DC: Author.

Burns, R., & Kaufman, H. (1972). *Action style and symbols in kinetic family drawing.* New York: Brunner/Mazel.

Doumanis, M. (1983). *Mothering in Greece: From collectivism to individualism.* New York: Academic Press.

Georgas, J. (1984). *Psychological and psychosomatic reactions to stress in Greece.* Presented at the Second European Conference on Personality Psychology, University of Bielefeld.

Georgas, J. (1989). Changing family values in Greece: From collectivist to individualist. *Journal of Cross-Cultural Psychology, 20,* 81–91.

Georgas, J. (1991). Intrafamily acculturation of values in Greece. *Journal of Cross-Cultural Psychology, 22*(4), 445–457.

Georgas, J. (1993). An ecological-social model for indigenous psychology: The example of Greece. *Indigenous psychologies: Theory, method and experience in cultural context.* Newbury Park, CA: Sage.

Georgas, J. (1999). Family as a context variable in cross-cultural psychology. In J. Adamopoulos & Y. Kashima (Eds.), *Social psychology and cultural context.* Beverly Hills: Sage.

Georgas, J. (2000). Psychodynamics of the Greek family: Similarities and differences with other countries. In A. Kalantzi-Azizi & E. Bezevegis (Eds.), *Training and sensitivity issues for mental health professionals working with children and adults.* Athens: Ellinika Grammata.

Georgas, J., Giakoumaki, E., Georgoulias, N., Koumandakis, E., & Kaskarelis, D. (1984). Psychosocial stress and its relation to obstetrical complications. *Psychotherapy and Psychosomatics, 41,* 200–206.

Kaftantzis, B. (1997). *The Greek systemic field.* Second Panhellenic Meeting of Family Therapy-Systemic Therapy, Salonica, Greece.

Katakis, C. (1976). An exploratory multi-level attempt to investigate intrapersonal and interpersonal patterns of twenty Athenia families. *Mental Health and Society, 3,* 1–9.

Katakis, C. (1978). On the transaction of social change processes and the perception of self in relation to others: A study of Greek preadolescents. *Mental Health and Society, 5,* 275–283.

Katakis, C. (1980). Changing patterns of the marital relationship in Greece. *Mediterranean Journal of Social Psychiatry, 1,* 7–11.

Katakis, C. (1984). *I tris taftotites tis Ellinikis ikogenias* [*The three identities of the Greek family*] (3rd ed.). Athens: Kedros.

Katakis, C. (1989). Stages of psychotherapy: Progressive reconceptualizations as a self-organizing process. *Psychotherapy, 26*(4), 484–493.

Katakis, C. (1990a). The self-referential conceptual system: Towards an operational definition of subjectivity. *Systems Research, 7,* 91–102.

Katakis, C. (1990b). Coexisting and conflicting self-referential conceptual systems: A model for describing malfunctioning in the contemporary family: Implications for therapy. *Contemporary Family Therapy, 12,* 343–362.

Katakis, C. (1991). Reflections on the self-reference of family therapy. *The International Connection, 4*(2), 7–12.

Katakis, C. (1995). *To mov ygro [The purple liquid].* Athens: Ellinika Grammata.

Katakis, C. (1998). *I tris taftotites tis Ellinikis ikogenias [The three identities of the Greek family]* (8th ed.). Athens: Ellinika Grammata.

Katakis, C. (2000, October). *Systemic group therapy: Family therapy without a family.* Presented at the SIPPR-VI International Congress, Milan, Italy.

McGoldrick, M., Gerson, R., & Shellengerger, S. (1999). *Genogram: Assessment and intervention.* New York: Norton.

Sakkas, D. (1994a). A discussion with psychiatrist George Vassiliou: Family and group therapy in the context of Social Psychiatry. *Psychiatry Issues,* 4–6.

Sakkas, D. (1994b). An interview with the Vassilious: The development of family therapy as we experienced it. *Tetradia Psychiatrikis, 45,* 11–21.

Softas-Nall, B. (1991). *The changing self-perceptions of young Greek men.* Panhellenic Research Symposium, Athens, Greece.

Softas-Nall, B. (1998). *Family therapy in the Greek systemic reality.* Athens: Laboratory for the Study of Human Relations.

Softas-Nall, B. (2000). Introduction to B. Softas-Nall and T. Baldo, *Dialogues within a Greek family: Multicultural stories of a couple revisited. The Family Journal: Counseling and Therapy for Couples and Families, 8*(4), 394–395.

Softas-Nall, B., & Baldo, T. (2000). Dialogues within a Greek family: Multicultural stories of a couple revisited. *The Family Journal: Counseling and Therapy for Couples and Families, 8*(4), 396–398.

Softas-Nall, B., Bardos, A., & Fakinos, M. (1993). *Fear of rape and its impact: An empirical study with Greek women.* Presented at Kansas Series Conference on Women's Psychological and Physical Health, Lawrence, Kansas.

Softas-Nall, B., Bardos, A., & Fakinos, M. (1995). Fear of rape, its perceived seriousness and likelihood among young Greek women. *Violence Against Women, 1*(2), 174–186.

Softas-Nall, B., & Stylianoudi, L. (1996). *Diversity and strength through "Back to the Roots" cultural genograms: Implications for therapists' identity and training in family therapy.* The International Family Therapy Association, 8th World Congress in Family Therapy, Athens, Greece.

Softas-Nall, B., & Tokumine, L. (1999). *Ethnicity and the Greek family in therapy: Recent research and implications.* Rocky Mountain Psychological Association Conference, Fort Collins, Colorado.

Tomaras, B. (2000). *The Greek systemic field—additional.* Scientific Conference [Epistimoniki Imerida], Athens, Greece.

Triandis, H., & Vassiliou, V. (1972). A comparative analysis of subjective culture. In H. Triandis (Ed.), *The analysis of subjective culture* (pp. 89–117). New York: Wiley.

Triandis, H., Vassiliou, V., & Nassiakou, M. (1968). Three cross-cultural studies of subjective culture. *Journal of Personality and Social Psychology, 8*(4), 1–41.

Vassiliou, G. (1970). Milieu specificity in family therapy. In N. W. Ackerman, J. Lieb, & J. Pearce (Eds.), *Family therapy in transition* (pp. 81–88). Boston: Little, Brown.

Vassiliou, G. (1990a). On studying-researching family and group processes for thirty-five years. *Psychiatriki, 1,* 283–288.

Vassiliou, G. (1990b). The product of a new epistemology in the sciences of the anthropos. *Journal of Psychiatric Notebooks, 30,* 69–71.

Vassiliou, G., & Katakis, C. (1980, July). *On the therapeutic contract.* Presented at the Eighth International Congress of Social Psychiatry, Zagreb, Yugoslavia.

Vassiliou, V., & Vassiliou, G. (1973). The implicative meaning of Greek concept of philotimo. *Journal of Cross-cultural Psychology, 4,* 326–341.

Vassiliou, G., & Vassiliou, V. (1983). On the Diogenes search: Outlining a dialectic systemic approach concerning the functioning of Anthropos and his suprasystem. In M. Pines (Ed.), *The evolution of group analysis* (pp. 359–380). London: Routledge & Kegan Paul.

PART III

Family Therapy in Africa

CHAPTER 11

Indigenous Family Work in Nigeria

The Yoruba Experience

MARY ADEKSON

NIGERIAN ETHNIC GROUPS

Nigeria has a rich heritage deriving from its indigenous ethnic elements as well as from Middle Eastern and Western cultural influences. Most African countries can trace their origin from very diverse, heterogeneous backgrounds with a rich mixed ethnic heritage. Some African countries have as many as 250 ethnic groups. Nigeria is one of the most ethnically diverse countries in Africa and, relative to its size, in the world. The four dominant groups, Igbo in the East, Yoruba in the West, and the Hausa and Fulani in the North, constitute 60% of the population. The Igbo have a population of 16.6 million (17%), whereas the Hausa and Fulani have a population of 29.5 million (30%), and the Yoruba have a population of 20.3% million (20%) (World Almanac, 1995).

YORUBALAND AND THE YORUBA

Yorubaland, located within the tropics, is much nearer to the equator than to the Tropic of Cancer. The roughly east-west coastline is on the average about 60' 22'N of the equator, where the coastline swings southward toward the delta. The great achievement of Yoruba settlements is their remarkable urban centers, unparalleled anywhere else in tropical Africa (Africa Yearbook, 1995; Mabogunje, 1962). The Yoruba are characterized by their indigenous economies—hunting, fishing, farming, and craft industries—as well as their settlements with their long tradition of living in towns and cities (Africa Yearbook, 1995; Ojo, 1967).

Epega and Neimark (1995) pointed out that

> one of the great powers of the Yoruba tradition is its ability to translate basic truth and wisdom through time, so that its application in our world of instant communication, high technology, and material goals and aspirations can be as accurate and beneficial today as it was thousands of years ago. (p. xvii)

The Yoruba have their own distinct, systematic [sic], and rationalized ideas about the mysteries of the world; their philosophy is life affirming, be it true or mythical, scientific or not.

Makinde (1974) noted that

> The material endowment of the Yoruba is a fund of invaluable information for the scientist. That the Yoruba are so immeasurable above the apathy peculiar to the denizens of Western Africa in general, so vivacious and alert, so skillful in the management of life that they may very well be called the nation of practical philosophy of dusky African people who are ready with an apt illustration of whatever may be under discussion as the thoughtful peasant of Europe. (p. 322)

The Yoruba are a people with their own philosophy of counseling with the *babalawo* as the medium through which healing and counseling are practiced. *Babalawo*, the traditional healers of Yorubaland, are comprise of diviners (*Ifa* priests) and herbalists (*Onisegun* or *Adahunse*).

Yoruba Traditional Healers

Traditional Yoruba family therapy is as old as the Yoruba of Nigeria. The Yoruba, who love children and women, are keenly interested in maintaining stability in the family, and cherish the foundation that the family gives to the culture (Adekson, 1997). Yoruba traditional healers, diviners, and herbalists, or *Babalawo,* work with families to stabilize family ties and continue the evolution and survival of new families for generations.

Traditional family therapy techniques, as old as traditional healing in Yorubaland and other parts of present-day Nigeria, are as ingrained in the culture as marriage. They were developed during constant interactions with clients over the years and have remained until today. These techniques recreate Yoruba traditions during counseling sessions by emphasizing parental roles vis-à-vis their children's. The healers explain these roles by sharing examples, including some from their own lives. In so doing, the healers enable their clients to understand that their problems are solvable. Healers also encourage parents who come to them for family counseling to act as role models for their children, train them in character development, and live exemplary lives (Adekson, 1997).

Babalawo employ different skills, such as encouragement, empathy, caring, kindness, humility, and esteeming others. During traditional family therapy, a climate of trust is created by the healers in their interactions with clients through relaxation, love, respect, an atmosphere of positive acceptance, receptivity, and unparalleled mercy. During the course of my fieldwork conducted in Nigeria in 1994, healers stated that a serene climate assists families in moving toward healing (Adekson, 1997). There are three kinds of healing: divining, which employs divining beads to inquire from the *Orunmila* a representative of Almighty God (*Olodumare*) about clients' problems; counseling, which involves listening to and helping clients solve their problems; and herbalism, which is healing with herbs and plants (Adekson, 1997). This climate of trust, peace, acceptance, love, and mercy creates a positive restorative effect that commences before the healing process can actually begin (Adekson, 1997). Yoruba families from all walks of life visit the *babalawo* with faith that they will obtain help for their problems. It is further held that the families' faith in traditional healing and counseling helps restore hope on matters relating to getting married, staying married, raising children, solving family problems, having children, and interacting positively with spouses and children.

Yoruba traditional healers cordially interact with and assist families in finding solutions to their problems, while paying special attention to the clients' needs and treating them as unique individuals. The healers study and inquire about the underlying problems prevalent with their clients before assisting the family members who become involved in the counseling and healing process. Hopefully, the clients have full confidence in the healers' abilities to resolve both marital and family problems. Good character (*iwa rere*) is one of the skills healers highlighted as being of utmost importance in working with families. Good character is of utmost importance in any healing relationship. Caring (*sise aajo*), willingness to help others (*riran ni lowo*), empathy (*fifi ara eni si ipo enikeji*), hard work (*sise ise kara*), endurance (*ifarada*), perseverance (*iforiti*), considerateness (*gbigba ti elomiran ro*), and being observant (*nini emi iwoye*) are some fundamental forms of *iwa rere*. Other skills and expertise that are used regularly are: respectfulness, inquisitiveness, giving others preference over oneself, humbleness, kindness, and receptivity to others (Adekson, 1997).

Healers also consult other healers who are experienced in certain areas of care to get to the core of clients' problem. Consultation, especially with the deans of healers and with diviners, enables Yoruba traditional healers to properly counsel older and younger families. The experience that the deans of healers and diviners (*Ifa* priests) have accumulated while working with families over the years qualifies them as consultants. Consultation with trusted colleagues, *Ifa* priests and deans of healers about the families' progress; status; background; and psychological, social, religious, medical, and emotional concerns helps bring out the best in the treatment mode.

Healers assist families by listening, and showing empathy and genuine love. They give advice when necessary, are attentive, and treat all of their clients' secrets with the utmost confidentiality. They accomplish this task by taking care of their clients lovingly and honestly. *Babalawo* follow specific treatment goals in line with the families' problems and encourage clients that everything will be fine. They also show mercy, by listening to their clients, cooperating with families, and admonishing all family members to be active in finding solutions to the issues that they bring for counseling.

Healers often have to help solve family problems by exercising the virtue of mercy, which is a unique part of the *babalawo* culture. Once the families know that the healer shows mercy toward them, they open up, discuss their problems honestly, and listen to the healers' suggestions and advice. Mercy is shown through healers' constant presence with their clients. Healers are there for the clients at all times to answer questions and offer suggestions for improvements in their families. Caring, empathy, compassion, and sympathy with parental compassion are also helpful skills that bring out the best of clients in family therapy.

Yoruba traditional healers have a wide knowledge of human personality because they have worked with different families over the years. This knowledge is readily available when families bring in their problems for therapy. The healers also rely on their knowledge of Yoruba culture to help them interact positively and relate with Yoruba and other Nigerian families that they counsel. Yoruba traditional healers also live in the community with the families who come for counseling. Healers, therefore, are acquainted with the pattern of interaction that prevails in different families within their community. The fact that they are conversant with this pattern helps healers make appropriate suggestions for improvement in family counseling. Knowledge of the families' likes and dislikes also enables healers to get to the root of their problems and counsel appropriately.

CORE CONDITIONS IN INTERVENTION

Yoruba healers take the task of family work and healing very seriously. The task is not for amateurs; it has been taught from one generation of healers to another with precision, detail, and selectivity. The process demands seriousness and complete preparation, with certain conditions having to be achieved both by healers and family. The traditional belief is that if these conditions are not achieved, the healing process cannot be effective.

Physical Presence

Healers' physical presence, which occurs when traditional healers are there to assist the families that come for therapy, helps alleviate problems and enhances treatment. Physical presence adds value and is advantageous to the families' healing and growth as individuals within their family and society. Concern (*aniyan*), love (*ife*), compassion (*ibakedun*), empathy (*fifi ara eni si ipo enikeji*), an exhibition of parental interaction with families, confidence, trustworthiness, and wisdom are forms that physical presence take (Adekson, 1997). The ability to discern, diagnose, and identify problems early in the counseling sessions, offer advice, and display a willingness to offer precautions against future family problems are other skills used by successful traditional healers.

Wisdom

Adekson (1997) discovered during field research that traditional healers pass accumulated wisdom to their clients through songs, proverbs, folklore, and witty sayings, which they apply as they diagnose and treat family problems. Yoruba traditional healers employ direct approaches with families during interactions in line with the dictates of Yoruba culture where honor, prestige, and status are accorded to people who possess wisdom, understanding, and natural and supernatural powers to heal and counsel (Adekson, 1997). This direct approach allows Yoruba traditional healers to guide and introduce information, suggestions, content, and attitudes that govern and influence their clients toward proactive, positive healing and counseling. This directness also requires considerable wisdom according to the healers.

Preventive Measures

Healers also work diligently to teach their clients preventive measures against problems. They do this by asking them questions regarding what problems currently pervade their lives, and by giving them suggestions that help alleviate the problems and avoid similar problems in the future. Healers persevere with clients by leading them toward solutions to their problems through the use of different techniques. Yoruba traditional healers pray for the families that comes to them for therapy. This means that the healers still keep each family that comes to them "in their hearts" even after they have left weekly or monthly counseling sessions. Healers schedule appointments for clients according to the gravity of their problems. Less complicated problems usually take less time and are less intensive.

Humility

Adekson (1997) discovered during her case study that Yoruba traditional healers show humility in their work by practicing patience, kindness, endurance, and perseverance to get to the root of their clients' problems. They use their cordiality as a catalyst to aid families toward healing. *Babalawo* exhibit joy and faith in the fact that clients will get well as they prayerfully assist families to work through their problems with optimism. Yoruba traditional healers' knowledge of various techniques enable them to be successful as they help build clients' trust and confidence. They show genuineness, concern, and compassion for their clients. Their ability to ask probing questions also helps them to easily work through their problems.

Consultancy

Healers stand out as consultants and elders for solutions to personal, community, and city problems. Yoruba traditional healers are keenly sought for their knowledge and wisdom by dignitaries; other traditional healers; and clients within city, state, country, African continent, and different parts of the world. Traditional healers also are sought for their knowledge, wisdom, and understanding of herbs and healing methods by Western trained medical doctors, psychiatrists, professors of pharmacy and other disciplines related to healing and counseling. Lambo (1974) reiterated the importance of Yoruba traditional healers by noting the following:

> . . . In addition to being a medicine man, something of a social worker and probation worker, teacher, priest and Justice of the Peace (JP), Yoruba Traditional Healers tackle the problem, of which his patients' symptoms are only a part, with an across the board approach impossible to the fragmental social, penal, and medical services in the West. (Lambo, 1974, pp. 33–34)

Multifarious Functions

Traditional healers' roles within the Yoruba community have come to depend to a great extent on the expectation of the people regarding the different roles they should perform at different times (Adekson, 1997). The people look up to *babalawo* to be there for them at all times. Families expect healers to assist them in working through different problems, from infertility through having a successful delivery at birth, from enjoying fruitful marital interactions through solving parental problems, and from healing mental health problems through giving them advice on becoming an effective leader in the workplace and community. Clients bring different problems that the healers vigorously seek to resolve. Traditional healers take care of their clients' physical, spiritual, and psychological problems concurrently.

One of the traditional healers interviewed for the 1994 study pointed out that Yoruba traditional healers perform the roles of medical practitioner; psychiatrist; pharmacist; herbal dispenser; consultant; career counselor; orthopedist; pediatrician; obstetrician; anesthetist; mediator; justice of the peace; genetic, group, marital, and family counselor; mental health practitioner; psychotherapist, and interventionist in daily interactions with their clients (Adekson, 1997). The healers' abilities to perform these multifarious functions allows clients to gain holistic health and work through their physical, mental, psychological, and spiritual problems (Adekson, 1997). Healers help those who come to them promptly and effectively so that they do not have to come back again for the same problem, except to show gratitude or bring another relative or friend for therapy or healing. Traditional healers want their clients to be healed and assisted every time they come for help concerning different issues.

Yoruba traditional healers' techniques allow them to combine individual counseling where necessary with group and family counseling where applicable. Culture plays a significant role in healer–client interactions. Families consult healers and feel comfortable with Yoruba traditional healers, who share their worldview and speak the same language as they do. *Babalawo* combine the roles of teacher, seer, diviner, healer, adviser, listener, and parent. The fact that healers understand these roles from a cultural standpoint allows the interaction to yield fruitful results and steers the relationship toward positive results. Effective family counseling occurs because Yoruba traditional healers share the same culture, experience, understanding, worldview, and the same view of problems with their clients. Healers understand the cultural language of interaction. In the same vein, Adegbite (1991) explained that *Babalawo's* language is used with clients to serve "the purposes of persuasion, education, naming, greeting, entertainment, healing, conjuring and recording experiences" (p. 8).

Extended Family

Extended family members play an active role in healing among the Yorubas. Healing and questions relating to health and family problems are very often initiated by concerned relatives, who encourage families to go to traditional healers with their problems. Family members all "stick together" to help their relatives get counseling from healers. Yoruba traditional healers believe that if all members are healthy, then everyone will be happy and comfortable. The Yoruba believe that: *irorun eye ni irorun eku* (The comfort of the bird is also that of the rat). Healing and counseling, that is, helping to solve problems, is regarded as a family affair among the Yoruba. The family emerges as the major catalyst for sound health in Yoruba traditional healing. The Yoruba believe that: *ebi eniyan ni aso won* (Family members are as clothes that must be worn at all times) (Mabogunje, 1962). The belief in the importance of the family not only permeates the culture, standards, and values, but also extends successfully to healing and solving family problems across Yorubaland. The healers utilize community-oriented therapy, which involves families, neighbors, supervisors, distant relatives, and coworkers as a culturally fit method appropriate and suitable for Yoruba clients. The healers solicit the help of families and friends when counseling by asking them questions about the clients.

Cultivating Clients' Confidence

Yoruba traditional healers are relaxed and feel at home with their clients during counseling sessions. Clients develop confidence in the traditional healers' competence, authenticity, and efficacy because the initiative is always there to address the issues that clients require assistance for at any time of the day. Healers are always ready to assist their clients because families come with new problems every time. This readiness gives families confidence that they can obtain help 7 days a week. Traditional healers take time to cater to their clients' problems, demands, and needs. The healers are skillful, efficient, and capable and are always on time and attuned to their clients' problems. Healers' skills and confidence coupled with their ability to help their clients work through their problems promptly enable them to help as many families as possible.

TECHNIQUES IN INTERVENTION

The myriad techniques of sacrifice, dream interpretation, folk tales, proverbs, prayer, herbarium, entreating and invoking the gods and ancestors, and therapeutic dances and songs are part of Yoruba culture. These techniques are widely used and recognized by clients as they come to consult Yoruba traditional healers for their problems. Families understand healers' basic traditional approach to healing, and consult healers with confidence and peace of mind because Yoruba traditional healers assist them with their problems utilizing the same worldview, culture, religion, and traditional base that they have grown up to understand. It is pertinent to note that Yoruba culture plays a predominant role in clients' beliefs; healers' diagnoses; and the techniques of healing and counseling, curing diseases and illnesses, and helping to solve problems (Adekson, 1997).

Diviners' Team Approach

Diviners (*Ifa* priests) sometimes use the team approach that brings about effectiveness, thoroughness, and the ability to get to the root of the problem by inquiring from *Orunmila* through *Ifa* divination into the source of families' problems. The duration of time spent with each family depends on the nature of the problem. Epega and Neimark (1995) maintained that, "once the correct interpretation has been presented to the client, he/she and the *babalawo* can explore specific solutions or alternatives" (p. x). Yoruba traditional healers do not limit their clients to any specific time when they start working with them. Healers do not worry about time as Western trained professionals do, because they have plenty of time to assist their clients: "Our ultimate goal is not how many clients we see per day, but how many families get their problems solved and do not have to come back to us with the same problem(s)" (Adekson, 1997, p. 327). Traditional healers work from dawn to dusk assisting their clients and family members. Their ability to ungrudgingly spend much-needed time with families makes them discharge their duties effectively. The healers discharge their counseling duties with humility, love, endurance, and genuine care.

Divining and Diagnosis

Techniques of divining include counting, throwing, and using the divining chain (*opele, ikin,* or *opon ifa*) to inquire about families' problems from *Orunmila*. Throwing the divining chain (*opele*) on a mat allows healers to probe into families' problems by asking *Orunmila* (the father of all gods) the question for which an answer is sought. Families bring their problems to diviners (*Ifa* priests), who use the divining chain to inquire about these problems from *Orunmila*. The diviner interprets families' problems.

The first two parts of *Ifa* divination are done in a monologue as incantations by the diviners, whereas the last part is done with the family's participation. Diviners throw the divining chain (*opele*) to invoke *Orunmila* about the nature of the family's problems during the first part of the counseling process. Yoruba traditional healers disclose the interpretation revealed by *Orunmila* to the family during the second part.

Yoruba traditional healers use divining to help diagnose problems presented by families. They throw the divining chain after they have asked the head of household who brought his or her family to counseling to whisper secretly into the chain. The head of the household holds the divining chain to his or her lips while secretly whispering what brought them to therapy. The healer collects the chain from the client and throws it on the floor. The healer interprets what the chain signifies to the family by telling them precisely why they have come to counseling and what the head of the household whispered into the divining chain. The family head agrees with the diagnosis as counseling commences with the healer. Counseling is in the form of finding a solution to what brought the family to counseling. They do this by offering suggestions and using different traditional techniques.

Sacrifices

Sacrifice is considered by Yoruba traditional healers to be the core of healing and it enables healers to solve their clients' problems. Families are of the opinion that the ability to follow through with making the sacrifices the healer suggests determines their ability to attain sound health. Animals and objects used as sacrifices and that aid in helping clients solve their problems include, chickens, goats, cows, snails, kola nuts, palm oil, water, and money. Yoruba traditional healers interviewed during field research pointed out that in some cases sacrifices are performed before proceeding to find out the source of families' problems (Adekson, 1997). Sacrifices could be performed in the healer's compound, in families' homes, outside the city limits, near a river or forest, or on a mountain.

The type of sacrifice, where it is to be performed, how it is to be performed, and for and by whom it is performed, depend on the gravity of the problem. Families typically follow healers' instructions promptly because they believe that they are supernatural mediators between them and their ancestors.

Herbal Therapy

Yoruba traditional healers utilize herbs and different plants to cure different ailments. The healers continue to refine experiments, and test and conduct research to find better methods. Healers prescribe herbs to families who come to them for therapy if needed in addition to counseling. The herbalists possess innate and acquired knowledge of appropriate herbs that cure different mental health, physical, and gynecological conditions.

Therapeutic Dances

Therapeutic dances assist families to work through and gain independence from stressors associated with their problems. Music is an important part of daily living among the Yoruba in particular and Africans in general. Music and dancing are used during different occasions such as childbirth, religious observances, marriages, initiations, and funerals. Music adds grace to every merrymaking occasion among the Yoruba, aids families to find solutions to some problems, and is used by clients for relaxation and as a means of working on their problems.

Diviners assist families when they sing a song that depicts a story with a character similar to that of the head of household or the family that has problems. Diviners choose a song to highlight a conflict resolution approach appropriate to the family's problems to enable it to solve its own issues (Adekson, 1997). Yoruba traditional healers also use songs to help families solve their problems by choosing protagonists that are similar to the families in counseling.

Prayer

Prayer is the mainstay of Yoruba traditional healers' profession. Prayer and sacrifice are of equal weight in Yoruba healing; to Yoruba traditional healers, prayer is equivalent to sacrifice.

> Prayer, in the form of entreating God Almighty (*Olodumare*) or invoking the ancestors or the gods, as each client or family understands them; or offering sacrifices to God Almighty, ancestors, the gods, or the elders who are wiser, can give families needed comfort and wisdom to work through their situations. (Adekson, 1997, p. 188)

Prayer helps the healers to get to the root of the family's problems and give them insight into those problems in order to identify the diagnosis through divining. Yoruba traditional healers pray for their clients, prospective clients, and all their family members both before and after each counseling session. Traditional healers use prayers and sacrifices to appease *Olodumare*, the gods and ancestors, as a process of making healing and counseling final for their clients. Prayer to God Almighty completes the healing process for the healers and their clients. Healers believe that God Almighty, the ultimate source of answered prayers and the chief ruler of the Universe, makes positive things happen by answering all prayerful invocations made on the families' behalf. In essence, Prayer to God Almighty completes healing.

Entreating and Invoking the Gods and Ancestors

Traditional healers advise families to entreat and invoke the gods and the ancestors when *Orunmila* entreats them to do so through the *Ifa* oracle. Healers appease God Almighty on behalf of families that come to them for counseling, and healers believe that some clients have problems because they refuse or forget to pay homage to their ancestors or because they disrespect God Almighty (*Olodumare*), *Orunmila* or the gods, supernatural beings, and ancestors who are vital parts of Yoruba culture. Invoking and entreating God Almighty, the gods, and the ancestors, which is done with the aid of the healer, can take the form of sprinkling palm oil; the blood of a chicken, goat, or cow; or going to a burial place to say prayers or make certain requests of ancestors.

Dreams and Dream Interpretation

Some Yoruba traditional healers sharpen their healing knowledge and get instructions about how to solve difficult client problems from dreams. Certain Yoruba traditional healers learn how to divine, heal, and counsel through dreams and meetings with supernatural beings. They ask their clients about their most recent dreams during counseling sessions, and make recommendations that enable their clients to relate their dreams to solutions of the problems they bring to counseling as families and individuals. Dreams assist Yoruba traditional healers to learn more about their clients' problems and gain insight into hidden mysteries that can only be revealed by God Almighty.

Proverbs

Yorubas regard proverbs as intellectual maps that assist the wise to find lost paths in the world. A Yoruba proverb is referred to as *owe*. Proverbs direct language, and if a word is confusing, proverbs are used to make its meaning clearer or to find solutions to it.

The Yoruba believe that the spoken word has hidden symbolic and inexplicable implications, or importations with its utterance producing the desired effect (Adegbite, 1993). Yoruba traditional healers use proverbs to instill wisdom into their clients. Traditional healers inform wives who come to marital counseling that patience, perseverance, and endurance can cook a stone until it becomes soft and tender (*Suuru le se okuta jinna*). This proverb means that perseverance, hard work, and endurance can assist a wife to enjoy a fruitful marital life. Healers use proverbs as successful traditional healing and counseling tools, and to instill wisdom and get their points across to their clients.

Folk Tales and Stories

Folk tales (*aalo*, *itan*) are common ways of transmitting tradition, knowledge, and wisdom in Yorubaland. Most teachers and traditional healers utilize folk tales to instruct their students and clients and to pass traditions on from older to younger generations without writing.

Yoruba traditional healers assist families through delicate and problematic situations by reenacting stories about what they have seen happen, or telling stories from *Ifa* oracle, from their healer fathers or mentors, or using stories to point out the actions of main characters as role models or teachers. Diviners use folk tales and stories from ancient Yoruba literature when revealing secrets to families during counseling. Epega and Neimark (1995) support the preceding point that diviners communicate and interpret the *odus*, the sacred stories of *Ifa*, which have survived through Yoruba literature. These two authors added that, "each *odu* carries with it hundreds of tales that have accumulated in the oral tradition of *Ifa* through thousands of years" (p. xvii). Most of the techniques used by Yoruba traditional healers are attributed to God Almighty (*Olodumare*). The Yoruba believe that God is the giver of all supernatural and natural powers. The healers believe that their techniques, which allow for positive healer–client interactions, are given through dreams by God Almighty. These are inherited characteristics and skills learned from *Orunmila* and their superiors, or as part of Yoruba tradition and culture.

FAMILIES AND HEALING

Families from different socioeconomic backgrounds consult healers concerning their problems. Additional support for families' confidence is provided by the fact that Western-trained professionals in Yorubaland who hold Yoruba traditional healers in high esteem also consult them for assistance in solving their clients' medical and psychological problems. Traditional healing and counseling occupy a larger place within the Yoruba cultural milieu. Families in Yoruba land believe that traditional healers are God Almighty's (*Olodumare's*) messengers and their chief source for acquiring healing and counseling. Clients believe that healers' power to heal is supernaturally endowed, and Yoruba traditional healers refer to this supernatural component as the foundation that gives Yoruba families faith to consult and believe in the efficiency and authenticity of traditional counseling (Adekson, 1997). Healers regard families that consult them as members of their own families as they utilize care, empathy, mercy, and respect with them.

Yoruba traditional healers transmit the social, political, moral, and educational norms of the Yoruba culture to families who come for counseling. Torrey (1986) supports this fact with the following:

> Regardless of what one believes about the desirability of promoting or not promoting the use of indigenous therapists in the third world cultures, the fact remains that such therapists are today the only psychotherapeutic and available source of health care for the majority of the world's population. (p. 185)

Empathy, mercy, respect, friendliness, unconditional love, and the climate of trust are what all healers repeatedly refer to as necessary fundamental attitudes that help in the healer–client relationship. These basic attitudes help Yoruba traditional healers as they use different techniques with the families—specifically, the techniques of divining; diagnosis; sacrificing; herbal therapy, therapeutic dance; prayer; entreating and invoking God, the gods, and ancestors; dreams and dream interpretation; and using proverbs, folktales, and stories.

CONCLUSION

To most outsiders, working with problematic families in the traditional Yoruba way appears to be strange and objectionable. It is hard to understand how such ancient practices are still acceptable in our cyberage. The reality is that this is the only way of helping families in this culture. Most foreign systemic intervention techniques do not work with the Yorubians, whose culture is entrenched in years of traditions and ancient beliefs. The most important element here is that families feel that they have been helped and that whatever problems they brought to the healers have been relieved.

Unfortunately, it is not an easy task to predict the future of the work with Yoruba families because they are a very closed and isolated culture. My qualitative work with them appears to be the latest, and one of the few attempts to understand how they work with families. My hope is that there will be more future attempts to understand other aspects of family work with them.

REFERENCES

Adegbite, W. (1991). Aspects of language use in Yoruba traditional medicine. *African Notes, 15*(1–2), 7–19.

Adegbite, W. (1993). Some features of language use in Yoruba traditional medicine. *African Languages and Culture, 6*(1), 1–10.

Adekson, M. (1997). *The interpersonal techniques used by Yoruba traditional healers of Nigeria: A case study*. Ann Arbor, MI: UMI Dissertation Services.

Africa yearbook and who's who. (1995). London: African Journal Limited.

Epega, A., & Neimark, P. J. (1995). *The sacred Ifa oracle.* San Francisco: Harper.

Lambo, T. A. (1974). Psychotherapy in Africa. *Psychotherapy and Psychosomatics, 24,* 311–326.

Mabogunje, A. L. (1962). *Yoruba towns: Problems of a pre-industrialized urbanization in West Africa.* Ibadan, Nigeria, Ibadan University Press.

Makinde, O. (1974). The indigenous Babalawo model—Implications for counseling in West Africa. *West Africa Journal of Education, 18*(4), 319–327.

Ojo, G. J. (1967). *Yoruba culture.* London: University of Ife and University of London Press.

Torrey, E. F. (1986). *Witch doctors and psychiatrists: The common roots of psychotherapy and its future.* New York: Harper & Row.

The world almanac and book of facts. (1995). Mahwah, NJ: Funk and Wagnalls.

CHAPTER 12

Finding Our Own Voice

The Development of Family Therapy in South Africa

CLARA GERHARDT

South Africans call themselves the *Rainbow Nation*, descriptive of the diversity found among its people. Eleven national languages are instrumental in communicating the hopes and desires of this nation. South Africa also has the distinguished honor of being one of the relatively few nations in history that changed hands of power in a peaceful manner. This momentous achievement is the product of people from many different cultural backgrounds working together for peace and harmony. The first President of the *New South Africa*, as it is often referred to, Nelson Mandela, was awarded the Nobel Prize for Peace, together with the last President of the *old regime*, F. J. de Klerk. Mandela's memoir, *Long Walk to Freedom* (1994), has become a classic and personal documentation of this transitional process, highlighting human dignity and human rights. This cooperation between people from very different backgrounds, in the name of harmony, speaks volumes.

South Africa has also known darker days when it was torn apart by intolerance and injustice, and *Apartheid* is the one word in the South African vocabulary that is loaded with pain and regret. Much like a hateful and violent divorce rips apart a family, this regime ripped apart a nation. With his *Truth and Reconciliation* hearings, Bishop Desmond Tutu (another Nobel Peace Prize winner) has been weaving together the strands of a torn nation into a new united Rainbow Nation, who symbolically have adopted a new flag integrating both the past heritage and the future hopes of all concerned.

In many ways, this reunification of the people of South Africa has been both a macro- and micro-systemic effort, a giant process helped along by countless individuals, which has touched the lives of all involved. As

Ingoldsby and Smith (1995) point out, relationships can become more satisfying as exchanges become mutually rewarding and responsive. Against this dramatic political and social backdrop of change, family therapy was developing in South Africa, with its tender and informal beginnings in the late 1960s and early 1970s. The interest in family therapy grew as social workers, especially, became concerned with the implications of social forces within the country, and they conducted interviews in home settings. Some of the earliest references to work in a family context was in the work of Geismar (1961, cited by Mason & Shuda, 1999), who focused on a family project in an impoverished area near Durban, a coastal town in Kwa-Zulu. As therapists who worked with family systems, these early pioneers in the field of family therapy revealed a reconciliatory force that had to be strong to go against the social norms of the day. Family therapists were metaphorically color blind, and professional groups, even the small informal ones of the early years, were multicultural, and diversity was cherished and respected.

THE UNIQUENESS AND UNIVERSALITY OF CULTURE

South Africa is in the somewhat unique position of being truly multicultural and multilingual, with a heritage of African people belonging to numerous tribes, a white population group that is subdivided into predominantly English and Afrikaans backgrounds, Malay, Asian Indian, and a number of smaller minorities who immigrated to South Africa from the date of its official colonization by the Dutch in 1652. If culture is regarded as a type of "mental blueprint or programming" (Matsumoto, 1996, p. 307) with which we are imprinted and that shapes our lives, then it follows that a multicultural awareness is crucial in helping us separate "*emics*, or culture-specific concepts, from *etics*, or universal or culture-general concepts" (Gardiner, Mutter, & Kosmitzki, 1998, p. 7). We need to find a balance between the uniqueness and universality of behaviors and to find mutual respect and understanding in order for all the subgroups who make up the whole to live optimally and harmoniously. Gardiner et al. (1998) describe a cyclical model of cultural identity whereby individuals can move from *cultural dependence*, where an understanding and appreciation for one's own culture have been formed as part of their unique developmental niche, to *cultural independence*, where they step outside the ecological setting of their culture to engage in new cross-cultural experiences, to *multicultural interdependence*, where they share with their native culture new ways and experiences of viewing the world, and by doing so influencing the ecological settings that make up the native culture. In other words, we cherish our own cultural identity as it is shaped by unique origins, but we respect and learn from other cultures and can incorporate what we learn by moving back and forward between being culturally dependent and culturally independent.

When groups segregate themselves from other socioracial groups (as has been the case in the Apartheid system) it may allow the dominant group to "hold onto and enhance elements of the cultures of their forbearers" (Helms & Cook, 1999, p. 101). However, it also hampers the valuable process of multicultural interdependence described by Gardiner et al. (1998). As Helms and Cook (1999, p. 238) state: "In the social microcosm of the real world, people must coexist in the world with other people who may have differing belief systems regarding race. Recognition of this reality and development of skills to cope with it are aspects of social learning that can take place in group interactions." Therapists "who are sensitive to cultural dynamics will be able to respond better to clients in counseling" (Axelson, 1999, p. 4). As family therapists we could make a valuable contribution in facilitating this learning process.

ROOTS: THE EARLY DEVELOPMENT OF FAMILY THERAPY IN SOUTH AFRICA

During the two decades (1960s and 1970s) prior to the formal founding of a Family Therapy Association in South Africa, several important international teachers had come to South Africa, usually by invitation of universities or smaller study groups. Between 1969 and 1972 Ginnot and Hirschowitz visited. Haim Ginott had written bestsellers on childrearing techniques and was eminent as the author of *Between Parent and Child* and later *Between Parent and Teenager*. He was attached to the New York and Adelphi Universities and together with Hirschowitz, a psychiatrist from Harvard University, they lectured at two early conferences at Tara Hospital, Johannesburg. These conferences were titled *Psychopathology and the Mental Health of the Family,* indicating that the formal family therapy movement had not quite taken off in South Africa.

Some other early visitors were Donald Bloch and Jessie Turberg from the Ackerman Institute in New York, who visited in 1974, and the late Avner Barcai of the Philadelphia Child Guidance Clinic and Haifa University, who conducted training courses for graduate students in psychiatry at the University of Cape Town. I attended Turberg's training sessions in Johannesburg, and as the audience, we were starved for what she had to offer; it was fresh and novel in a field where little formal training was locally available. She introduced us to genograms and family sculpting and we loved what we heard. I remember the sense of connectedness she created among us; slowly we were aligning ourselves with a therapeutic approach that had its own identity, different from the models we had been exposed to in our earlier university training.

It needs to be pointed out also that only a few years previously, legislation had been passed giving psychology its own professional identity, and making it subject to formal licensure procedures supervised by the South African Medical and Dental Council. Psychologists still did not have their own professional licensing body and they were adopted by a subsection of the medical and dental regulatory body, with clinical and counseling psychology as two of five possible subsections; the others being industrial, educational, and research or experimental psychology. Family therapy, on the other hand, promised to be interdisciplinary, embracing several helping professions, just as it currently does in the United States.

Another important international name from these early days was that of Florence Kaslow. Kaslow guided us to international links, encouraging formal affiliation as members of the International Family Therapy Association. Her work was invaluable and gave South Africans a sense of belonging at a time when they were excluded from many groups as a result of international pressures to exert economic and academic sanctions in an effort to speed up the transition process. She published an article entitled, *A South African Odyssey: Family Style* (Kaslow, 1981), reflecting some of the issues of the day. This year, 1981, became the key date for future developments. In 1981 family therapists, under the leadership of Jean Mason, founded the South African Institute of Marital and Family Therapy (SAIMFT) and the organization became a mouthpiece for interdisciplinary professionals within the field and an organizing body that invited foreign teachers, and organized national and international conferences (Mason & Shuda, 1999). Later the word *Institute* was replaced with *Association*, to become the South African Association of Marital and Family Therapy (SAAMFT) as we now know it.

THE INTERNATIONAL DIALOGUE

As family therapists know, describing the development of family therapy in South Africa in a linear fashion is an oversimplification. A number of factors interacted simultaneously, preparing the soil for the formal paradigm shift of the 1980s to occur. "An extended family formed around the nucleus of emerging family therapists" (Mason & Shuda, 1999, p. 157). And so it happened that South Africans went abroad and studied with therapists from the United States, Italy, and Great Britain, to name some of the leading destinations. They attended conferences internationally and were strengthened in their beliefs. Several therapists who had studied independently overseas were virtually matched by Salvador Minuchin and the late Anver Barcai. After one such training session at the Philadelphia Family Therapy Center, Jean Mason, a social work educator, and Norma Altman, a clinical psychologist, returned to South Africa "imbued with a mission to forge links with emergent family therapists in their home country" (Mason & Shuda, 1999, p. 157). The therapists they linked up with were Judith Landau, a psychiatrist, and Carol Phillips, a clinical social worker. Of that early quartet, Altman, Mason, Landau, and Phillips each went on to donate a substantial piece of herself to the field, and family therapy was the *leitmotiv* of their lives. Landau subsequently immigrated to the United States where she has done valuable work.

Norma Altman (1927 to 1996) became the nucleus of a family therapy group based in Johannesburg of which I was a member. She traveled to the United States regularly and brought back fresh ideas and renewed enthusiasm. She was also national president of the association. Her manner of organizing the Johannesburg subgroup was gentle and democratic. We met on a monthly basis in an empty classroom of the Witwatersrand University, even in the most dismal weather. These small meetings gave us a connectedness that inspired us in our work. Not only did we feel connected with each other, but also with the wider international community of family therapists. Norma had a wealth of knowledge. She was a respected therapist who never flaunted her expertise. In a way she was the mother figure we needed, a constant point of reference, who helped us fledgling therapists to find our own wings and applauded us when we found we could fly.

A sprinkling of therapists emigrated from South Africa in the turbulent years between the mid-1980s and mid-1990s, but they maintained their links with South Africa and a valuable communication network ensued. South African trained therapists can be found in a number of English-speaking countries, including Australia, New Zealand, Great Britain, Canada, and the United States. The late Julian Rubenstein went to Australia and returned to South Africa, where he documented many of the activities of the Family Therapy Association, including the first two books covering early conference procedures. Both Pieter le Roux and Clara Gerhardt took up positions with universities in the United States, but returned regularly to South Africa, maintaining their links with their former colleagues. Le Roux was the keynote speaker at the International Conference on Family Therapy in 1990, held at Broederstroom near Johannesburg, where the audience was touched by his message concerning "realness" or authenticity, a metaphor that was drawn from the classic children's book *The Velveteen Rabbit* (Williams, 1983) and that was so apt for a country immersed in the throes of transition (Le Roux, 1992).

Therapists in teaching positions were also influential in training the next generation of therapists. Rick Snyders of the University of South Africa

(UNISA) was exposed to the work of Andolfi in Italy, and this university became the main training institute according to a family systems model. Other therapists involved with the training of the next generation were Pieter Le Roux, who had been trained at the Ackerman Institute in New York; Ricky Mauer, who occupied leadership positions in the corporate world and psychology; Dave Beyers, who became chair of psychology at two universities sequentially; Suzanne Shuda, who was national president several times; and Clara Gerhardt, whose expertise was eating disorders in a systemic context (Gerhardt, 1992), to mention only a few in a long list. Gerhardt also attended workshops by Mara Selvini-Palazzoli in Italy, whose work with anorexia nervosa was renowned. At the Natal Technikon, in Kwa-Zulu, Frida Rundell did powerful work with students in a residential childcare program, work that had a unique cross-cultural flavor that was badly needed (Rundell, 1996). She also became a leading figure in the local branch of the South African Marriage and Family Therapy Association. Jeff Cumes from the University of Witwatersrand, Chris Venter from Potchefstroom University, Hester van Rooyen, later of Stellenbosch University, Jackie Meyerovitz, and many others all added their expertise. The movement gained in momentum, had numerous spokespersons, and made unique contributions.

LEARNING TO SING IN HARMONY

The first three conferences of the South African Association for Marriage and Family Therapists invited impressive lists of foreign therapists. The first International conference, held in Durban in 1981, opened with the keynote address of Donald Bloch. Maurizio Andolfi brought his Italian charisma. I clearly remember attending Carl Whitaker's session, where Carl tied a handkerchief and put it on his head during the session, baffling clients and audience alike with his paradoxical style. Nevertheless, his own family rootedness, as well as his wisdom and caring shone through clearly in the vignettes concerning his own family interactions, such as conversations with grandchildren. This somewhat unconventional session lives on videotape and by now has taken on almost mythic qualities when it is used with fledgling therapists. Florence Kaslow showed us with her strong personal example that cross-cultural blocks need not exist. Duke Stanton highlighted new meanings in symptomatic behavior, drawing from his work in the field of addictions. Many of these presentations were recorded on video and have become unique training tools, and as a therapist who was present at that momentous conference, I recall the event with gratitude and humility. To have been an observer of family therapy sessions with the legendary Carl Whitaker was a privilege, the magnitude of which dawned on me many years later when I read his obituary in the *Family Therapy Networker*. He had brought something truly his own to the therapy session and we were there as witnesses, without knowing that it was to become a moment of historical significance in the development of family therapy in South Africa.

The Second International Conference on Family Therapy (1983), held in Sun City, Bophutswana, again brought a wave of international expertise in the form of Maurizio Andolfi, Mony Elkaim, Edgar Auerswald, Carlos Sluzki, Duke Stanton, and Judith Landau. Auerswald emphasized his ecological approach, very appropriate within this time context. The setting of the conference was symbolic as well. Bophutswana was an island of a country within South Africa, with its own ruler and rules. The dreaded word *Apartheid* was not part of their vocabulary and it was reaffirming to be within another ecosystem and know that it functioned. This conference allowed momentum to gather as South African therapists became more aware of their unique ecosystem, which represented cultural diversity, a rich and mixed heritage of people from many backgrounds, creeds, and races. On a minor but nevertheless significant note: The conference buffet had a multicultural theme and food from different cultures was served. All these minor aspects amplified each other, and gave a sense of empowerment, encouraging therapists to find their unique African voices.

By the time the third conference was held in 1985 in Johannesburg, the organizers felt confident that another approach could be followed. Instead of inviting representatives from various approaches within the field, they focused on the Milan school and welcomed three Milan systemic therapists—Luigi Boscolo, David Campbell, and Rosalind Draper. Even so, we were feeling the pressures of the academic boycott. The invited keynote speakers who had accepted invitations, Jay Haley and Cloe Medanes, canceled in February before the conference, stating that the antiapartheid movement and sanctions made it impossible for them to fulfill their engagement (Altman, 1991, p. 4). With such pressures, it was important that we could empower ourselves with the uniqueness of the African context and find new ways of moving forward.

When the fourth conference was held in Cape Town (1988) a distinct shift was occurring in the family therapy movement in South Africa. While South Africa was facing major social and political upheavals, therapists in Southern Africa had to find meaning and strength within these transitions. The invited speakers—Margaret Robinson from Great Britain and Val Velkes from Israel—shared the vision and again subtly amplified our voice, which was getting stronger. We were beginning to grasp the systemic principles of greater systems, as we experienced them in our own environment: Namely, in order for reorganization to occur we had to go through a period of seemingly chaotic transition, hopefully to find a new balance or homeostasis at the end of the tunnel. This period would prove to be stressful and taxing to emotional resources. Many social issues were questioned and needed to be reassessed. One of these was education. It became imperative that therapists from all races, backgrounds and creeds be trained to find their place within the multicultural nation. We needed to address uniquely African belief systems and incorporate them into a therapeutic context (Bakker & Snyders, 1999). A number of students with truly multicultural backgrounds were graduating and taking up leadership positions to train the next generation of therapists who could speak in the metaphorical mother tongues within a nation that has 11 official languages. As far as the training of students in a multicultural context was concerned, it was important to think multidimensionally without being caught up in restrictive and reductionistic ways of perceiving human relationships (Marchetti-Mercer, Beyers, & Daws, 1999).

Rubenstein (1988), who had a gift with words, who chronicled our progress and was the driving force behind many of the publications of the Family Therapy Association, summed it up this way:

> In retrospect, 1988 may well be considered the year of coming of age of family therapy in South Africa. The 4th National conference in Cape Town was the first that utilized primarily South African participants sharing their work and ideas—without a major dependence on overseas family therapists telling us what to do and how to do it. We have said, it seems, that it is time to look at ourselves, to ask who we are, what we want and need and what it is we have to offer. What in fact is the role of family therapy in general and the South African Institute for Marital and Family Therapy in particular, in the climate currently prevailing in this country.

THE 1990S: FROM DIVERSITY TO HEALING

At the end of the 1980s we were very concerned, but at the beginning of the 1990s, the instability of the society escalated even further. The 1990 fifth conference in Broederstroom (near Johannesburg) took place against a backdrop of boycotts, making themselves felt in economic, sport, cultural, and academic domains. At some of the international meetings—including the previous Olympic Games of 1988—we were no longer welcome. The door had been slammed shut in our faces, and with a reason—the international community was becoming impatient. To admit that one was South African was to admit that one was part of a system that represented injustice; a system that had allowed inadequate and unequal healthcare, housing, and educational facilities; just the tip of the iceberg of the many problems the country faced. "The fabric of South African society had been torn apart and lay in shreds . . ." (Shuda, 1992, p. vii).

In a move to put our money where our mouth was, the organizers of this conference, under the leadership of Suzanne Shuda, distributed a number of scholarships to health care–related professionals to open our doors in a truly multicultural manner. This approach had been started on a small scale at previous conferences, but now it was expanded drastically. It became a tradition and in subsequent conferences many invited attendees were the guests of the organizing committee and were sponsored by grants generated by fully paying members and other supportive organizations. If we wanted to be an association for marriage and family therapy, we had to ensure that those helping professionals in the community, who dealt with these issues on a daily basis, would be able to be a part of the gathering and that we could grow together.

By the time the sixth meeting was held in the Valley of the Thousand Hills, near Durban Kwa-Zulu, the sense of collegiality was expanding into new avenues again. Colleagues from neighboring countries Namibia and Zimbabwe attended; the community (through a local high school) and the Vuleka trust were involved. Tarboton (cited in Mason & Shuda, 1999, p. 165) wrote about this event:

> . . . Bridges were built, creating a different ethos to the "problem saturated" history . . . there was talk of a spirit of hope, the healing and affirming nature of the experience, the openness and sharing, the sense of inclusiveness and togetherness. All these qualities which, together with others, represent the essence of family, contributed to a feeling of unity and a sense of growth along the progress path.

The seventh conference focused on narrative therapy, with Michael White from Australia as the keynote speaker. It was held in Helderberg, Gauteng. It was the first conference that was held after President Mandela's inauguration and renewed optimism and a sense of hope had resurfaced in the new South Africa. As Mason and Shuda (1999, p. 165) summed up the events at the conferences:

> These were not dry events where papers were read, but they were special rituals for a group of people who became more and more like family members and an external kinship network themselves.

In April 2000, the eighth conference was held in Cape Town, organized by the current SAAMFT president, Suzanne Shuda and her team. Invited guests were Kathy Weingarten, Peggy Papp, and Marianne Walters. In some ways the choice of these speakers completed a cycle. The late Norma Altman, the doyenne of family therapy in the 1970s and 1980s, had had strong links with the Philadelphia Child Guidance Clinic, and Walters is the founder and director of this unit. Papp, of the Ackermann Institute of Family Therapy, had worked with yet another of the South African pioneers, Pieter Le Roux. Weingarten is the cofounder of the narrative therapies program, an approach that lent itself perfectly to our multicultural setting. I had the privilege of attending, and realized that I had attended all the conferences except for one. I had witnessed the birth, early childhood, and adolescence against a backdrop of turbulent times, and finally the debutante-like coming of age of the South African Association of Marital and Family Therapy. It gave me a deep sense of homecoming. Having left South Africa in the early 1990s, I reconnected with colleagues who had walked the family therapy path with me over the past 25 years. It was a silver anniversary of sorts. We looked deep into each others' eyes, could not see the difference in time, and felt reconnected at the same point we had last taken off; just as children do when they return to the fold. What impressed me profoundly was that South Africans had found their own voices, voices appropriate for the Southern African context. Frida Rundell presented a workshop, *Community in Caring,* in which her students from Kwa-Zulu each added a voice to an a cappella choir, singing spontaneously and harmonizing in a way that brought tears to our eyes. Each one of these young therapists found a metaphor that came from her own background and that she could apply to her own people and be understood (Kelly, 1986). I looked at the group and thought that we could only have dreamed about this harmony and cooperation when the first conference was held in 1981 in Durban. Here were young people of many religious backgrounds: Islamic, Buddhist, Judeo-Christian, and traditional African. Their first language frequently was not English: They spoke Xhosa, Sotho, Zulu, Afrikaans, Gudjerati, and Hindi. Many of these young therapists shared their own stories of lost childhoods while the country was burning. And yet they found hope, they moved forward to reach out and be part of a healing system. They held hands as their communal singing grew louder and we all joined in what sounded like a hymn. Each one of us knew in our hearts that in this diversity lay strength, and hope and that this was the way of the future.

> If you heal the family, you will heal the nation.
> *Virginia Satir*

ACKNOWLEDGMENTS

The author dedicates this chapter to all the pioneers of marriage and family therapy in South Africa, not mentioned by name but whose work set up the loom to produce the woven product that family therapy is today. I also gratefully acknowledge the work of Jean Mason, the founder and former president of the SAAMFT and the late Julian Rubenstein, psychiatrist, whose various articles on the history of family therapy in South Africa represent the bulk of formally published work documenting the beginnings of the movement. The current chapter is largely based on information from these sources, the published work of Shuda, and the personal recollections of the author. I am thankful for the constructive comments by South African pioneer and marriage and family therapist, Pieter le Roux, of the Department of Psychiatry, Rochester University, Rochester, New York.

REFERENCES

Altman, N. (1991). Looking back. *SAIMFT Newsletter*. September, pp. 3–4.

Axelson, J. A. (1999). *Counseling and development in a multicultural society* (3rd ed.). Pacific Grove, CA: Brooks/Cole.

Bakker, T. M., & Snyders, F. J. A. (1999). The (hi)stories we live by: Power/knowledge and family therapy in Africa. *Contemporary Family Therapy, 21*(2), 133–154.

Gardiner, H. W., Mutter, J. D., & Kosmitzki, C. (1998). *Lives across cultures: Cross-cultural human development*. Boston: Allyn & Bacon.

Gerhardt, C. (1992). Marriage and weight: Eating disorders and intimate relationships. In J. Mason, J. Rubenstein, & S. Shuda (Eds.), *From diversity to healing*. Durban: South African Institute of Marital and Family Therapy.

Helms, J. E., & Cook, D. A. (1999). *Using race and culture in counseling and psychotherapy.* Boston: Allyn and Bacon.

Ingoldsby, B. B., & Smith, S. (1995). *Families in multicultural perspective*. New York: Guilford Press.

Kaslow, F. W. (1981). A South African odyssey: Family style. *Journal of Marital and Family Therapy, 7*, 89–92.

Kelly, J. G. (1986). Context and process: An ecological view of the independence of practice and research. *American Journal of Community Psychology, 14*(6), 581–594.

Le Roux, P. (1992). Diversity and dialogue. In J. Mason, J. Rubenstein, & S. Shuda (Eds.), *From diversity to healing*. Durban: South African Institute of Marital and Family Therapy.

Mandela, N. (1994). *Long walk to freedom*. Boston: Little & Brown.

Marchetti-Mercer, M., Beyers, D., & Daws, L. (1999). Training family therapists in a multicultural setting. *Contemporary Family Therapy, 21*(2), 187–201.

Mason, J., & Shuda, S. (1999). The history of family therapy in South Africa. *Contemporary Family Therapy, 21*(2), 155–172.

Matsumoto, D. (1996). *Culture and psychology*. Pacific Grove, CA: Brooks/Cole.

Rubenstein, J. (1988). Introduction: Family therapy in South Africa today. In J. Mason, J. Rubenstein, & S. Shuda (Eds.), *Family therapy in South Africa today.* Durban: South African Institute of Marital and Family Therapy.

Rundell, F. (1996). The dream catcher! *Family Therapy Review: A publication of the South African Association of Marital and Family Therapy.* December: 14.

Shuda, S. (1992). Introduction: From diversity to healing. In J. Mason, J. Rubenstein, & S. Shuda (Eds.), *From diversity to healing*. Durban: South African Institute of Marital and Family Therapy.

South African Association of Marital and Family Therapy. (1982–2000). Published newsletters for members and unpublished minutes of meetings. From the private collection in the archives of the South African Association of Marital and Family Therapy. Cape Town.

Williams, M. (1983). *The velveteen rabbit*. New York: Little Simon.

PART IV

Family Therapy in Other Countries

CHAPTER 13

Family Therapy in a Multicultural Society

The Case of Israel

YOAV LAVEE

In his introduction to a special issue of *Contemporary Family Therapy* on the state of family therapy in Israel, the editor, William C. Nichols wrote:

> Israel represents one of the more interesting places in the world in which to examine the development and current status of family therapy theory, practice, and research. The emergence of Israel as a new state occurred only a few years before the advent of family therapy in the United States of America as a revolutionary approach to dealing with human problems. Today, Israel provides a setting in which not only the "hot issues" of culture and ethnicity are part of the everyday scene, but also one in which immigration and continuing rapid change are abundantly evident. (Nichols, 1995, p. 351)

Indeed, one cannot fully grasp the development of family therapy in this country without being aware of its unique characteristics. Therefore, this chapter begins with a brief overview of Israeli society. The rest of the chapter provides a description of the development and current status of family therapy in Israel and a discussion of some specific issues for family therapists in this country.

THE CONTEXT: ISRAEL AND THE ISRAELI SOCIETY

Israel is a small country in the Middle East (slightly smaller than New Jersey), flanked by the Mediterranean Sea on the west, Jordan and Syria on the east, Lebanon on the north, and Egypt on the south. The population numbers approximately 6 million, of whom about 80% are Jewish and the rest are non-Jewish, primarily Arabs (Central Bureau of Statistics, 2000). In addition to its mix of Jewish and Arab populations, Israel is home to immigrants coming from more than 70 countries around the world and speaking many different languages. It is a land of contrasting cultures, lifestyles, and family patterns: traditional family patterns alongside modern lifestyles, the influence of Western culture together with Middle-Eastern heritage, values and practices ranging from secular to ultraorthodox religions among both Jews and Arabs.

As a young and dynamic country, Israel has always been characterized by a rapid rate of increase in population, with the demographic composition of the Jewish population constantly changing as a consequence of massive immigration waves. In the last 50 years there has been a sixfold increase in the population. In 1948, when the State of Israel was established, the population amounted to 873,000. Two large influxes occurred shortly thereafter: Holocaust survivors from Europe and Jews from Islamic countries (mainly North Africa, Iraq, Syria, and Yemen). The 1950s saw a relatively large wave of immigrants arrive from Europe and North Africa, whereas the 1960s were characterized by immigration from the affluent West (the United States, Canada, and the United Kingdom), and the 1970s and 1980s by immigration from the USSR. In the 1990s there was massive immigration (about 700,000) from the former Soviet Union. Jews from Ethiopia (about 56,000) immigrated in two waves: first in the mid-1980s and again in the early 1990s (Central Bureau of Statistics, 2000).

For both Jews and Arabs, different ethnic and religious groups coexist, with immigrants from various countries of origin living alongside veteran Israelis. The Jewish majority today is composed of two main ethnic clusters: "Orientals," or Sephardim (meaning Spanish), who themselves or their ancestors originated from the Near East, North Africa, Yemen, Ethiopia, the Balkans, Iran, Iraq, India, and the Muslim republics of the former Soviet Union; and Ashkenazim, whose origin is in American or European continents. At present, 33.5% of the Jewish population is Asian-African–born or children of Asian-African origin; 40% are European-American–born or children of European-American origin; and 26.5% were born in Israel to Israeli–born parents. In addition, the Arab population is composed of several religious groups—Moslems (75%), Christians (16%), and Druze and others (9%) (Central Bureau of Statistics, 2000).

The diversity and pluralistic nature of the population make for a wide variety of family patterns and lifestyles, including different types of couple formation and marital dynamics, gender relations within families, intergenerational relationships, and ways of coping with internal and external sources of stress (Lavee & Katz, in press). Another important aspect of Israeli life is its continuous state of conflict with the neighboring Palestinian people and Arab countries. Wars, terrorist acts, and security threats are at the core of Israel's existential reality. In its 50 years of existence, Israel has fought seven wars and suffered a ceaseless chain of hostilities, including repeated shelling on border settlements and random terrorist activities inside the country, such as suicide and car bombings. The armed conflict between Jews and Arabs in Palestine has resulted in thousands of military and civilian casualties. The percentage of Israeli families who have suffered injury or loss themselves, or who have close relatives or personal friends who have experienced this suffering approaches 100% (Milgram, 1993). Besides the loss of life and serious injury caused by terrorist attacks, they also disrupt the routine life of families, put limitations on leisure activities, and increase the anxiety level of children and adults alike. Yet, at the same time, most Israelis live their lives normally, going about their daily business. Israelis enjoy all of the institutions that characterize modern democratic states: a well-developed health care and social welfare system, a vibrant art and literary community, and an advanced educational system. Within this context of Israeli society, we now move on to describe the development and place of family therapy in Israel.

THE HISTORY OF FAMILY THERAPY IN ISRAEL

The development of the field of family therapy in Israel was strongly influenced by the development and growth of family therapy in North America, which coincided with the need of Israeli professionals for more effective intervention modalities with multiproblem families. However, as in other revolutions, the "family therapy revolution" in Israel cannot be separated from its leaders—psychiatrists, psychologists, and social workers—who took a lead in introducing family therapy, establishing family therapy clinics, and educating generations of new family professionals.

The beginning of family therapy in Israel can be traced to the early 1960s, when Mordechai Kaffman, a child psychiatrist, introduced systemic assessment and family intervention in treating a variety of emotional and behavioral problems. Kaffman, who was trained in family therapy with Nathan Ackerman in New York, began practicing and teaching family therapy at the Kibbutz Child and Family Clinic (KCFC), which he headed, and at the mental health department of Kupat Holim (a major HMO) in Haifa. In 1963, Kaffman published the first account of the short-term family intervention that he developed in these two centers (Kaffman, 1963). The model consisted of an intake process, including an interview with the entire family in order to assess relationship patterns, followed by 10 sessions focusing on family dynamics related to the child's symptoms, and a closing assessment. The introduction of this mode of intervention initially faced many difficulties and objections from the psychiatric establishment (Kaffman, 1985). However, the rate of success of this model has influenced many professionals to adopt systemic therapy, first at the KCFC centers (which by the mid-1970s consisted of two major clinics and a number of smaller ones throughout the country) and later in other institutions. The pioneering work of Kaffman and his colleagues was described in a number of publications in international family therapy journals (Kaffman, 1965, 1972). Kaffman was later joined by Avner Barcai, who was trained with Salvador Minuchin at the Philadelphia Child Guidance Clinic. Barcai joined the Kibbutz Child and Family Clinic and began teaching family therapy by introducing the one-way mirror, in which he first served as a model therapist and later as a teacher of live supervision. Psychologists and social workers at the KCFC, trained by Kaffman and Barcai, were the first generation of family therapists who later continued to practice, teach, and develop MFT into a well-respected mode of treatment in this country.

A second major force in the development of family therapy in Israel consisted of social workers in social welfare agencies. In the late 1960s, social workers were disillusioned by the child-centered ideology and began adopting the idea that "children live in families" (Wertheimer & Wertheimer, 1988). Social workers also needed new solutions for families in distress other than taking children out of their families and placing them in institutions. Thus began the trend of dynamically oriented family intervention, catalyzed by Wertheimer, a social worker who was trained with Nathan Epstein in Canada. In the early 1970s, Wertheimer developed a family therapy program at the Institute for the Training of Social Workers. The program included courses of family dynamics, sociology of the family, psychopathology in the family context, and treatment of multiproblem families. It also included field experience in family therapy and supervision. In the first 10 classes, more than 200 social workers were trained, which helped spread the approach in the social welfare system.

The application of family therapy by the young graduates of the Institute was not without its difficulties, however. Not only was the new way of treating families perceived as a threat to the established system, but heavy case loads and lack of adequate physical conditions presented serious obstacles to the conduct of long-term family therapy (Slonim-Nevo & Wagner, 1991; Wertheimer, 1979). Nevertheless, the steadfast enthusiasm and interest in developing family therapy in social welfare agencies have proven worthwhile. Today, more than 70 public family therapy clinics are spread throughout the country.

The next phase in the development of family therapy training was the establishment of academic family therapy programs within major universities. The first program was established at Tel Aviv University in 1984 by Israel Charny as an extension of the Institute for the Training of Social Workers program. This program was developed as postgraduate family therapy training. It was interdisciplinary in content as well as in its faculty and student makeup. In 1987, the program led to the development of a family therapy specialization within the masters program in social work at Tel Aviv University. A year later, a masters program in family studies and family therapy was established in the School of Social Work at the University of Haifa, and in 1993 a program was opened in integrative marital and family therapy and individual psychotherapy at the Hebrew University of Jerusalem (Charny & Friedlander, 1996).

THE ISRAELI ASSOCIATION FOR MARITAL AND FAMILY THERAPY

The Israeli Association for Marital and Family Therapy and Family Life Education (IAMFT) was established in 1977. It is an interdisciplinary association, composed of psychologists, social workers, family physicians, psychiatrists, lawyers, educational counselors, and other helping professionals who conduct marital and family therapy, divorce mediation, systemic consultation, and family life education. The IAMFT maintains professional contacts with other marriage and family therapy associations worldwide, is a member of the European Family Therapy Association (EFTA), and was among the founding group of the International Family Therapy Association (IFTA).

The IAMFT conducts a range of professional activities in order to continue the development of family therapy in Israel. These include an annual conference, training workshops, and miniconferences with Israeli and international family professionals, a bimonthly newsletter, *Inyan Mispachti* (Family Matters), and a journal, *Ba'Mishpacha* (Inside the Family). In addition, professional meetings are held by three regional branches in Jerusalem, Haifa, and Rehovot. The Association has also hosted six international family therapy conferences since 1977, gathering thousands of family professionals from around the globe.

Five ongoing committees are in operation to promote family therapy in Israel, to enrich family therapists and maintain professional standards. These include the Professional Training Committee, Public Relations Committee, Accreditation Council, Ethics Committee, and Audit Committee. A divorce mediation council is also affiliated with the IAMFT, conducting miniconferences and workshops for family professionals and lawyers who engage in divorce mediation.

The IAMFT is governed by a board, composed of the association's president, secretary-general, executive director, treasurer, legal advisor, committee chairpersons, branch chairpersons, a representative of the divorce mediation council, and the editors of the newsletter and journal. The board meets regularly (usually every 6 weeks) in order to discuss professional and executive matters. With the exception of the executive director, all members of the board, as well as all committee members, are volunteers. The IAMFT assembly, in which all members have voting power, meets once a year to approve the financial report, make changes in the Association's bylaws, and discuss plans for the development of the organization.

The IAMFT certifies family therapists and approved family therapy supervisors through the Accreditation Committee. Those eligible to become Certified Marriage and Family Therapists include helping professionals (e.g., psychologists, social workers, and school counselors) who hold a master's or doctoral degree; graduates of MFT graduate programs abroad; and physicians with an adequate specialty (e.g., psychiatrists and family practitioners). In addition to their respective professional training, candidates for Certified Marriage and Family Therapists should have a graduate or post-graduate training in marital and family therapy. Specific requirements for training include courses in theoretical models of marriage and the family; transitions and crises across the family life cycle; individual dysfunction from a systemic perspective (e.g., sexual dysfunction, eating disorders, learning disabilities, family violence); family therapy intervention methods, skills, and techniques; theory and practice of marital therapy; and ethical issues in marriage and family therapy. In addition to these courses, candidates are required to have at least 750 hours of direct client contact in family and marital therapy conducted over a 3-year period, and to have received at least 250 hours of supervision from two or more approved supervisors. In order to be eligible for an Approved Supervisor status, family therapists must have at least 3 years of experience after receiving Certified MFT status. Requirements for this certification include advanced courses in family therapy and family therapy supervision, 200 hours of supervising two supervisees, and at least 75 hours of supervision from two or more Approved Supervisors.

FAMILY THERAPY TRAINING

Today, family therapy training is provided by academic institutions, public clinics, and private clinical institutes. Within the Israeli academic infrastructure, there are no academic departments specializing in marital and family therapy. Instead, family therapists are trained within master's programs in schools of social work (at the universities of Tel Aviv and Haifa) or in a program affiliated with the department of psychology (at the Hebrew University of Jerusalem).

The programs at the University of Haifa and Tel Aviv University have both a general family studies component (family theory, research, and methodology; family policy; and courses on a variety of family issues, such as violence, parenting, aging, and others) and a heavy emphasis on family therapy. Courses in the latter area cover various marital and family therapy approaches, the therapist's own family of origin, assessment and diagnosis, as well as a structured program of practicum and supervision. These programs make use of public family therapy clinics as field sites for gaining experience in family therapy, and all students are supervised by approved supervisors, both at the university (as part of their course of study) and in the field site. The Program for Advanced Studies in Integrative Psychotherapy at the Hebrew University of Jerusalem (Charny & Friedlander, 1996) is an integrative, interdisciplinary diploma program that emphasizes the integration of different modalities of intervention at the individual, family, and community levels. It consists of core and elective courses in psychotherapy, theories, and techniques of marital and family therapy, clinical seminars, and a clinical practicum under supervision.

In addition to the academic programs described in the preceding, family therapy courses are taught in schools of social work and psychology departments at other major universities in Israel (such as Bar Ilan and Ben Gurion University of the Negev). Family therapy training programs, including clinical courses, practicum, and supervision, are also provided by a number of public family therapy clinics as well as private family therapy institutes around the country (Slonim-Nevo & Wagner, 1991).

FAMILY THERAPY AND FAMILY THERAPISTS IN ISRAEL

Family therapy is alive and well in this country. There are currently about 980 members in the Israeli Association for Marital and Family Therapy, that is, one family therapist per 7,000 population (as compared with one per 10,000 in the United States). Family therapists are employed both in public services and in private institutes, as well as maintain private practice. Small private clinics and a number of larger family therapy institutes have been established throughout the country.

One of the most convincing indications for the place of marital and family therapy in Israel is the widespread existence of public clinics. Today, there are 71 such clinics available around the country. These clinics are run under the auspices of the Ministry of Labor and Social Affairs and are staffed primarily by social workers who are certified family therapists or family therapists in training. All of these clinics offer therapy on a sliding-scale basis, making it affordable to all. Many of the clinics provide training and supervision for family therapy students, including family therapy courses and live supervision.

In addition to clinics specializing in family therapy, family counseling units are included within other public agencies. There are six agencies that provide counseling for family courts and eight drug-and-alcohol treatment centers that include family counseling in their program. Family therapy is also provided as part of adult and youth probation services; units for family support and counseling exist in medical centers; and many school psychologists trained in family therapy provide counseling and intervention for families within the system of municipal psychological services.

Family therapy has gained widespread public acceptance owing, in part, to radio talk shows and television programs, as well as regular columns in daily newspapers and weekly magazines that focus on family and marital relationships. These media programs and columns regularly feature family practitioners who discuss parent–child interactions and interpersonal couple relationships. Given the high value placed on family integrity in Israel and the high reliance on the media in this country, these programs have been significant in bringing family therapy to the public's awareness and enhancing the visibility of family therapy as a mode of assistance for families (Halpern, 2001).

RESEARCH ON FAMILIES AND FAMILY THERAPY

Dozens of Israeli family professionals—researchers and therapists—regularly conduct research and publish theoretical and practice-related articles on marriage and family functioning as well as on intervention with couples and families. Most of the research is conducted by family scholars in various fields (psychology, social work, education) in the five research universities: the Hebrew University of Jerusalem, Tel-Aviv University, the University of Haifa, Bar-Ilan University, and Ben-Gurion University of the Negev. A number of family research institutes serve as host for interdisciplinary research on marriage and the family, including the Center for Research and Study of the Family at the University of Haifa, the Peleg-Bilig Center for Research on Family Well-Being in Bar-Ilan University, and the Bandy Steiner's Center for Family Life at Ben-Gurion University. In addition, research is conducted and theoretical and clinical essays are published by scholars in a number of public academic colleges (e.g., Yezreel Academic College and Tel-Hai College), mental health institutes (e.g., Eitanim, Talbieh, and Shalvata), and psychiatric departments in medical centers (e.g., Kaplan, Hadassa, and Rambam). Research is also conducted by practitioners in public agencies (Kibbutz Child and Family Clinic, Youth Aliyah Psychosocial Service, and the Israel Defence Forces Mental Health Department) and private family therapy institutes (e.g., Shiluv Institute for Family and Couple Therapy, Shinui Institute for Family and Personal Change, Barcai Institute for Family Therapy, and Tomer Institute for Medical Psychology).

Because of the small size of the academic community in this country, Israeli family researchers and practitioners most often publish their work in international journals to make it available to family scholars worldwide. However, a sizable amount of research is also published in Hebrew in a number of Israeli journals (*Sihot*, *Society and Welfare*, *Psychologia*, and *B'Mishpacha*), research monographs, and master's theses and doctoral dissertations.

A review of family treatment studies in Israel, in both Hebrew and English (Rabinowitz, 1996), shows the breadth of topics researched by Israeli family scholars. My own review of the literature indicates that the most frequently studied phenomena are those that relate to family effects of the Israeli–Arab conflict (security and war-related problems, terrorist activities, loss, and trauma), families of Holocaust survivors, immigrant families, and special considerations of treatment of Arab families in Israel. These issues, which are perceived as relatively unique to Israeli society (Good & Ben-David, 1995; Halpern, 2001; Lavee & Katz, in press) are addressed in more detail in the next section.

In addition, research has been conducted on more universal family issues, such as life-cycle transitions and life events (e.g., transition to parenthood, fertility problems, divorce and remarriage, neonatal death, and death of a child); families with special needs (e.g., parents with children with mental retardation or Down's syndrome, multiproblem families, families in extreme economic distress, and prisoners' families); families with members suffering from a range of mental disorders (e.g., depression, paranoid disorders, psychosomatic illnesses, eating disorders, alcoholism, and drug abuse); families with children and adolescents who have emotional problems (e.g., school phobia, elective mutism, stuttering, or conduct disorders); families with chronic illnesses; and family violence, primarily child abuse and wife battering. Researchers have also studied "normal" couple and family functioning, including support and coping within couples, management of work and home conflicts, patterns of parent–child attachment, parenting stress, adult attachment, and marital relationships.

Family researchers and practitioners also report on intervention methods and models (e.g., dialectical approach in couple therapy, use of biofeedback and hypnosis in couple and sex therapy, psychodrama and play therapy, use of art and photography in therapy, cognitive family therapy, enrichment programs for newlyweds, and psychoeducational programs for couples), as well as treatment effectiveness. Finally, reports have also been published on marriage and family training programs and supervision.

SPECIFIC ISSUES FOR FAMILY THERAPISTS IN ISRAEL

For the most part, Israeli families face life challenges similar to those faced by families in other industrialized countries: normative, developmental transitions, such as transition to parenthood, raising children, and retirement, in addition to non-normative life events, such as illness, disability, and death. Families struggle with an array of daily hassles and with conflicting demands of the workplace and the family, as well as with chronic stressors, such as caring for a disabled or chronically ill family member, raising a child with a developmental disability or mental illness, or caring for an elderly parent. Families must also cope with stresses and strains that stem from inside the family itself—parenting stress and parent–child conflicts, marital crises, divorce, and violence. A review of literature on family treatment studies in Israel (Rabinowitz, 1996) confirms that Israeli family therapists deal with universal sources of family stress, such as life cycle transitions and other life events, as well as marital violence, child abuse, extramarital affairs, sexual dysfunctions, and a host of illness- and child-related problems.

There are, however, several unique characteristics of Israeli society that can compound the stress with which individuals, families, and communities are faced and that have specific relevance for the work of family therapists. Most notable are stresses and strains inflicted by the Israeli–Arab conflict—repeated wars, terrorist acts, and other security-related sources of stress. In addition, particular stresses exist in certain families and not in others—such as those of immigrants and Holocaust survivors—but in Israel these are so prevalent that they should be viewed as characteristic Israeli stresses. In this regard, we must consider the multicultural nature of Israeli society and its implications for family therapists.

WARS, TERRORISM, AND SECURITY-RELATED STRESS

The armed conflict between Jews and Arabs has had multiple effects on families in Israel: The effect of war on combat soldiers and their families (Solomon, 1993; Solomon, Mikulincer, Fried, & Wosner, 1987; Waysman, Mikulincer, Solomon, & Weisenberg, 1993); the impact of a soldier's death on his or her family (Rubin, Malkinson, & Witztum, 1999); and the consequences of warlike hostility on civilians, such as the shelling of border settlements and the perpetration of random terrorist acts (Ayalon, 1993). Combat stress reaction (CSR) and posttraumatic stress disorder (PTSD) have long-lasting effects on the social aspects of the army veteran's life (Solomon, 1993). CSR casualties report more problems in social, family, sexual, and work functioning. A number of PTSD symptoms, such as numbing of responsiveness; reduced involvement with the external world; diminished interest in previously enjoyed activities; feelings of detachment, alienation, constricted affect, and increased hostility, have adverse effects on family relations and intimate marital relationships (Solomon et al., 1987). In addition, secondary posttraumatic symptoms leading to severe marital distress have been found among wives of CSR veterans (Waysman et al., 1993).

War-related loss and bereavement have a major impact on families in Israel. In its 50 years of existence, more than 19,000 soldiers have lost their lives. Needless to say, the loss of a spouse, parent, sibling, or child has a major effect on the life course of all family members, especially on parents. Research on bereaved parents has shown that a heightened level of bereavement responses is demonstrated beyond the number of years normally expected following such a loss (Rubin, 1993, 1996). In fact, Rubin and his colleagues (1999) suggest that such terms as coping, adaptation, and resolution are inadequate for describing the experience of the majority of bereaved parents. War and security-related stress can also have a direct effect on civilians through acts of terrorism, shelling targeted against border communities, and threats of chemical and biological warfare against the Israeli general population.

Terrorist acts throughout Israel are not a new phenomenon. These threats to the civilian population, resulting in trauma and loss of life, have come to define the reality of Israeli families who have long experienced violent attacks on passenger cars and school buses. More recently, violent attacks on civilians have been occurring in a variety of urban settings, such as discotheques, restaurants, and open-air markets. Especially for families in the West Bank, this constant sense of threat has been coupled with feelings of being "imprisoned in their own homes" and of being isolated from friends and members of the extended family because of travel limitations (Lavee, Ben-David, & Azaiza, 1997). Families in the West Bank as well as in the Gaza Strip and the Golan Heights continue to live under conditions of prolonged uncertainty even in the face of the "peace process" among Israel, the Palestinians, and neighboring countries (Ben-David & Lavee, 1996; Lev, 1998; Lev-Wiesel & Shamai, 1998; Shamai & Lev, 1999).

Shelling targeted against border communities, particularly in northern Israel, has been an ongoing source of stress for families over the past 30 years. In addition to the threat to life and limb involved in these incidents, families must be confined to the small space of a shelter during such attacks. Likewise, during the 1991 Gulf War, when the civilian population throughout the country was exposed to missile attacks with potential chemical weapons, families were repeatedly confined to hermetically sealed rooms. The forced closeness under stressful conditions sometimes created or intensified interpersonal tension in families (Ben-David & Lavee, 1994a; Lavee & Ben-David, 1993), with an increased need for help with marital distress (Rabin, 1995).

Family Therapy and War-Related Family Needs

Operating in an environment where war and security-related stress are an integral part of Israeli experience, family therapists, like their counterparts in other mental health professions, are often faced with the need to provide help for bereaved families, families with a member in military service, families traumatized by a terrorist attack, or families with a member suffering from PTSD. Family therapists are called upon to provide help for families both in acute stressful situations and under conditions of prolonged distress and uncertainty. Many communities are now organized to provide support and intervention to victims and their families—for the sake of the injured individuals themselves as well as for the entire affected community (Ayalon, 1993). In addition, there is known to be an upsurge of volunteer activity by professionals in times of crisis.

Family therapists have responded to the unique needs of families under war-related stress by developing specific intervention programs. For example, Ayalon (1993) suggests a strategic method of short-term family therapy for survivors of terrorist attacks involving kidnapping and face-to-face killing. Dreman and Cohen (1982, 1990) report on a family intervention program for children of victims of terrorist activities that is concentrated on promoting family strengths and coping while deemphasizing individual pathology. Margalit and his colleagues (Margalit, Ezion, Rabinowitz, & Guri, 1993) present an integrative, multifaceted treatment model for surviving POWs and their families, and Levy and Neumann (1987) illustrate how families should be involved in the treatment of acute combat reaction casualties. In accordance with their report that family involvement enhances the speed and completeness of the victim's recovery, the emphasis in their program is on the victim's reaffirmation within the family. Shamai (1994) describes a unique mode of family crisis intervention by phone that was intended to help families deal with the impact of tension and insecurity during the Gulf War. Because of the special conditions of war, family therapy agencies must adjust to the needs of families that are unable to attend sessions.

An important element in the work of therapists with families affected by war and security-related crises is that therapists themselves are likely to be influenced by the same sources of stress. In all likelihood, the therapists themselves have been touched by war or terrorism through the loss of a family member, close relative, or close friend, or they are living under the same threat as their clients. Family professionals in the West Bank, for example, may be both part of a therapeutic system and members of the same community living in political uncertainty (Shamai, 1998, 1999).

HOLOCAUST SURVIVORS AND THEIR FAMILIES

Although the Holocaust happened more than five decades ago, it is still a central theme in the existential reality of Israeli society (Charny, 1990). Its legacy persists not only in the survivors who continue to be haunted by their experiences but also in their children and grandchildren, who often need help because of the multigenerational transmission of unresolved issues of anger, guilt, grief, loss, abandonment, and a host of other powerful emotions (Good & Ben-David, 1995; Harel, Kahana, & Kahana, 1993). The traumatic wounds of the survivors are made more difficult as they grow older. The losses and disabilities associated with aging interact with the unhealed psychic wounds, and chronic health problems create a situation that places strain on family members (Harel et al., 1993). The entire family system may be dynamically affected by a reciprocal effect in which the children of these survivors enact a pattern of transference and experience many of their parents' problems in a personal way (Mazor & Mendelsohn, 1998; Mazor & Tal, 1996; Steinitz, 1982). Furthermore, the offspring of Holocaust survivors are often committed to a heritage that they cannot fully understand, which they absorbed either by overexposure or through the protective cover of silence (Mor, 1990).

For the most part, the literature on the long-range effects of the Holocaust on survivors and their children points to their conspicuous adaptive and reintegrative capacities. Similarly, although there is evidence indicating that children of survivors presented specific psychological problems, there is also considerable evidence to indicate that large numbers of survivors' children enjoy healthy family relationships (Klein-Parker, 1988). Nevertheless, the legacy of the Holocaust may be manifested when families deal with major traumatic life events. For example, the threatened use of gas warheads in the Gulf War brought to the surface Holocaust survivors' collective memory of gas extermination. A loss in general, and loss of a child in military service in particular, also has a unique meaning for survivors (Gay, 1982). Furthermore, research has shown that children of Holocaust survivors suffer higher rates of PTSD than other soldiers (Solomon, Kotler, & Mikulincer, 1988–1989). In working with Holocaust survivors as well as with the second (and now third) generation of Holocaust survivors, family therapists need to take into consideration the many facets of this traumatic experience and the ways in which it may affect marital and family relationships.

IMMIGRATION AND IMMIGRANT FAMILIES

As was noted earlier in this chapter, Israel has been shaped by massive waves of immigration from all corners of the globe. More than 700,000 immigrants arrived from the former Soviet Union in the last decade alone, and about 56,000 immigrants came from Ethiopia in the mid-1980s and early 1990s. Although immigration is not unique to Israel, its proportions require family therapists to attend to the wide range of difficulties faced by immigrant families. It also requires family therapists to consider the suitability of models of therapy to different populations.

Immigration poses major stress for the families involved in a number of ways: movement from one geographical location to another, often requiring changes in climate and lifestyle; disengagement from a familiar network of social relations, with the disruption of longstanding ties and the accompanying sense of loneliness, isolation, and lack of support; and the need to abandon old norms and values and adopt new ones (Levenbach & Lewak, 1995; Shuval, 1993). Differences between family members in their willingness to immigrate and differences in their rate of absorption sometimes intensify interpersonal conflicts. New work conditions and living arrangements create shifts in patterns of closeness–distance regulation and changes in patterns of conflict resolution (Ben-David & Lavee, 1994b). Additionally, migration often results in changes in family structure and a shift in the balance of power, both between spouses and generations (Sharlin & Elshanskaya, 1997). For example, a father who traditionally wielded the power in the family may find himself stripped of his accustomed role, and role reversal may occur, as children become "socializing agents" and mediators in their parents' relations with authorities.

For family therapists, the challenge posed by immigration is twofold. First, they are often called upon to treat families whose norms and values are different from their own. Second, they need to adapt models of family therapy, which were developed primarily in the United States and Western Europe, to a population that may not respond well to such therapeutic methods. These challenges are addressed in the following section.

FAMILY THERAPY IN A MULTICULTURAL SOCIETY

There are two characteristics of Israeli society that make it unique with respect to multiculturalism. First, there is a sizable minority group (about 20%) of Arab citizens, whose family lifestyle and values may be different from the dominant culture. Second, as a country of immigrants, Israel is host to a large proportion of newcomers relative to veteran Israelis.

In recent years, the awareness of cultural sensitivity in Israeli society has been growing. A number of Arab family professionals have examined cultural values of contemporary Arab society in Israel (Haj-Yahia, 1995), unique family forms among certain Arab groups (Al-Krenawi, 1998; Al-Krenawi, Graham, & Al-Krenawi, 1997), the gap in the understanding of cultural terminology (Al-Krenawi, 1999), and the relevance of these aspects to intervention. Abu-Baker (1999a) describes how the assimilation and integration within the dominant culture may lead to disharmony and disintegration within the home culture and suggests that therapists be aware of the complexity of acculturation and its interfamilial, intrafamilial, and social levels.

Culturally related issues of treating Arab families have also been raised by other family professionals. Savaya (1995) found that Arab women express readiness to seek professional help for problems with their children, but much less so for problems with their spouses. According to Lavee (1991), difficulties in treating sexual dysfunction in Arab couples may be encountered when commonly used techniques are employed, and he offers some guidelines for providing sex therapy to non-Western clients. In describing "an intervention that almost failed," Rubin and Nassar (1993) discuss a case in which a Moslem Arab family was treated by a Christian Arab woman therapist, who was supervised by a Jewish man of American origin. They concluded that knowledge of the client's cultural reference to the problem may help the therapist in diagnosing difficulties and directing intervention by understanding when intervention runs counter to tradition or in line with it.

Awareness of cultural norms and their relevance for treating immigrant families has also been raised in regard to Ethiopian families (Ben-David, 1993; Ben-David & Good, 1998) and families from the former Soviet Union (Bardin & Porten, 1996). There seems to be a growing recognition among Israeli family therapists that they have an obligation to meet the unique needs of ethnic minorities by offering systemic intervention services that are culturally sensitive (Abu-Baker, 1999b; Ben-David & Good, 1998; Slonim-Nevo, Sharaga, & Mirsky, 1999). In a comprehensive book of competent family therapy, Ariel (1999) integrates family therapy theories and culturally oriented therapy and presents techniques that are modified to fit the character of families from different cultures.

CONCLUSION

The development of family therapy in Israel has been strongly influenced by models, approaches, and techniques developed in North America and Europe. In many respects, these models are well suited to the training and scientific orientation of clinical and school psychologists, social workers, and psychiatrists in this country. Although Western approaches to treating families are still quite influential (in part, because of ongoing contact with family professionals in Europe and North America), indigenous sociocultural and geopolitical characteristics of Israeli society are evident in both research and clinical work. In terms of family research, Israeli scholars have been among the leaders in studying war-related stress and trauma, the impact of immigration on family relationships, and intergenerational issues for Holocaust survivors. They also add original conceptualizations to established theoretical formulations of family systems (Halpern, 2001). At the same time, family practitioners have developed culturally congruent modes for intervention that better suit the multicultural nature of Israeli society and its unique circumstances.

REFERENCES

Abu-Baker, K. (1999a). Acculturation and reacculturation influence: Multilayer contexts in therapy. *Clinical Psychology Review, 19*, 951–967.

Abu-Baker, K. (1999b). The importance of cultural sensitivity and therapist self-awareness when working with mandatory clients. *Family Process, 38*, 55–67.

Al-Krenawi, A. (1998). Family therapy with a multiparental/multispousal family. *Family Process, 37*, 65–81.

Al-Krenawi, A. (1999). Integrating cultural rituals into family therapy: A case study with a Bedouin-Arab patient in Israel. *Journal of Family Psychotherapy, 10*, 61–74.

Al-Krenawi, A., Graham, J. R., & Al-Krenawi, S. (1997). Social work practice with polygamous families. *Child and Adolescent Social Work Journal, 14*, 445–458.

Ariel, S. (1999). *Culturally competent family therapy: A general model.* Westport, CT: Praeger Publishers/Greenwood Publishing Group.

Ayalon, O. (1993). Posttraumatic stress recovery of terrorist survivors. In J. P. Wilson, & B. Raphael (Eds.), *International handbook of traumatic stress syndromes* (pp. 855–866). New York: Plenum Press.

Bardin, A., & Porten, D. (1996). Culture change: A training program for recent immigrant professionals from the former Soviet Union. *Contemporary Family Therapy, 18,* 61–67.

Ben-David, A. (1993). Culture and gender in marital therapy with Ethiopian immigrants: A conversation in metaphors. *Contemporary Family Therapy, 15*, 327–339.

Ben-David, A., & Good, I. J. (1998). Ethiopians and the Hmongs: A comparative study in cultural narrative from a family therapy perspective. *Journal of Family Psychotherapy, 9,* 31–45.

Ben-David, A., & Lavee, Y. (1994a). Families in the sealed room: Interaction patterns of Israeli families during SCUD missile attacks. *Family Process, 31,* 35–44.

Ben-David, A., & Lavee, Y. (1994b). Migration and marital distress: The case of Soviet immigrants. *Journal of Divorce and Remarriage, 21*, 133–146.

Ben-David, A., & Lavee, Y. (1996). Between war and peace: Interactional patterns of couples under prolonged uncertainty. *American Journal of Family Therapy, 24,* 343–357.

Central Bureau of Statistics. (2000). *Statistical Abstracts of Israel*. Jerusalem: Israel.

Charny, I. W. (1990). To commit or not to commit to human life: Children of victims and victimizers—all. *Contemporary Family Therapy, 12*, 407–426.

Charny, I. W., & Friedlander, D. (1996). Program for advanced studies in integrative psychotherapy: Family, couple, and individual therapy (An interdisciplinary program). *Contemporary Family Therapy, 18,* 85–94.

Dreman, S. B., & Cohen, E. C. (1982). Children of victims of terrorist activities: A family approach to dealing with tragedy. *American Journal of Family Therapy, 10*(2), 39–47.

Dreman, S. B., & Cohen, E. (1990). Children of victims of terrorism revisited: Integrating individual and family treatment approaches. *American Journal of Orthopsychiatry, 60,* 204–209.

Gay, M. (1982). The adjustment of parents to wartime bereavement. *Series in Clinical and Community Psychology: Stress and Anxiety, 8*, 243–247

Good, I. J., & Ben-David, A. (1995). Family therapy in Israel: A review of therapy done under unusual circumstances. *Contemporary Family Therapy, 17*, 353–366.

Haj-Yahia, M. M. (1995). Toward culturally sensitive intervention with Arab families in Israel. *Contemporary Family Therapy, 17,* 429–447.

Halpern, E. (1985). Training family therapists in Israel: The necessity of indigenous models. *American Journal of Family Therapy, 13*, 55–60.

Halpern, E. (2001). Family psychology from an Israeli perspective. *American Psychologist, 56*, 58–64.

Harel, Z., Kahana, B., & Kahana, E. (1993). Social resources and the mental health of aging Nazi Holocaust survivors and immigrants. In J. P. Wilson & B. Raphael (Eds.), *International handbook of traumatic stress syndromes* (pp. 241–252). New York: Plenum Press.

Kaffman, M. (1963). Short-term family therapy. *Family Process, 2*, 216–231.

Kaffman, M. (1965). Family diagnosis and therapy in child emotional pathology. *Family Process, 4*, 241–258.

Kaffman, M. (1972). Family conflict in the psychopathology of the Kibbutz child. *Family Process, 11*, 171–188.

Kaffman, M. (1981). Community care for the kibbutz chronic psychiatric patient. *International Journal of Family Therapy, 3*, 193–204.

Kaffman, M. (1985). Twenty years of family therapy in Israel: A personal journey. *Family Process, 24*, 113–127.

Klein-Parker, F. (1988). Dominant attitudes of adult children of Holocaust survivors toward their parents. In J. P. Wilson, Z. Harel, & B. Kahana (Eds.), *Human adaptation to extreme stress: From the Holocaust to Vietnam* (pp. 193–218). New York: Plenum Press.

Lavee, Y. (1991). Western and non-western human sexuality: Implications for clinical practice. *Journal of Sex and Marital Therapy, 17*, 303–313.

Lavee, Y., & Ben-David, A. (1993). Families under war: Stresses and strains of Israeli families during the Gulf War. *Journal of Traumatic Stress, 6*, 239–254.

Lavee, Y., Ben-David, A., & Azaiza, F. (1997). Israeli and Palestinian families in the peace process: Sources of stress and response patterns. *Family Process, 36*, 247–263.

Lavee, Y., & Katz, R. (in press). The family in Israel: Between tradition and modernity. In C. B. Hennon & T. H. Brubaker (Eds.), *Diversity in families: A global perspective*. Belmont, CA: Wadsworth.

Lev, R. (1998). Coping with the stress associated with forced relocation in the Golan Heights, Israel. *Journal of Applied Behavioral Science, 34*, 143–160.

Lev-Wiesel, R., & Shamai, M. (1998). Living under the threat of relocation: Spouses' perceptions of the threat and coping resources. *Contemporary Family Therapy, 20*, 107–121.

Levenbach, D., & Lewak, B. (1995). Immigration: Going home or going to pieces. *Contemporary Family Therapy, 17*, 379–394.

Levy, A., & Neumann, M. (1987). Involving families in the treatment of combat reactions. *Journal of Family Therapy, 9*, 177–188.

Margalit, C., Ezion, T., Rabinowitz, S., & Guri, S. (1993). Israel Defence Forces experiences with treatment of POWs and families: An innovative multifaceted treatment model. *Military Medicine, 158*, 376–378.

Mazor, A., & Mendelsohn, Y. (1998). Spouse bereavement processes of Holocaust child survivors: Can one differentiate a black frame from a black background? *Contemporary Family Therapy, 20*, 79–91.

Mazor, A., & Tal, I. (1996). Intergenerational transmission: The individuation process and the capacity for intimacy of adult children of Holocaust survivors. *Contemporary Family Therapy, 18*, 95–113.

Milgram, N. (1993). War-related trauma and victimization: Principles of traumatic stress prevention in Israel. In J. P. Wilson & B. Raphael (Eds.), *International handbook of traumatic stress syndromes* (pp. 811–820). New York: Plenum Press.

Mor, N. (1990). Holocaust messages from the past. *Contemporary Family Therapy, 12*, 371–379.

Nichols, W. C. (1995). Introduction. *Contemporary Family Therapy, 17*, 351.

Poskanzer, A. (1995). The Matryoshka: The three-generation Soviet family in Israel. *Contemporary Family Therapy, 17*, 413–427.

Rabin, C. (1995). The use of psychoeducational group to improve marital functioning in high-risk Israeli couples: Stage model. *Contemporary Family Therapy, 17,* 503–510.

Rabinowitz, J. (1996). Review of family treatment studies in Israel. *Contemporary Family Therapy, 18,* 161–193.

Rubin, S. (1993). The death of a child is forever: The life course impact of child loss. In M. S. Stroebe, W. Stroebe, & R. O. Hansson (Eds.), *Handbook of bereavement: Theory, research and intervention* (pp. 285–299). Cambridge: Cambridge University Press.

Rubin, S. (1996). The wounded family: Bereaved parents and the impact of adult child loss. In D. Klass, P. Silverman, & S. Nickman (Eds.), *Continuing bonds: Understanding the resolution of grief* (pp. 217–232). Washington, DC: Taylor and Francis.

Rubin, S., Malkinson, R., & Witztum, E. (1999). The pervasive impact of war-related loss and bereavement in Israel. *International Journal of Group Tensions, 28*(1/2), 137–153.

Rubin, S. S., & Nassar, H. Z. (1993). Psychotherapy and supervision with a bereaved Moslem family: An intervention that almost failed. *Psychiatry: Interpersonal and Biological Processes, 56*, 338–348.

Savaya, R. (1995). Attitudes towards family and marital counseling among Israeli Arab women. *Journal of Social Service Research, 21*, 35–51.

Shamai, M. (1994). Family crisis intervention by phone: Intervention with families during the Gulf War. *Journal of Marital and Family Therapy, 20*, 317–323.

Shamai, M. (1998). Therapist in distress; Team-supervision of social workers and family therapists who work and live under political uncertainty. *Family Process, 37,* 245–259.

Shamai, M. (1999). Beyond neutrality: A politically oriented systemic intervention. *Journal of Family Therapy, 21,* 217–229.

Shamai, M., & Lev, R. (1999). Marital quality among couples living under the threat of forced relocation: The case of families in the Golan Heights. *Journal of Marital and Family Therapy, 25,* 237–252.

Sharlin, S., & Elshanskaya, I. (1997). Parental attitudes of Soviets in Israel to the immigration process and their impact on parental stress and tensions. In S. Dreman (Ed.), *The family on the threshold of the 21st century: Trends and implications* (pp. 229–244). London: Erlbaum.

Shuval, J. T. (1993). Migration and stress. In L. Goldberger & S. Breznitz (Eds.), *Handbook of stress: Theoretical and clinical aspects* (2nd ed.) (pp. 641–657). New York: The Free Press.

Slonim-Nevo, V., Sharaga, Y., & Mirsky, J. (1999). A culturally sensitive approach to therapy with immigrant families: The case of Jewish emigrants from the former Soviet Union. *Family Process, 38,* 445–461.

Slonim-Nevo, V., & Wagner, R. (1991). Family therapy in Israel: Historical development. *B'Mishpacha, 34,* 11–17 (in Hebrew).

Solomon, Z. (1993). Immediate and long-term effects of traumatic combat stress among Israeli veterans of the Lebanon war. In J. P. Wilson & B. Raphael (Eds.),

International handbook of traumatic stress syndromes (pp. 321–332). New York: Plenum Press.

Solomon, Z., Kotler, M., & Mikulincer, M. (1988–1989). Combat related post-traumatic stress disorder among the second generation of Holocaust survivors: Transgenerational effects among Israeli soldiers. *Psychologia: Israel Journal of Psychology, 1,* 113–119 (in Hebrew).

Solomon, Z., Mikulincer, M., Fried, B., & Wosner, Y. (1987). Family characteristics and posttraumatic stress disorder: A follow-up of Israeli combat stress reaction casualties. *Family Process, 26*, 383–394.

Steinitz, L. Y. (1982). Psyco-social effects of the Holocaust on aging survivors and their families. *Journal of Gerontological Social Work, 4*(3-4), 145–152.

Waysman, M., Mikulincer, M., Solomon, Z., & Weisenberg, M. (1993). Secondary traumatization among wives of posttraumatic combat veterans: A family typology. *Journal of Family Psychology, 7*, 104–118.

Wertheimer, D. (1979). Family therapy training in Israel. *Society and Welfare, 2,* 71–79 (in Hebrew).

Wertheimer, J., & Wertheimer, D. (1988). Family therapy in Israel in the 80's. *Bulletin of the International Family Therapy Association, 1*(1), 2–4.

CHAPTER 14

Family Therapy in Brazil

Memoir and Development

JÚLIA BUCHER
ILENO I. DA COSTA

Not much has been written about the history of family therapy in Brazil. In 1989, we sought to systematize what there was in the field of family therapy in Brazil (Bucher, 1989). A few years later, a survey was taken of what was happening in the area (Macedo, 1993). After that, few efforts were made to trace the evolution of what had happened in the area. Recently, Kaslow (2001) published an article entitled "History of Family Therapy: Evolution Outside of the U.S.," which was made available on the home page of the International Family Therapy Association (IFTA). However, the article carries information on family therapy in just one of the states of Brazil.

An attempt to relate the history of a movement is never easy. Generally, historical reconstructions are limited to identifying the personalities who initiated or transformed the movement. In this chapter, we intend to describe these aspects, which constitute the living memory of the family therapy movement in Brazil, considering that such a record will help identify the theoretical and conceptual issues that underlie the structural and dynamic transformations in families today and in therapeutic practice. Therefore, the recording of attainments provides an important opportunity to gather recollections of what has been done and accomplished with regard to family therapy in Brazil.

For three decades, as we shall see, family therapy in Brazil followed in the theoretical tracks of the North American and European continents. It may be stated that we are facing two fundamental questions, which must be better investigated: (a) How do family therapists, in practice, construct subjective and collective meanings regarding Brazilian families; and (b) What is the reality of Brazilian families, considering the continental dimensions of Brazil and its diverse regional, social, and cultural manifestations?

In the first part of this chapter we outline a brief history of FT in Brazil, with the aim of describing the historical context in which family therapy developed. Next, we present a history of the encounters, congresses, themes, publications, theses, and dissertations in the area. Finally, we introduce the institutions working with family therapy in the country and make a few critical-epistemological remarks regarding this development.

SOME ASPECTS OF THE FAMILY IN A BRAZILIAN CONTEXT

Traditional family patterns in Brazil have been changing, especially in recent decades. The fecundity rate declined substantially. Following changes in the law, the establishment and dissolution of marital ties led to a significant increase in new forms of family organization, divorce, and remarriage. There has been a steady increase in the number of single-parent households (almost exclusively maternal). All of these factors imply alterations in the organization and composition of family structures. Furthermore, new complex family structures have begun to appear, such as those of homosexual couples, with their struggle to legitimize their union and be permitted to adopt children. As for heterosexual couples, the 1988 Brazilian Constitution not only legitimizes new and emerging forms of family organization, but also eliminates certain barriers that had made it hard to obtain recognition for family constellations that had been considered illegal, such as concubine and the figure of the bastard child, thus altering social and legal relationships.

Longer life expectancies and the large number of adolescent pregnancies, in turn, have contributed to extensive modifications in the dynamics of family functioning, highlighting the influence of the grandparents in everyday family life and giving a new lease on life to the extended family. The complexity of Brazilian families poses a challenge not only to public and social policy, but also to professionals in the social and health arenas. The structuring of fields of specialization such as family therapy has acquired fundamental importance in new forms of studying the family in Brazil, dealing with families and intervening in social reality. In this chapter, we outline the concomitant evolution of family therapy in Brazil, as a way to point up the challenges to this field of specialization in a Brazilian context.

A BRIEF HISTORY OF FAMILY THERAPY IN BRAZIL

Although the structure of family therapy in Brazil has taken as its starting point the dissemination of ideas developed in other countries (especially the United States), there already existed studies of the Brazilian family that attempted to describe it from a historical, anthropological, sociological, and/or legal perspective, without a systematic psychological approach. Among these, mention must be made of the internationally known Brazilian anthropologist Gilberto Freyre, who inaugurated the study of the patriarchal family in Brazil, from an anthropological-historical perspective, in the colonial period. In those days, the Brazilian family, consisting of a patriarch and his wife, children, concubines, and a broad network of relatives, came to be of great interest to researchers in the fields of sociology and anthropology, and much later, psychology. Those studies emphasized the patriarchical values, position of women, relationships between the sexes, double standard, and machismo, as well as affective and emotional relations (Candido, 1951; Correa, 1982; Freyre, 1993; Levi, 1974; Nogueira, 1962; Williams, 1954). The system of kinship was also studied, considering the extended family as a peculiar characteristic of traditional Brazil (Lewin, 1979; Nizza da Silva, 1976; Pereira de Queiroz, 1975; Ramos, 1978; Santos, 1979). Today, the modern family has been the topic of numerous studies in the universities. Among these are studies of the family and schizophrenia (Costa, 1990); the family and the life cycle (Cerveny & Berthoud, 1997); families and ways of life; gender, generations, and identity (Lago, 1998); the family and contemporaneousness (Costa, 1990); and the family and AIDS (Bucher, 1999), as well as the collection organized by Féres-Carneiro, *Casal e família entre a tradição e a transformação* (Couple and family between tradition and transformation) (Féres-Carneiro, 1999). Thus, in this past decade, there was a significant increase in scientific production regarding couples and families and especially how to deal with this reality, beginning with the structuring of the Brazilian family therapy movement, as described in the following.

Prior to the structuring of the family therapy movement, several support groups were organized by the Catholic Church ("Couples with Christ," encounters of engaged couples and newlyweds, etc.). With that same concern, Protestant churches have done similar work. Today there are countless religious groups working with married couples. Many of these counselors seek undergraduate and special graduate programs specializing in the family.

At the same time, under the influence of the family therapy movements that have developed, especially in the United States, a great deal of interest in the area of family studies in Brazil from a psychological and therapeutic perspective began to be manifested. The first master's theses, the product of theoretical studies and empirical research, were presented.

There were three pioneering university institutions that started up research and therapy for couples and families in Brazil: the Catholic University of Sao Paulo, under the leadership of Mathilde Neder; the University of Brasilia, under the orientation of Júlia Bucher; and the Catholic University of Rio de Janeiro, where the program was directed by Terezinha Féres-Carneiro.

At the same time, in Sao Paulo, Matilde Neder, who was working in the Hospital das Clinicas, where she treated couples and families in a hospital context, was concerned with the growing demand in this area. She organized the first family therapy encounters promoted by the Program of Graduate Studies in Clinical Psychology of the Pontifical Catholic University of Sao Paulo. Among the participants were psychologists, social workers, psychiatrists, psychoanalysts, and other professionals interested in the area.

In Belo Horizonte, Maria José Ulhoa, who had recently arrived from France, also started training family therapists from other states, with the aim of opening up possibilities for undergraduate education concentrating on couples and families. These were the first recorded initiatives, which started a process leading to the organization of nationwide events for professionals in the area.

THE ORIGINS AND STRUCTURES OF THE FAMILY THERAPY MOVEMENT IN BRAZIL

Family Therapy Institutes, Societies, and Centers

In the late 1980s, Bucher (1989) recorded the birth and structuring of family therapy institutes, societies, and centers that laid the groundwork for the therapy movement. In the northern region, for example, some family therapy work was done by the Integrated Psychology Cluster (NIP), in Belem, Pará. Countless problems are being faced by families in that region in recent years. The deforestation of the Amazon region, the large-scale migration from other parts of the country to that region, the construction of big dams, and panhandling have, in a disorderly way, transformed the behavior of people in the region, often provoking difficulties in interaction among husband and wife, parents and children, and other family members. Although there is an awareness of the family problems derived from this situation, any work with these families in the region to help solve their problems remains, as pointed out almost ten years ago.

Continuing on to the northeast region of the country, family therapy is present in a significant portion of the states here. The work carried out at the Center for Family Studies (CEF), in Ceará, stands out: The center put into place a community therapy endeavor aimed at family issues in the barrio of Pirambu, under the organization and coordination of Adalberto Barreto, who today is internationally recognized and has several publications in French. In Bahia, the Center for Studies of Marriage and the Family (CEFAC), which is basically run by social workers, offers educational courses to prepare family therapists and provides therapeutic care. In other states, several research and study groups are working with family therapy and family therapist education. One example is the recent program in Recife, Pernambuco, which is one of the first family therapy associations in Brazil.

In the center-west Region, and especially in Brasilia, the capital of Brazil, there exists the Brazilian Center for Family Therapy (CEFAM), which started up in 1978. It conducts study groups and courses to prepare family therapists, as well as providing service to low-income families. At the present time, there are countless other groups with diverse approaches working in the capital (including psychodrama) as well as the efforts of the family courts and public defenders (mainly using a family mediation mechanism). The latter got underway in the late 1970s, via the Department of Clinical Psychology at the University of Brasilia. Under the influence of CEFAM, structured family therapists developed education programs and study groups in Goiania, the capital of Goias. Family therapy has indeed developed rapidly and spread widely throughout this state.

It is the southeast region where the greatest number of groups and institutions working with family therapy with a broad range of theoretical approaches are to be found. Given the amount and intensity of work undertaken there, it is considered a pioneer region in the vanguard of the movement, with several family therapist education programs, research groups, and publications such as: The Family Institute (INFA), in Minas Gerais; the religiously oriented Family Institute (INFA), in Rio de Janeiro; the Cluster on Marriage and the Family, in the state of Rio de Janeiro; the Family Therapy Institute (ITF), in Rio de Janeiro; Mosaico (Mosaic), in Rio de Janeiro; Delphos, in Rio de Janeiro; the Family Studies Society (SEFAM), in Sao Paulo; the Institute for Psychotherapy and Psychiatry of Childhood and Adolescence (IPPIA), in Sao Paulo; the Center for Studies of Marriage and the Family (CECAF), in Sao Paulo; the Institute for Family Education and Orientation (INEF), in Sao Paulo; and the Family Therapy Institute (ITF), in Sao Paulo. Of course, this list is not complete; nor is it possible to lengthen it, given the scope of this chapter.

In the southern region, an extensive amount of family therapy work was done in the states of Rio Grande do Sul, Paraná, and Santa Catarina, such as the pioneering Clinical Psychology Cluster of Curitiba, Paraná; the Center for Studies, Care and Research on Childhood and Adolescence (CEAPIA), in Rio Grande do Sul; and the Santa Catarina groups today joined together in the Santa Catarina Family Therapy Association (ACATEF), as well as several other groups in the region grounded in the courses and study groups structured by the states of Rio Grande do Sul and Paraná.

In all the states, many other groups are engaged in family therapy activities. Furthermore, professionals in private offices serve families, whether from a psychoanalytic or integrative perspective. Thus, not only the number of groups, but also the number of courses, and types of attention and studies, are steadily increasing and diversifying. The family approach, disseminated throughout all the states of Brazil, is growing in importance, not only for the area but also for the country itself, as we see in the historic evolution of the encounters that have structured the family therapy movement in Brazil.

The National Encounters, Congresses, and National Association

The first national encounter, chaired by Matilde Neder, was held at the Graduate Studies Program in Clinical Psychology of the Catholic University of Sao Paulo in 1982. For the first time, marriage and family therapists from various regions of Brazil met to exchange experiences, discuss theories, and identify what each was doing in this new field. Therapists, professors, researchers, and students participated in this significant event.

Two years later, Matilde Neder organized the Second National Family Therapy Encounter, this time bringing together professionals who had been working in isolation or small groups until that time. Participants in that encounter included not only those family therapists working in a systemic perspective, but also Luiz Meyer, a psychoanalyst who had received his degree in London and was also an acclaimed writer. Also present were pioneers of family therapy such as Terezinha Fez Carneiro (CECAF and PUC/RJ), Nelida Simonelli (an Argentinian living in Brazil, founder of the INEF/SP), Silvia Alonso (Sedes Sapiencia), Fiorangela Desiderio (SEFAM/SP), Clea Palatinik Pilnik (IUP/SP), Maria José Ulhoa (Belo Horizonte, UFMG), Júlia Bucher (UnB/DF), Sonia Alves (INEF/SP), Lia Alexander (SEAF/SP), Almira Rosetti, and Madalena Ramos (PUC/SP), among others. At that encounter, discussions were mainly focused on the theoretical and methodological aspects of family therapy, social implications, and the theory of technique. These themes also generated the first publications in these areas.

Two years later in 1986, the Third National Encounter was held, also convened by Matilde Neder from the Pontifical Catholic University of Sao Paulo. At the third encounter, 13 institutions working with family therapy were represented, such as, for example, Ileno Costa (CEFAM/DF); Luiz Carlos Prado, Olga Falceto, and José Ovídio Waldemar (CEAPIA/RS); Janice Rechulski (PUC/SP) and Maurício Knobel (PUCCAMP/SP), each of whom came to make a contribution, going more deeply into issues raised in previous encounters.

Although in a way they constituted a "silent movement" in Brazil, the national encounters hosted by the PUC/SP, under the coordination of Matilde Neder, encouraged systematization and the expansion of the circle of family therapists then scattered around the country. In recognition of that effort, we may affirm with certainty that these encounters gave rise to the family therapy movement in Brazil. After the Third National Encounter, there was a consensus to initiate the First Brazilian Encounter of Family Therapists in 1988 in Salvador, Bahia, where approximately 100 family therapists from the different regions of Brazil were to meet. The main objective of that encounter was to maximize professional interchange and demonstration of family therapy work throughout the country. At that same time, a rich and complex network of professional, affective, and institutional ties was being formed in Brazil. The organizing institution was the Center for Families and Couples (CEFAC), in Bahia, in the northeast of the country. The coordinators were Margarida Rego and Maria Luiza Timóteo; logistic support was provided by Guatemalan family therapist Carlos Arturo Molina-Loza. In addition to several simulations of therapy sessions, a course for therapists and educators present at the encounter was given by Italian family therapist Maurizio Andolfi.

At that point, it was decided to hold biannual encounters aimed at exchanging ideas, updating information, and deepening our understanding. The state of Minas Gerais, in southeastern Brazil, was chosen to host the Second Brazilian Encounter in 1990. Present at that encounter were about 500 people, including educators, therapists, and others interested in family therapy. The organizing committee consisted of Maria Beatriz Rios Ricci, Juliana Aun, and Maria José Vasconcelos.

Brasilia, the capital of Brazil, was the place selected for the Third Brazilian Encounter in 1992. Leadership was provided by Ileno Izídio da Costa (University of Brasilia). A partner institution, the Brazilian Center for Family Studies (CEFAM), in the Federal District, cohosted the event. The approximately 650 participants divided up and congregated in various activities such as conferences, round table discussions, open discussions, workshops, experiences, and thematic encounters. In view of its structure, the Brasilia meeting amounted to the first experience with a national encounter, although it was not identified as such. It was in Brasilia that the first challenge was launched to consider the formal (legal and associative) organization of a possible Brazilian family therapy association, at a gathering of leading family therapists, brought together by the then-president of the congress, Ileno Izídio da Costa. On that occasion, the state of Sao Paulo was chosen to host the next encounter.

In 1993, after a prior meeting of several representatives of family therapy institutions throughout the country, it was decided that, in view not only of the growth of the movement but also of the structure developed in Brasilia and the interest generated throughout the country, the Sao Paulo event would constitute the First Brazilian Congress of Family Therapy.

The First Brazilian Congress of Family Therapy was born in 1994, organized by several family therapy centers in the state of Sao Paulo under the presidency of Maria Rita Seixas. With the participation of family therapists representing all parts of the country, it was decided also to create the Brazilian Association of Family Therapy (ABRATEF). Basic guidelines were produced at that encounter, in the form of the first statutes to be approved and registered on the occasion of the Second Brazilian Congress, set for Rio Grande do Sul, under the responsibility of the first directorate to be chosen, the first elected president which was José Ovídio Waldemar Copstein.

The multifarious Rio Grande do Sul congress was organized in the city of Gramado in 1996 and had approximately 900 participants. With regard to the organization of the movement, it fell to Rio Grande do Sul to put the final touches on the legal proceedings of registration of ABRATEF and move ahead with the process. The details and final form of what is now called the Brazilian Family Therapy Association were the focus of deliberations. At the time of the congress, the following regional associations were already legally registered: the Family Therapy Association of Rio de Janeiro (ATF/RJ), the Sao Paulo Family Therapy Association (APTEF), the Bahia Regional Family Therapy Association (ARTEF), the Minas Gerais Family Therapy Association (AMITEF), and the Rio Grande do Sul Family Therapy Association (AGATEF). Although the center-west region was represented by papers and participants from Brasilia and Goiania, under the leadership of Ileno Costa, it did not as yet have a formally constituted association.

In 1998, ATF/RJ (via the second elected ABRATEF board of directors) hosted the Third Brazilian Congress of Family Therapy, under the responsibility of ABRATEF, which was chaired by family therapists Tereza Cristina Diniz and Lia Baptista Carvalho. Together with the congress, the First Latin American Encounter and a National Encounter of Family Therapy Educators were held separately. The aim of the former encounter was to bring together colleagues from Latin America who were not only working with family therapy but had also been keeping in contact and exchanging information with their Brazilian colleagues. In the latter case, the goal was to meet the growing demand for family therapy educators to have their own space for discussion of and reflection on the family therapist education programs offered in Brazil. It was in Rio de Janeiro that it became clear to the educators in the area that there was a need for a specific encounter to discuss the training of family therapists and the challenge of integration with the rest of Latin America. The final legal registration of ABRATEF took place thanks to the Rio de Janeiro congress.

On that occasion, through a written proposal unanimously approved by the general assembly, Brasilia was selected to host the Fourth Brazilian Congress. The Regional Directorate of the Center-West (ACOTEF), presided over by Professor Ileno Izídio da Costa of the University of Brasilia, was elected to constitute the National Directorate of ABRATEF and organize the Fourth Brazilian Congress. This was the first time that had happened in a general assembly of the national association.

Thus, in 2000, the Fourth Brazilian Congress of Family Therapy was held, with approximately 700 participants. The congress was chaired by Cláucia R. S. Diniz (then Vice President of ABRATEF), and had as its main theme "The family in times of transition: Social justice, ethics and citizenship." Simultaneously, the Second Latin American Encounter was held and chaired by Maria Fátima Sudbrack. In both events, there were participants from the United States, Germany, France, Canada, Belgium, Colombia, and Argentina.

As president of ABRATEF, Ileno Costa organized and, together with the directorate of ARTEF/BA (especially Maria Margarida Rego and Maria Luiza Timóteo), realized in Salvador, Bahia, in 1999, the Second Encounter of Family Therapy Educators (in recognition of the first encounter—organized by family therapist Rosana Rapizzo, together with the congress held in Rio de Janeiro). To be sure, the second encounter was the first to be held separately from the Brazilian congress, as had been suggested previously.

When the president-elect took a leave of absence to pursue doctoral studies in Europe, the vice president, Gláucia Diniz, a family therapist who received her degree from United States International University, assumed the presidency of ABRATEF and not only led the process of organization of the congress and the movement, but also did the networking for holding the Third National Encounter of Family Therapy Educators in 2000 in Santa Catarina. The latter was organized by the newest association, which had just been formed—the Santa Catarina Association of Family Therapy (ACATEF), the president of which was Dalmo de Oliveira, a family therapist.

In the Brasilia congress, the Bahia regional association was chosen to constitute the fourth directorate of ABRATEF, under the responsibility of ARTEF, the president of which was Maria Luiza Timóteo. ARTEF committed itself to holding the Fifth Brazilian Congress of Family Therapy in 2002.

THE PRINCIPAL CHARACTERISTICS OF FAMILY THERAPY IN BRAZIL

Publications in the Area

Gradually, the study of the family was transformed into published articles and books with an anthropological or sociological focus. Little by little, interest grew in the clinical application of the family. At that point the articles, which until then had been published in psychological journals or general magazines, came to have a space of their own. The first journal on family therapy, *Família: Temas de Terapia Familiar e Ciências Sociais*, was published in 1986 in Fortaleza by family therapist Carlos Aturo Molina-Loza, at the Center for Studies of the Family. In it were discussed the various applications of family therapy work in Brazil. However, the journal was discontinued because of financial difficulties.

At present, there is one journal that publishes research articles, essays, clinical studies, and surveys related to marital and family therapy, as well as disseminating current theories. This journal—called *Nova Perspectiva Sistêmica*—is published by the Family Therapy Institute of Rio de Janeiro under the initial editorial responsibility of family therapist Gladis Brun.

Meanwhile, several special issues focusing on the married couple or the family have been published in Brazil, in the following magazines, for example: *Psicologia: Teoria e Pesquisa*, of the University of Brasilia; *Revista Brasileira de Enfermagem*, of the Federal Nursing Council; *Psicologia: Reflexão e Crítica*, of the Federal University of Rio Grande do Sul; and *Texto Didático—Série Psicologia,* of the Catholic University of Brasilia. Beginning in the 1970s, studies and research at the universities were transformed into master's theses, doctoral dissertations, articles in Brazilian and international publications, and several books.

With the creation of courses on the family and family therapy in the universities, and the development of countless degree programs in the area, written production has greatly increased; more detailed examination of this specific production is called for. This is one of our challenges for the future.

A BRIEF CRITICAL-EPISTEMOLOGICAL EVALUATION OF THE FAMILY THERAPY MOVEMENT IN BRAZIL

Based on this historical overview of the development of family therapy in Brazil, a few brief critical-epistemological considerations may be put forth. Historically, just for pedagogical purposes, we may divide this process of development into three distinct periods. The first period, constituted by family therapists with degrees and training from abroad, mainly the United States and Europe (the 1970s), fits into the theoretical-epistemological context that today we call the first cybernetics.

The second phase may be broken down into two others. The first refers to dissemination and diversification of teaching, research, and service-providing, with the principles of the second cybernetics as a theoretical reference point; the second refers to the structuring of the first nationwide groups and encounters, as described in the preceding.

The third phase is characterized by the restructuring of the national movement with the organization of related activities in the 1990s. This further consolidated the movement throughout the country. One may say that included in this period is the evolution of a globalized movement and the latest theoretical-epistemiological discussions and positions, such as social constructionism, the narrative approach, and constructivism.

CONCLUSION

To speak of a typically Brazilian family therapy implies taking into account the social and cultural reference points that support family structures. There are certain indicators that family therapy practice and research in Brazil have particular characteristics that need to be investigated in greater depth. We may, for example, cite the papers on the northeast region that have taken into account the specific beliefs, values, and language patterns of a typical portion of the Brazilian reality; these papers have focused on communities. Likewise, we may call attention to experiences derived from family health movements in the Southeast region, involving the training of medical professionals and paramedics focusing on family care, for example.

Data are still lacking that might make it possible to affirm that there exists a typically Brazilian family therapy. Nevertheless, we have seen that techniques and approaches uniquely adapted to studying and providing care within a Brazilian family context have been created. In our view, a characterization of this phenomenon is to be the next step in investigation and recognition of the Brazilian movement as unique and able to make a contribution at the worldwide level. There is no doubt that the family, as a reference today, constitutes one of the most important and widely disseminated models of work and study of human relations in our country. With that in mind, a critical discussion has begun in certain groups of theoretical and practical points of reference, not just concerning studies done abroad, but also, and foremost, regarding the typically Brazilian experience.

Finally, it may be said that the greatest challenge facing the family therapy movement in Brazil is to find appropriate and satisfactory ways to deal with the complexity and diversity of the different expressions of family life. There is no simple answer to the current situation. The challenge before us is to find a balance.

REFERENCES

Bucher, J. (1989). Terapia Familiar: su enseñanza e investigacion en el contexto brasileño. (Family therapy: Its teaching and investigation in the Brazilian context.) Revista Interamericana de Psicologia/Interamerican. *Journal of Psychology, 23*, 33–51.

Bucher, J. (1999). O Casal e a família sob novas formas de interação. (Couple and family therapy and their new modes of interactions.) In éres-Carneiro (Ed.), *Casal e família entre a tradição e a transformação* (pp. 82–95). Rio de Janeiro: Nau Editora.

Candido, M. (1951). The Brazilian family. In L. Smith & A. Marchand (Eds.), *Brazil, portrait of half a continent* (pp. 82–95). New York: The Drydend Press.

Cerveny, C., & Berthoud, C. (1997). *Família e Ciclo Vital nossa realidade em pesquisa.* (Family and life cycle: Our reality in research.) São Paulo: Casa do Psicólogo.

Correa, M. (1982). Repensando a família patriarcal brasileira (notas para o estudo das formas de organização familiar no Brasil). (Rethinking the Brazilian patriarchal family). In M. S. N. Almeida (Ed.), *Colcha de Retalhos: Estudo sobre a família no Brasil* (pp. 37–46). São Paulo: Ed. Brasilense.

Costa, I. (1990). *Família e esquizofrenia: um estudo transgeracional.* (Family and schizophrenia: A transgenerational study). Dissertação de Mestrado não publicada. Brasília, DF: Universidade de Brasília.

Féres-Carneiro, T. (1999). *Casal e família entre a tradição e a transformação.* (Couple and family between tradition and transformation.) Rio de Janeiro: NAU.

Freyre, G. (1993). *Casa Grande e Senzala.* Rio de Janeiro: Livraria José Olympio Editora.

Kaslow, F. W. (2001). *History of family therapy evolution outside of the U.S.* Retrieved from http://www.ifta-familytherapy.org/journal/kaslow_article.htm

Lago, M. C. S. (1998). Famílias e modos de vida: gênero, gerações e identidade. (Families and modes of life: Gender, generation and identity.) *Cadernos de Psicologia e Educação, 8*(14/15), 33–43.

Levi, D. E. (1974). *A família Prado.* (Prado's family.) São Paulo: Cultura Livraria Editora.

Lewin, L. (1979). Some historical development of Knishipo organization for family based politics in the Brazilian Northeast Comparative Studies. *Society and History, 21*(2), 36–44.

Macedo, R. M. S. (1993). A pesquisa sobre família em Psicologia a partir da década de 80. (Research about family in psychology from 80's.) In Rosa Maria S. Macedo (Ed.), *Mapeamento da pesquisa em Psicologia no Brasil.* Cadernos da: ANPEPP.

Nizza da Silva, M. H. M. (1976). Sistema de Casamento no Brasil colonial. (Marriage systems in colonial Brazil). *Ciência e Cultura, 28*(11), 382–390.

Nogueira, O. (1962). *Família e Comunidade. Estudo Sociológico de Itapetininga.* (Family and community: Sociology study of Itapetininga.) Rio de Janeiro: CBPE.

Pereira de Queiroz, M. O. (1975). *O coronelismo numa interpretação sociológica: O Brasil republicano.* São Paulo: Dijel editora S.A.

Ramos, D. (1978). City and country: The family in Minas Gerais, 1804–1838. *Journal of Family History, 3*(4), 78–92.

Santos, A. (1979). Os Medeiros: Uma família pioneira na ocupação do Sertão Parapanema. (Medeiros: A pionner family in the occupation of Sertao Parapanema.) *Ciência e Cultura, 31*(8), 373–382.

Williams, F. (1954). A estrutura da família brasileira. *Sociologia, 16*(4), 90–98.

CHAPTER 15

Observing the Growth and Development of Family Therapy in Ecuador

INGEBORG E. HAUG

The practice and profession of marriage and family therapy have their roots and history in the United States. It is interesting to note, however, that a large number of pioneering theoreticians and clinicians were born in other countries—from Gregory Bateson to Paul Watzlawik, from the original Milan group to Michael White, to name a few. Family therapy has always had an international flavor, much as North Americans want to claim it as their own.

The influence of voices from South American countries on the development and practice of family therapy is especially pronounced. The field is built on the contributions of Salvadore Minuchin's structural approach, Chloe Madanes' expansion of strategic family therapy, Carlos Sluzki's postmodern reflections, Huberto Maturana's theories, and Celia Falicov's multicultural model. Most of these innovators ultimately worked in the United States. However, they traveled back to their home countries to teach family therapy concepts and practices, and since 1970 they have attracted South Americans and professionals worldwide who traveled to the United States to study with them. In South America, family therapy initially took root in Argentina and Chile and then spread to Brazil and other countries (M. Brepohl, personal communication, 2001). Charismatic and dedicated mental health professionals started advocating the "systemic revolution" in their South American context and created family therapy teaching institutes and clinics. At this writing, family therapy training and practice are flourishing in most South American countries.

It has been a privilege for this author to participate in the growth and development of family therapy in Ecuador by serving as collaborator and consultant to Ecuadorian colleagues for more than a decade. Over those years, I gained tremendous respect for Ecuadorian culture, admiration for the dedication and commitment of Ecuadorian family therapy pioneers, and love for this small country of geographic beauty and complex socioeconomic and political problems. Ecuadorian colleagues also collaborated with the research in this chapter. It nevertheless constitutes a subjective and very limited description of the Ecuadorian experience through the eyes of an outsider. All errors and omissions are the author's.

HISTORICAL PERSPECTIVE AND CONTEXTUAL FACTORS

Over the past centuries, the peoples of Ecuador have experienced repeated invasions and conquests, particularly by the Incas from the south and the Spaniards from Europe. Each conquest led to displacement and oppression of the indigenous Indian population, cultural relativism through intermarriage, economic and social upheaval, and a profound loss of common cultural and national identity. These dynamics appear to continue to characterize and plague Ecuadorian society.

Ecuador's twelve and a half million population is currently comprised of 25% Indians, 10% Blacks, 10% Whites, and 55% mestizos (people of mixed race) (Armour & Haug, in press). There are over 18 different ethnic groups with almost as many languages or dialects, and 22 provinces, which maintain distinct traditions. The history of conquest and the resulting multiracial and multicultural composition of Ecuador have contributed to rigid class distinctions and the oppression of non-White people. Among the groups most affected are indigenous Indians, who predominantly live in the countryside. This group is poor and less politically organized and represented than Whites. The mounting economic crisis, which led to a 90% inflation rate in 2000, propelled many Indians to migrate to urban centers and many men to emigrate to Europe or other countries in search of jobs. Natural disasters forced further relocation and uprooting of large numbers of rural, mostly indigenous families. As a result, many Ecuadorian families are living in ghetto-like urban "barrios" cut off from their roots and traditions. They face a crisis of poverty, inadequate housing, joblessness, violence and gang activity, lack of continuity, loss of traditional support structures, and a painful generation gap, which is ever-widening as young people gravitate toward Western dress, grooming, entertainment, and values. Many households are headed by women who grieve the loss of family members, mostly men, many of whom have emigrated overseas. Because it is generally easier for women to find work, particularly as domestic aids, women tend to be overburdened with multiple roles and children are often left alone to fend for themselves (H. Braun, personal communication, 2001). The traditional "machismo" culture, however, accords them little power in their relationships with men. Suffering from unemployment, poverty, and loss of hope, symptoms and problems such as substance abuse and violence (mainly wife battery) are not uncommon.

Societal, economic, and political upheaval, however, have not erased the gentleness, friendliness, and politeness that characterize the Ecuadorian way of life. The efforts by governmental agencies and nongovernmental organizations (NGOs) to support family cohesion and resiliency, cultural diversity and traditions, and to improve the quality of life in this third-world nation are ongoing. Survival of indigenous villages and traditional ways of life and access for all citizens to resources such as education, jobs, or medical assistance are seen as a matter of great national importance (H. Braun, personal communication, 2001). However, border wars with Peru; political corruption and upheaval; and natural disasters, such as the widespread flooding in the early 1990s, the earthquakes near Quito in 1989 and near Salcedo in early 1996, or the eruption of Tunguragua volcano in 1999 and 2000 add to the hardships Ecuadorians have to surmount.

THE DEVELOPMENT OF FAMILY THERAPY IN ECUADOR

In Ecuador, as in many third-world countries, the last century has seen a shift in the delivery of mental health services. Once the domain of shamans, elders, priests, and pastors, these services became increasingly the responsibility of physicians, especially psychiatrists, and psychologists. In contrast to the age-old traditions, which were based on family and community involvement in healing, these "new" approaches to persons in distress were individually and medically oriented. Side-by-side, however, help for families continued to be provided through traditional channels and persons. Given this history, it seems understandable that systemic therapies, particularly family therapy, caught the interest of Ecuadorian professionals, particularly members of the clergy.

The beginnings of the family therapy movement in Ecuador may be traced back to the 1982 founding of "la asociacion Latinoamericana de asesoramiento y pastoral familiar" (Latin American Association of Family Counseling and Family Ministries). This organization was founded by a group of Protestant clergy and psychologists from several Latin American countries. One of the founders of this new association was Jorge Maldonado from Quito, Ecuador, a clergy and pastoral psychotherapist who had just returned from the United States, where he received training in systemic family therapy. The organization's goals were to: (a) advance family based services in Latin

American communities; (b) define training requirements for a certification program for family counselors; and (c) share and coordinate resources, such as experiences, textbooks, and research. They closely affiliated with the non-profit Christian human service association EIRENE Internacional (Greek for "peace") with headquarters in Quito, the Ecuadorian capital. In 1984, 300 clergy and professionals from 7 Latin American countries, interested in learning a systems perspective and family therapy approach, gathered in Bogota, Colombia, at the Second International Symposium on the Systems Approach.

In 1982, Jorge Maldonado began offering workshops in family systems under the auspices of EIRENE in Quito. In 1985, Margareth Brepohl, a clinical psychologist who had trained in family therapy in Brazil and Switzerland, joined EIRENE and helped establish the Centro de la Familia—EIRENE, a family therapy clinic and training center. Together with several other professionals they sought further training in structural-strategic family therapy by traveling to the United States and attending month-long seminars with Carlos Sluzki, Salvadore Minuchin, Jorge Colapinto, and Celia Falicov. In 1986 they were able to equip their treatment room with a one-way mirror. With remarkable dedication and enthusiasm, instructors and students read literature together and, with their books in hand behind the one-way mirror, supervised each other in translating theory into practice. The group began to follow a Milan-style protocol of a presession, session with session break and message to the family, and postsession format. The work of trainers received the same scrutiny and feedback as the work of trainees. This collaborative learning approach between trainers and trainees helped create exceptional group cohesion and greatly furthered professional creativity and integration. The excitement and passion generated by these dynamics are still dominant features of the family therapy movement today.

Structured training monetarily began in 1988. Maldonado and Brepohl devised a 3-year program, which progressed from first-year emphasis on didactic course work and self-of-therapist focus (genogram) to 2 years of primarily clinical work and supervision. The model taught was primarily structural-strategic family therapy, heavily influenced by the work of the original Milan group. Graduates of the program received a certificate of training in family therapy issued by EIRENE. They applied their new skills in prior community settings such as schools, neighborhood councils, Indian Affairs Bureaus, churches, and hospitals.

Student recruitment efforts and admission criteria reflected the founders' commitment to train individuals who would serve indigenous and economically/socially disadvantaged populations. Reminiscent of the 1960s training model at the Philadelphia Child Guidance Clinic, approximately one-third of trainees were laypeople who did not necessarily have an academic degree.

A special effort was made to reach out to laypersons from various indigenous and marginalized groups so that they could become providers of family services in their own communities. These laypersons had to meet specific admissions criteria, including demonstrated personal integrity and maturity, intellectual abilities, life experiences, involvement in community affairs, and dedication to serving families in their communities.

Access to professional literature was, and to some degree continues to be, problematic. First, most texts were written in languages other than Spanish without being available in translation. Therefore, they were inaccessible to most students as primary sources. Second, financial constraints made it difficult for students as well as the Centro to purchase family therapy texts published by an Argentinean company. Sharing resources, including photocopies of texts and "homespun" translations through "la asociacion Latinoamericana de asesoramiento y pastoral familiar" became crucial to further development. This situation is reminiscent of the situation in the former Soviet Union, where an underground exchange of photocopied and earmarked psychotherapy texts, including family therapy materials, fed the fledgling interest and understanding in the officially prohibited field of psychotherapy.

The Quito courses originally attracted mainly members of the Protestant minority who sought training in family systems theory and approaches. As word spread, however, leaders from other religious or secular backgrounds, individuals already working with families in a variety of settings, and health professionals such as physicians, social workers, psychologists, and psychiatrists, applied for admission. Over the years, fewer instructors and students came from a formal theological background. However, they all shared a common commitment to helping families in distress, with particular emphasis on serving disadvantaged families and underserved communities. They saw and still see their work as a mission, a calling, and a service that enables them to put their beliefs and values into practice. This missionary commitment to service created a unique ideological context for training and family therapy practice. For example, trainers and trainees alike often made significant financial sacrifices to obtain and further their training and offer their services. They often provided free or low-cost assistance to families without resources and donated tremendous amounts of time and energy without direct financial rewards. Therapists' engagement included and continues to include, to this day, a high level of personal involvement in the form of advocacy for families, particularly minority and disadvantaged families. Several students in the late 1980s and early 1990s lived and worked with Quechua Indians; others established a family clinic in Solanda, then the poorest part of Quito; and still others traveled to sites of natural disasters to offer services free of charge.

Clients were referred for clinical services by social service agencies, clergy, or word-of-mouth recommendations. Reflecting the international composition and language abilities of the trainers, the group reached out to the English-, Portuguese-, and German-speaking communities in Quito. At the end of the 1980s, a significant number of clients were internationals from the diplomatic corps, NGOs, or corporations; and family therapy was offered in Spanish, English, Portuguese, and German. Their fees and donations constituted crucial support to the ongoing operations.

FORMATION OF THE CENTRO INTEGRAL DE LA FAMILIA

In the early 1990s J. Maldonado and a few years later M. Brepohl moved overseas. Responding to the growing interest in clinical services and training, five exceptional graduates—Helen Braun, Margarita Teran, Martha de Camas, and Gloria and Oto Dannemann—formed the Centro Integral de la Familia (Centro), which became independent from EIRENE in 1993/1994 and incorporated a year later. EIRENE continued to provide some training workshops in family therapy.

Because almost every one of the trainers and trainees at the Centro had to maintain other "daytime" jobs to pay their bills, therapy and classes took place only during prearranged time slots. Teaching and providing family therapy to the community was the passion of all involved, and they pursued it with astounding zest and dedication, squeezing late afternoon, evening, and weekend appointments into their busy lives.

Boundary violations had been inflicted on the Ecuadorian population not only centuries ago but also in recent history, perpetrated by politically repressive regimes, widespread corruption and racism, and the "invasion" of Western influences through the media and third-world aid programs. Individuals have little expectation that their privacy, confidentiality, and boundaries will be protected. Trainers and trainees struggled to find culturally appropriate ways of setting and abiding by professional limits that empower their clients. Respect for each client's dignity and right to self-determination initiate profound changes in attitude and behavior and have far-reaching consequences in many other areas of life. Therapy has the potential to become an empowering political act. A similar effect may result in challenging clients' preconceived notion that they will be told what to do by the therapist, the authority figure (H. Braun, personal communication, 2001). Training students and educating clients that therapy is a collaborative effort in the service of empowering families to uncover and increase their competencies and resources is a necessary part of teaching and of every first counseling interview at Centro (Haug, 2000).

From the late 1980s on, EIRENE and then the Centro invited family therapists from outside its borders to provide continuing education, supervision, and administrative consultation. Early collaborators were Hans Burki and his colleagues from Switzerland, as well as Michelle Bograd and Ingeborg and Siegfried Haug from the United States. In the late 1990s and 2000, Cathi Tillman, Catherine Ducommun Nagy, and Rhea Almeida from the United States provided training and opportunities for collaboration.

Similar to professionals in many other countries, the Ecuadorian pioneers were interested in learning Western approaches and also apprehensive of uncritically adopting ideas developed in very different cultural and societal contexts. Given both the Ecuadorian history of conquest and subjugation and the Western history of colonization and export of a Western way of life, these apprehensions were appropriate. They propelled Ecuadorian colleagues to closely examine Western theories and practices, challenge their universality, and adapt them to their unique cultural context. Attempting to undermine "colonizing practices" (McCarthy, 1994), every class included a critical evaluation of material presented as to its appropriateness for the Ecuadorian context, what J. Grimes later termed "hermeneutics of suspicion" (J. Grimes, personal communication, 2001).

INITIATING A DEGREE-GRANTING ACADEMIC FAMILY THERAPY PROGRAM

During the 1990s, training at the Centro became more rigorous and formalized. As graduates sought professional recognition in the wider mental health community, the Board of Directors decided after lengthy discussions to admit only students who had previously obtained an undergraduate academic degree. The Centro continued to offer workshops on a continuing basis to community workers who could not afford training or meet the academic criteria for admission, but needed specialized training from the Centro. Some of these initiatives are elaborated on in the following.

As applications for training from professionals and from outlying communities increased, the leadership of the Centro felt that there was a critical need in Ecuador to establish an academic training program in systemic family therapy. Helen Braun and Margarita Teran, codirectors of the Centro, contacted human services departments at major universities in Quito but found departments disinterested in expanding their individually and medically oriented training programs and apprehensive of embracing a systemic paradigm.

In 1995 the Salesian Community, a Catholic order with the mission to provide educational opportunities for disadvantaged and marginalized youths and adults, established the Universidad Politecnica Salesiana with its main campus in Cuenca and additional branches in Quito and Guayaquil. The university, legalized by the state in 1995, grew rapidly and in 2001 educated a total of approximately 6,000 students.

In response to a request by the Centro leadership, Vice Rector Padre Juan Bottasso, who then served as director of the Quito campus, reviewed international developments in family therapy training in degree-granting institutions. He concluded that pioneering such training in Ecuador would serve the community and also be consistent with the mission of the University. He encouraged the Centro leadership to develop a proposal for a master's level graduate program in family therapy.

In consultation with the author and support from Fairfield University in Connecticut, Helen Braun, Margarita Teran, and Martha de Camas from the Centro researched educational requirements and administrative policies for master's programs in family therapy. They reviewed materials from the U.S. Commission on Accreditation for Marriage and Family Therapy Education and from the master's program at Fairfield University. They subsequently proposed a unique 2½-year program of intensive study and clinical and supervisory experience, tailor-made to their cultural context. Numerous conferences with authorities at Salesian University required diplomacy, determination, and conviction. The Centro team had to repeatedly explain the value of family therapy, the rigor of the planned curriculum, and the teaching and program responsibilities of faculty. An array of difficult details concerning accountability, budget, and integration of the new program into the university structure needed to be worked out, among them the following questions:

- Are the training requirements, especially the research and thesis component, rigorous enough to constitute advanced academic achievement? The University review of the proposed curriculum affirmed the high standards of the program. The Academic Council also placed value on the ongoing consultation and program review with the accredited family therapy program at Fairfield University.
- How can legal, administrative, and budgetary concerns be reconciled with the unique program requirement that students acquire direct clinical experience as part of their education? The program emphasis on supervised clinical training and experience was novel and required unique arrangements. The university agreed to a contract with the Centro to serve as off-campus clinical training site.
- Who will qualify as teaching faculty? As in other countries, most family therapy pioneers at the Centro had received their family therapy training in nonacademic settings. All were university graduates and most held

master's or doctoral degrees in related fields. Accepted as teaching faculty were trainers who held both, a related advanced academic degree and a certificate in family therapy. These included Helen Braun, M.A., Marcos Maldonado, M.D., and John Grimes, Ph.D., a Catholic priest and Massachusetts licensed psychologist trained in family systems who had recently relocated to Ecuador. Additional teachers in subjects such as research were drawn from the psychology and social work departments of the Salesian and several other universities. Dorys Ortiz, a family therapist trained at Lovaine University in Belgium, was retained to provide clinical supervision of students. In addition, the university made a commitment to invite each semester international teachers for additional learning opportunities for both students and faculty.

- What requirements for excellence in teaching, scholarship, and service to the University, profession, and community at large will be expected of faculty? Because of budgetary constraints in this third-world country, the University had few full-time salaried faculty members. It placed a premium on excellence in teaching, demonstrated through student evaluations, and a secondary emphasis on service.
- How can the program become integrated into the life of the University? Program directors of the different departments served on a variety of university committees.
- Who will direct the program? John Grimes, who had been teaching at Boston College prior to relocating to Ecuador, accepted the position as program director. Helen Braun served as clinical director.
- Should this innovative graduate program be affiliated with the graduate school of psychology or education? Predictably, issues of program overlap, turf protection, and the legitimacy of establishing a new mental health discipline were complex. The decision was made to initiate the new degree program as a freestanding department under the direct supervision of the Vice Rector.
- How can tuition as well as teaching salaries be kept low, in keeping with the University's commitment to provide quality education at affordable cost to less privileged populations? The issue of providing low enough tuition to make training accessible to students and high enough salaries to retain teaching faculty needed to be revisited again and again as the economic situation in Ecuador worsened during the end of the 1990s. Financial sacrifices were borne by students and teachers alike. For both, their involvement was and continues to be a passionate pursuit.

In April of 1997 the Salesian University officially accepted the proposal and simultaneously signed a plan for ongoing academic consultation and collaboration with Fairfield University's master's program in marriage and family therapy. The first degree-granting graduate program in family therapy on Ecuadorian soil was becoming a reality.

THE FIRST GRADUATING CLASS AT SALESIAN UNIVERSITY

Over 90 students began classes in August of 1997 in the "Maestria en Intervencion Asesoria y Terapia Familiar Sistemica," the master's program in systemic family intervention, counseling, and therapy. They came from a variety of disciplines in which they had received their undergraduate ("grado terminal") or advanced university degree, including psychology, family medicine, psychiatry, law, journalism, and social work. Although all courses were taught at the university campus, students were provided client contact hours at the Centro and their places of employment, if deemed appropriate. Built on a core commitment to professional ethics that permeates all aspects of the program, the training is divided into three domains: (a) "ser," self-of-the-therapist, which includes personal genogram and life cycle work as well as the expectation that students receive a minimum of five sessions of personal therapy per semester; (b) "saber," didactic coursework in family therapy theories and their applications; and (c) "hacer," namely, clinical work and supervision. At graduation, students must have successfully passed all coursework, accumulated 600 hours of clinical service and 300 hours of supervision, and written and successfully defended their thesis.

Many difficulties emerged over the ensuing years. Teachers who commonly taught at the Centro in an egalitarian style now needed to follow university policies and procedures for evaluating students' performance according to strict criteria, a shift for both students and teachers alike. Some conflict arose around the culturally condoned practice of cheating, which, Ecuadorian colleagues explain, is a way to show solidarity with those less capable or fortunate. Although academic institutions decry the practice and have instituted (but rarely enforced) penalties, in day-to-day situations students tend to place a higher value on the sanctity of relationship bonds over individual recognition, even when the issue is framed as one of ethics. This cultural value embedded in cheating gives ethical action a very different meaning than it would in Western contexts.

The more anonymous and hierarchical atmosphere at the University and the higher cost of the program socialized students into a new attitude of entitlement as far as their training was concerned. The subtle shift among students from looking at their training as a calling, pursued at great personal cost, to training for a career was perceptible and caused friction among students, faculty, and administration as student demands and complaints rose.

Other major hurdles to be overcome were related to other contextual factors. The family therapy program became only the second master's degree program at the University, and administrative policies were not yet "tried and true" but at times developed "on the go." Turf wars among the disciplines led the administration in 1999 to house the family therapy program within the graduate program in education. In the same year the University decided that the arrangement with the Centro to serve as clinical off-campus site caused too many legal and financial problems. Negotiations are now underway to equip the University's student counseling center with one-way mirrors and observation capabilities and require students to accumulate most of their clinical hours on campus. Ecuador's worsening economic situation in the late 1990s made it difficult for students to afford tuition fees as well as for teachers to get paid according to contract. As the crisis worsened, the University restricted funds for program support and suspended acceptance of new admissions to the program. Equally disconcerting were the shifts in administrative leadership at the University. The numerous changes meant that the University's commitment to the family therapy program came under repeated scrutiny and needed to be reaffirmed again and again, with mixed results. At the present, the long-term survival of the program is not assured.

These growing pains notwithstanding, however, in August of 2000 the first 29 "made-in-Ecuador" family therapists graduated with the title "master en intervencion, asesoria y terapia familiar sistemica," namely "master's in systemic family intervention, counseling, and therapy." This was a milestone event for students and faculty, the program and University, as well as the public and profession at large. A particular achievement and large contribution to Ecuadorian social sciences constituted the theses students submitted. Containing a theoretical component and clinical application, topics covered issues such as models of working with families of Down's syndrome children and clinical work with families traumatized by the suicide of a family member. The University research committee was so impressed by the quality of these papers and their contribution to developing unique contextually appropriate approaches to families that it considers publishing them in the near future.

Graduates may call themselves "terapeuta familiar," "intervencionista familiar," or "asesor, asesora familiar." The terms terapia, asesoria, and intervencion are used almost interchangeably to denote therapy or counseling. Most graduates use their skill and experience in fields in which they had originally trained: psychology, education, psychiatry, family medicine, law, social work, and ministry. Many are pioneering innovative programs such as those for families with disabled children, for foster families, or for cancer patients and their families.

COMMUNITY INITIATIVES

Parallel to their teaching and administration of the master's program at the Salesian University, the Centro leadership and associates continue to provide therapy and workshops. In addition, they volunteer their services during natural disasters, training local community leaders in crisis intervention: After the earthquake near Salcedo in 1996, a team of four family therapists traveled to the area every weekend for several months as part of the NGO network that was led by Medical Assistance Program International. After the 1999/2000 ash fall from Tungurahua Volcano covered wide stretches of land and displaced many Quechua (Indian) families, the Centro leadership responded to requests from Catholic Relief Services to come to Penipe, Chimborazo and train professionals to help traumatized families in their communities. The group created crisis intervention training manuals, which might be published in the future.

In cooperation with a Catholic relief agency, members of the Centro in 1998 provided training for staff from several social service agencies to promote deinstitutionalization of children and their possible reintegration within their families. Parallel to these efforts the Centro offered parenting workshops in one of the poorest areas in south Quito, with many illiterate participants.

In June 1999, the Centro was approached by CONFIE, the Consorcio de Organizaciones No Gubernamentales a Favor de la Familia y la Infancia Ecuatoriana, a nongovernmental consortium devoted to helping families with young children, of which the Centro is a founding member. They were invited to train volunteers and paraprofessional social service providers in Catholic parishes in Santo Domingo de los Colorados, a buzzing commercial center beset with problems such as family disintegration and family violence, poverty, gang activity, drug abuse, and unwanted pregnancies. Under the direction of Margarita Teran a team of family therapists traveled biweekly 3 hours to Danto Domingo, southwest of the capital city. After 18 months the program graduated 43 participants as "systemic family facilitators" in 2000. A central objective of the courses consisted in teaching the impact of larger systemic contextual issues on individual families. Participants quoted in a news release were enthusiastic about the program and believed that the systemic lens will enable them to help families to decrease self-blame and hopelessness, to assist the community to work toward joint solutions to the common crisis, and support individual families in distress. A similar program, which trains volunteers as family facilitators, is slated for early summer 2001 in Quito, in conjunction with the YMCA. The program was very well accepted and planning for future programs is in progress.

CURRENT DEVELOPMENTS IN TRAINING AND PRACTICE

One year after the initiation of the master's program at the Salesian University, a second master's degree program in family therapy opened in 1998 in Quito as a branch of the Lovaine University in Belgium. Following Belgium requirements, the program accepts only students with a qualifying degree in psychology or psychiatry. This program has a more medical and less clinical orientation and graduated 28 students in 2001. In addition, the newly founded (1997) Universidad Cristina Latinoamericana initiated a 1-year diploma in family therapy for social workers in 1999. The respected Catholic University in Quito is currently initiating a 1-year postgraduate diploma in "intervencion familiar" and is currently negotiating with the Centro to propose a curriculum to extend training to the master's level. Academia's interest in systemic family therapy is increasing, and training opportunities are multiplying.

A further program in the planning stages is geared to train family mediators. In connection with the Law School of Catholic University in Quito, the Centro is preparing to launch a 12-month training program in family dynamics, interviewing skills, and conflict resolution for mediators.

Another major initiative concerns interventions to combat the widespread ill of family violence, mainly wife battery (H. Braun, personal communication, 2001). Violence toward women appears impacted by dispiriting poverty, the plight of joblessness among men, and the ingrained cultural attitude of "machismo," male entitlement and superiority over women. Machismo attitudes tend to keep women disempowered in couple relationships. In a discussion group on sexuality, Ecuadorian women shrugged helplessly when talking about how difficult it is for women to voice their sexual preferences and how common men's sexual infidelity and parenthood outside marriage are. With the support of CEIME, the Centro de Investigacion sobre la Mujer Ecuatoriana (Center for Research on Ecuadorian Women), and CEPAM, the Centro de Promocion y Apoyo a la Mujer (Center for Promoting and Supporting Women), the Centro in 2000 invited Rhea Almeida and her colleagues to train staff in the Cultural Context Model of domestic violence. This model uses group therapy and community sponsors to support men in nonviolent conflict resolution and recognition of "machismo" attitudes. It also includes therapy for women and children. Because in Ecuador no other "treatment" than jail is currently available for wife batterers, and only 1% of violent men are being jailed, legal and social agencies have a great interest in the further development of this model. More training and planning are currently underway.

The Centro has relocated to larger and more central quarters and is currently under the directorship of Gabriel Cuesta. The master's program at the Salesian University is currently co-led by Helen Braun, Diego Tapia Figueroa, Monica Bernal de Newton, Maria del Carmen Borrero de Muller, and Jeny Agila. Approximately 20 students graduated in 2001.

Although established mental health disciplines, mainly psychology and psychiatry, initially regarded family therapy with suspicion, turf wars seem to have abated and family therapy appears to be slowly gaining ground. At the same time, the early "modernist" belief in the superiority of the systemic perspective and zeal in its promulgation is giving way to a more integrative, postmodern understanding of the limits of any singular approach and facilitates multidisciplinary exchanges.

At the present, an Ecuadorian family therapy organization has been established, mainly with institutional membership and a mission to promote its members (Armour & Haug, in press). There is no current professional association that establishes training and membership requirements, ethical standards, continuing education, communication among family therapists, or advocacy for families. Such a professional association may develop in the future as the field and profession mature.

CONCLUSION

The growth and development of the practice and profession of family therapy in Ecuador seems to mirror, albeit in a condensed time frame, the evolution of family therapy in the United States and many other countries around the globe. In the United States a number of innovative and charismatic professionals began to develop the new paradigm and approach. They commonly shared a commitment to assist marginalized and underserved families. With passion, energy, and conviction these pioneers create family therapy clinics and over time, as theories and techniques evolve, offer training courses. Family therapy is initially received with apprehension by other mental health disciplines. As the "systemic revolution" and a concurrent sociopolitical focus on the family gain momentum, requests for services and training increase. Training becomes more formalized and then moves from freestanding institutes into academia and degree-granting education. As the practice and profession develop, a number of political issues surface, namely turf wars among the mental health disciplines and academic departments and the desirability of forming a professional organization that can establish standards of practice and training.

The Ecuadorian experience underscores for the field the importance of the cultural context in all our theories and approaches, be it models to address family violence, ethical guidelines, or qualifications for teaching faculties, to name but a few. It may at the same time serve as a reminder that our field had been devoted to assist underprivileged and stigmatized families from its inception. In the United States, this foundational commitment became obscured as family therapy "matured" into theories and applications for a White middle class. Over the past 20 years, the feminist critique, the challenges of addressing diversity in its many forms, and social constructionist thinking have begun to reorient the field (Haug, 2000). International dialogue and collaboration provide critical and crucial contributions to advance ethical practice that respects the diverse contexts in which families live, with particular attention to those who are disadvantaged and marginalized.

This account of the history of family therapy in Ecuador is colored and limited by the author's experiences. In all likelihood, many more initiatives of which the author is unaware deserve highlighting. Central to the modest but increasing success of family therapy in Ecuador are the awe-inspiring passion, dedication, and untiring commitment of a small group of professionals, charismatic pioneers, and visionaries in their corner of the world. They deserve much respect, admiration, and continued support.

ACKNOWLEDGMENTS

The author wishes to express her great appreciation to Helen Braun, faculty at the Salesian University and founding member and supervisor at Centro Integral de la Familia in Quito, Ecuador, for her substantial assistance in the preparation of this chapter. Many thanks also to Margareth Brepohl, clinical psychologist in Curitiba, Brazil, for her helpful contributions.

REFERENCES

Armour, M., & Haug, I. E. (in press). International roundtable on ethical norms and practices in psychotherapy. In R. F. Massey & S. D. Massey (Eds.), *Comprehensive handbook of psychotherapy, vol. III: Interpersonal, humanistic, existential approaches to psychotherapy.* New York: Wiley.

Haug, I. E. (2000). What in the world is happening? A glimpse at family therapy in Ecuador. *Family therapy News*, August/September.

McCarthy, I. C. (1994). Abusing norms: Welfare families and a Fifth Province stance. *Human Systems, 5*, 229–239.

About the Contributors

EDITOR

Kit S. Ng, Ph.D., is a graduate faculty member in the department of psychology at Kean University, Union, New Jersey. He also coordinates the marriage and family therapy (postgraduate) and the psychological services (master's) program. He obtained his Ph.D. (family therapy) from Texas Women's University and has been in different clinical positions for over a decade. He is a clinical member and an approved supervisor with the American Association for Marriage and Family Therapy. Currently, he also serves as editor of the *New Jersey Journal of Professional Counseling.*

Dr. Ng's research interests are in cross-cultural family therapy, supervision, Zen psychotherapy, treatment outcomes, and qualitative inquiry. He maintains a private practice in Montclair, New Jersey.

CONTRIBUTORS

Mary O. Adekson, Ph.D., earned her master's degree from Obafemi Awolowo University in Nigeria and her doctorate from Ohio University. She is currently an assistant professor in the counselor education department at St. Bonaventure University, St. Bonaventure, New York. Her areas of research are adolescents, youth at risk, and in counseling techniques by Yoruba traditional healers.

Paolo Bertrando, M.D., Ph.D., is a psychiatrist and family therapist practicing in Milan, Italy. He specializes in individual systemic therapy; his current research interests are in the history of family therapy and the nature of the therapeutic relationship. He coauthored with Luigi Boscolo, *The Times of Time*, in 1993.

Ileno Izídio da Costa, M.A., M.Sc., is a current doctorate student in clinical psychology. Besides being a clinical psychologist specializing in family therapy and psychopathology, he is also coordinator of the Psychological Clinic-School of Institute of Psychology at University of Brasília, Brasil.

Júlia S. N. Ferro-Bucher, Ph.D., born in Brazil, is a senior associate researcher at the University of Brasília—UnB, and professor at the University of Fortaleza, Ceará, Brazil. She studied at the Catholic University of Rio de Janeiro and at the University of Louvain in Belgium, where she completed her doctorate in 1975 in family sciences and sexology. She did postdoctoral studies at the University of Giessen and the University of Tübingen in Germany. She received a Fullbright fellowship exchange with St. Johns University in New York. She has written numerous papers on interpersonal relations and transcultural issues related to marriage and the family.

Clara Gerhardt, Ph.D., LMFT, is a clinical psychologist and associate professor of human studies in the family studies department of Samford University, Birmingham, Alabama. She originally received her training in South Africa and was a member of the South Africa Association of Marriage and Family Therapy from 1981 to 1992.

Ingeborg E. Haug, D.Min., is an associate professor of marriage and family therapy education at Fairfield University, Fairfield, Connecticut, and honorary visiting professor at Universidad Polytecnica Salesiana Sede Quito, Ecuador. She is a clinical member and approved supervisor with the American Association for Marriage and Family Therapy. Ingeborg has had many years of experience collaborating and consulting with family therapists in Europe; Asia; and North, Central, and South America. Her research interests include ethics and the inclusion of spiritual dimensions in family therapy.

Gerda Klammer, Ph.D., has worked as a psychologist at the Child Social Welfare in Vienna since 1979. He studied psychology in Salzburg and Memphis, Tennessee. He also received systemic family therapy training in Vienna and at the Galveston Houston Institute with Harry Goolishian. He currently does training in family therapy and mediation. He also is the coeditor of the *Journal of Association of Psychologists.*

Yoav Lavee, Ph.D., is Director of both the master's program (family studies track) and doctoral program (School of Social Work), University of Haifa. He is also senior researcher at the Center for Research and Study of the Family. He obtained his Ph.D. in family social science from the University of Minnesota. He is a certified marital and family therapist and supervisor (in Israel) and a clinical member of AAMFT. His research interests are in family stress and coping, couple relationships under stress, family patterns in Israeli society, and human sexuality.

Jean François Le Goff, M.D., is a psychiatrist and family therapist. He is also the head of Hospital Psychiatric and Mental Health Center near Paris.

V. Radha Prabhu, Ph.D., works on and researches different mental health issues related to the people in India. At the time of this writing, she is a postdoctoral associate in the department of psychiatry, State University of New York, Health Science Center at Brooklyn, New York. She plans to eventually move to Australia with her husband, who is a psychiatrist.

Basilia Softas-Nall, Ph.D., taught in a Greek University for 5 years and currently is a professor of counseling psychology at the University of Northern Colorado. She teaches core courses in marriage and family therapy. She coedits the Case Consultation Column of *The Family Journal: Counseling and Psychotherapy with Couples and Families*. She is a clinical member of the AAMFT.

Takeshi Tamura, M.D., M.Sc., is a child psychiatrist and family therapist and also associate professor at Tokyo Gakugei University. He researched and wrote extensively on adolescents in crisis, gender issues in family therapy, and cultural factors that shape human relations. He has collaborated and studied in Italy, England, and the United States. He also has presented at several major conferences around the world.

Augustine Tan, LL.B (Hons), M.A., has an active practice and provides consultations in different school systems and human services in Singapore. He also lectures and supervises interns at Tamasek Polytechnic, the National Institute of Education, and the University of South Australia.

Anna Varga, Ph.D., is currently chairperson of the board of the Society of Family Consultants and Therapists in Russia. She is also head of the Marriage and Family Therapy Program at the Institute of Practicing Psychology and Psychoanalysis. Anna has a private practice as a systemic family therapist in Moscow.

Index